D1234572

JOURNAL FOR THE STUDY OF THE OLD TESTAMENT SUPPLEMENT SERIES

59

Editors
David J A Clines
Philip R Davies

JSOT Press
Sheffield

CREATIVE
BIBLICAL
EXEGESIS

Christian and
Jewish Hermeneutics
through the Centuries

edited by
Benjamin Uffenheimer
and
Henning Graf Reventlow

Journal for the Study of the Old Testament
Supplement Series 59

Published by JSOT Press
JSOT Press is an imprint of
Sheffield Academic Press Ltd
The University of Sheffield
343 Fulwood Road
Sheffield S10 3BP
England

Typeset by Sheffield Academic Press
and
printed in Great Britain
by Billing & Sons Ltd
Worcester

British Library Cataloguing in Publication Data

Creative Biblical exegesis : Christian and
  Jewish hermeneutics through the centuries.
  1. Bible. Hermeneutics
  I. Uffenheimer, Benjamin   II. Reventlow,
  Henning Graf   III. Series
  220.6'01

  ISSN 0309-0787
  ISBN 1-85075-082-3

CONTENTS

PANEL DISCUSSION

PREFACE

The papers contained in this volume were presented at a conference on Creative Biblical Exegesis, which took place on 16th and 17th December 1985 at Tel-Aviv University under the joint auspices of the Rosenberg School for Jewish Studies, the Department of Bible, Tel-Aviv University, the Evangelisch-Theologische and the Katholisch-Theologische Fakultät, Ruhr-Universität, Bochum.

The initiators of this event pursued three major aims:

1. To make a modest contribution to research into various Jewish and Christian readings of the Bible throughout the ages, a task which can be carried out most effectively by close cooperation between scholars from both traditions. It is a commonplace that both Judaism and Christianity emerged and developed in the course of a long process of interpreting and reinterpreting the Bible which crystallized in the creation of Judeo-Christian tradition, the backbone of modern western humanist culture.

   This process starts with the interpretation of ancient biblical writings by their later editors or by the authors of the late literary layers of the Bible. It includes inter-testamental and Qumran studies, Rabbinics and the hermeneutics of medieval and modern approaches to the Bible, and last but not least the emergence of modern critical biblical studies. Scholarly research into these hermeneutic trends takes into account the respective homiletic, dogmatic, juridical etc. interests of the exegetes in their own historical-sociological setting.

2. The additional aim of that conference, perhaps the most conspicuous one in this context, lies in the field of Jewish-Christian relations. Since the rise of the emancipation during the eighteenth century, i.e. since the period of Moses

Mendelsohn and Gotthold Ephraim Lessing a new Jewish-Christian dialogue has been ushered in. This gained momentum especially after World War II, with the major representatives of western Christianity, the Catholic and Protestant churches alike, being committed to it. The main intellectual effort of the Christian partners aims to track down the Jewish heritage absorbed in their tradition. On the other hand, it is the impact of the Zionist renaissance movement and the establishment of the State of Israel which created the psychological setting for modern Jewish scholarship's move towards a new unbiased, open-minded appreciation of Christianity, free from apologetical constraints, such as is reflected in some contributions to this volume.

3.   Finally we hope that this conference will be a step towards close scholarly and scientific ties between Tel-Aviv University and Ruhr Universität, Bochum, thus taking another step toward the rebuilding of bridges between the Jewish and the German people, without forgetting the dark shadows of the recent past.

If the present volume meets at least some of these expectations, the efforts of all participants will have been worthwhile. In any case, we hope that it will constitute an intellectual challenge towards the above mentioned goals.

We would like to thank the sponsoring institutions for their support, which made possible the convening of the conference and the publication of this volume: Tel-Aviv University, especially the Rector, Professor Y. Ben-Shaul, and the deputy Rector, Professor Y. Orgler, for their sympathetic and encouraging attitude and their material support; the Dean of the Faculty of Arts Professor A. Cohen; the head of the Rosenberg School for Jewish Studies Professor A. Tal, and last but not least the secretary of the Rosenberg School Mr Gideon Spiegel for his relentless efforts in organizing the conference and for his technical assistance in preparing the papers of the Israeli participants for publication.

We thank the Deutsche Forschungsgemeinschaft for supporting the participants from Bochum with a grant in connection with the journey to Israel.

January 1987
Henning Graf Reventlow   Benjamin Uffenheimer
Bochum   Tel Aviv

EDITORS* AND CONTRIBUTORS

1. Menahem Banitt is Emeritus Professor of French, Tel Aviv University, Israel.
2. Pin'has Carny is Lecturer in the Department of Bible, Tel Aviv University, Israel.
3. Marcel Dubois is Professor of Ancient and Medieval Philosophy, The Hebrew University, Jerusalem, Israel.
4. David Flusser is Emeritus Professor, Department of Comparative Religion, The Hebrew University, Jerusalem, Israel.
5. Christopher Frey is Professor of Systematic Theology (Ethics), Evangelisch-Theologische Fakultät, Ruhr-Universität Bochum, Federal Republic of Germany.
6. Yair Hoffman is Professor in the Department of Bible, Tel Aviv University, Israel.
7. Jacob Levinger is Professor of Jewish Philosophy, Tel Aviv University, Israel.
8. Rüdiger Liwak is Associate Professor of Old Testament, Evangelisch-Theologische Fakultät, Ruhr-Universität Bochum, Federal Republic of Germany.
9. Konrad Raiser is Professor of Ecumenical Studies, Evangelisch-Theologische Fakultät, Ruhr-Universität Bochum, Federal Republic of Germany.
10. Heribert Smolinsky is Professor of Medieval and Modern Church History, University of Freiburg im Breisgau, Federal Republic of Germany.
11. Elazar Touitou is Chief Lecturer in the Department of Bible, Bar-Ilan University, Ramat-Gan, Israel.
12. Johannes Wallmann is Professor of Church History, Ruhr-Universität Bochum, Federal Republic of Germany.
13. *Benjamin Uffenheimer is Professor in the Department of Bible, Tel Aviv University, Israel.
14. *Henning Graf Reventlow is Professor of Exegesis and Theology of the Old Testament, Ruhr-Universität Bochum, Federal Republic of Germany.
15. Ze'ev Falk is Professor of Jewish Law, The Hebrew University, Jerusalem, Israel.

ABBREVIATIONS

AOAT	Alter Orient und Altes Testament
BK	Biblischer Kommentar
BWANT	Beiträge zur Wissenschaft vom Alten und Neuen Testament
BZAW	Beihefte zur Zeitschrift für die alttestamentliche Wissenschaft
Cath(M)	*Catholica* (Münster)
CThM	Calwer Theologische Monographien
Eph.Theol.Lov.	*Ephemerides theologicae lovanienses*
HK	Handkommentar zum Alten Testament
HUCA	*Hebrew Union College Annual*
JAC	Jahrbuch für Antike und Christentum
JBL	*Journal of Biblical Literature*
JCS	*Journal of Cuneiform Studies*
JR	*Journal of Religion*
JSOT	*Journal for the Study of the Old Testament*
JThS	*Journal of Theological Studies*
KHC	Kurzer Hand-Commentar zum Alten Testament
NTD	Neues Testament Deutsch
NTS	*New Testament Studies*
OBO	Orbis Biblicus et Orientalis
OLZ	Orientalistische Literaturzeitung
RSR	*Revue des sciences religieuses*
s.a.e.l.	sine anno et loco
SAT	Schriften des Alten Testaments in Auswahl
s.l.	sine loco
ThLZ	*Theologische Literaturzeitung*
TRE	*Theologische Realenzyklopädie*
VAW	*Verhandelingen der k. akademie van wetenschappen*
VNAW	*Verhandelingen der k. nederlands(ch)e akademie van wetenschappen*
VT	*Vetus Testamentum*
VTS	Vetus Testamentum Supplements
WA	D.M. Luthers Werke. Kritische Gesamtausgabe, Weimar 1883–
WMANT	Wissenschaftliche Monographien zum Alten und Neuen Testament
ZAW	*Zeitschrift für die alttestamentliche Wissenschaft*
ZEE	*Zeitschrift für Evangelische Ethik*

1

EXEGESIS OR METAPHRASIS

Menahem Banitt

It was very kind of Professor Uffenheimer to invite me to participate in this colloquy. My field is Romance philology, esoteric and profane. I was therefore apprehensive about the confrontation with real scholars of the Bible and its exegesis. As you see, vanity got the better of me.

This paper will consist of two parts: first, the conclusions inferred from the study of the Old French Jewish Glossaries of the Bible, while preparing their Corpus;[1] secondly, and in a more elaborate way, some examples that should illustrate these conclusions, as much as space allows. Mixing conclusions and examples runs the risk of losing the thread of argumentation.

From the outset, interest in the Old French glosses[2] scattered in Jewish commentaries and Biblical glossaries, especially those that adorn the *glossa* or *contèrs*, compiled by Rashi (on the part of scholars like Darmesteter and Blondheim),[4] resided mainly in the philological aspect of these vocables. True, Blondheim ventured, with great insight, upon the tradition of Jewish translations of the Bible, but nevertheless limited himself to lexicological matter.

Following in their steps, I approached the edition of the Glossaries with an almost exclusive consideration of the Old French language and its dialects. However, the editing of the very elaborate Biblical glossary kept at the Leipzig University[5] brought to the fore the fundamental interrelation between translation and interpretation. It should have been obvious from the beginning. A text that needs to be explained is a text that is not understood or is misunderstood, at least in the eyes of the master. It has therefore to be transposed into another language. This operation is *metaphrasis*. I preferred this term to *metaphrase*, which, in Modern English, seems to designate translation only. The lexical equivalents of the vocables in the text under study may be chosen from the same tongue, but then of a different social level or from a more modern usage, or again, in the case of a dead language, like Biblical Hebrew, by playing on synonyms, homonyms and paretymology, or, finally by translating the text into a different language, the one understood by the learner, where again paronomastic practice comes into play. *Paronomasia* here is used in its etymological sense, namely 'designation by a word derived from the same root, or considered as such for the sake of the discourse', or again, if you want 'explanation through what we now call *paretymology*'.

The Leipzig Glossary, composed at Rouen at the end of the thirteenth century, illuminates these methods as applied in biblical hermeneutics in some unexpected ways. Its very elaborate composition allows correlative observations both with the oldest biblical versions and with the extensive contemporary exegetical activities.

Beside the translation into Old French, more specifically Old Norman dialect, ranging from the word בראשית until the end of Chronicles, the Glossary offers:

a. a Hebrew gloss, which more often than not is no more than the Hebrew equivalent, called *calque* in French (*abklatsch*), of the Old French gloss. It also appears under the form of a binomial,[6] some of whose modalities will be reviewed later on;

b. a quotation from a verse, where the term, which serves as reference for the particular translation-interpretation, does occur. A technique different from the one of which Professor Hoffman has so thoroughly exposed the various modalities in his essay on 'The Technique of Quotation as an Interpretive Design';

c. a short Hebrew explanation, mostly taken from Rashi's *glossa*;

d. less frequently, a contextual commentary, especially on the book of Job and on Qohelet, where some chapters benefit from rather lengthy commentaries.[7]

The first evidence of the prominence of the translation in understanding the Scripture lies, of course, in the French glosses, which give their name to the book: ספר הפתרונות.[8] By studying them carefully we get to learn all the varieties of paronomasia used in rendering the Hebrew term in Old French. However, the other four categories, just mentioned, although written in Hebrew, reveal, in their way, the translational foundation of their wording as well as the use of French in the class. I referred already to the *calques* and the binomials: taken by themselves, without reference to the *la'az*, they are inane and could never be of any help in understanding the text. Even the quotations often refer to the French word and not to the root of the biblical term involved. Be it said, *en passant*, that the thousands upon thousands of quotations confer a fascinating insight into the mnemotechnic of the masters of the Bible beside an understanding of the intricacies involved in the application of the paronomastic methods.

As to the commentary, contextual or not, with the French word facing it, their interrelation becomes obvious, whether the rendition is due to Hebrew or to French metaphrasis. It clearly shows the extent to which paronomasia served in authenticating the lesson to be drawn from the particular verse under study, or, in other words, in enabling the master to enrich the divine message, not excluding, as you know, its so called *multiple interpretation*. The paronomastic acrobatics are the logical, indeed, the only valid outgrowth of the staunch faithfulness to the *letter*, the Word of God. This exegesis *ad litteram,* פשוט or מליצה,[9] is the foundation on which the lessons *ad mores* and *ad historiam* are built.

With the *realia*, the translation-interpretation stops there, except for halakhic purposes. With verbs and abstract notions, the lesson mainly deals with the history of the Jewish people, events past and present, but also of things to come.

There is one more distinctive feature marking the glossaries that strengthens the conviction about the major significance of the translation. They carry hundreds of biblical headings that have two or three meanings attributed to them. These alloglosses are of two types. Some offer a more modern word than the one obtaining in the traditional Vulgate version, which apparently had become obsolete.[10] To what extent the new term was accepted in the לעז העם, as the Vulgate version was called,[11] remains an open question. The effort though is noteworthy. The second type of allogloss represents a different interpretation, obtained either by a novel Hebrew etymological cognation or by taking advantage of French synonymy and paronymy.

These *novellae* would be of no great value, if, as some suggested, the glossaries were the work of minor teachers.[12] In fact, the Leipzig Glossary, for instance, names some thirty of the great masters of

Jewish medieval exegesis as source for its glosses. Next to the older
ones already quoted by Rashi and Rashi himself, it mentions the
most prominent names of the school of Rouen in the twelfth and
thirteenth centuries: RaShBaM, Rabbenu Tam, Avraham Ibn Ezra,
Eliezer of Beaugency, Berekhya, etc.[13]

This leads us to affirm, first, that metaphrasis was the accepted
method of exegesis at the French school, secondly, that Rashi's
commentary on the Bible contains mainly the traditional interpretation, and, as the glossaries show, that only when he adds a
French gloss, introduced by the formula בלעז, are we in the presence
of an innovation on his part. This, by the way, explains why he
should be wont to repeat the *la'az* at each recurrence of the Hebrew
vocable involved.[14] It also means that to really understand the
meaning of some, if not all of his comments, one has to trace the
underlying French translation.

This mobilization of all the paronomastic resources of the
language in which the Bible is taught, and through which, therefore,
the Holy Word is interpreted, has not, of course, occurred for the first
time on Gallic soil. We already find traces of it in the Midrash, but
even there it is manifest that it is mainly the Greek translations that
put their stamp on the interpretation of the Scriptures. In the French
Vulgate version, however, there are more than just traces of the
Greek methods of metaphrasis and its various modalities. Some
biblical terms benefit in their turn by the retranslation into Latin, the
substratum of all Romance versions.

Since I have scientific pretensions, I felt compelled to work out a
theory that would account for these facts. The recourse to metaphrasis
is imbedded, to my mind, in the belief that the true meaning of the
Word of God can be, or rather *should* be retrieved by searching for its
original meaning in any language that offers a like-sounding word
and which could give a more proper or profound significance to it.
The principle at the basis of this belief consists of a combination of
several myths: that the world was created in the Holy Tongue,
לשון הקודש,[15] in which also the Torah, was promulgated; that Adam
spoke that language and used it to name all things according to their
nature and essence;[16] that the primordial לשון הקודש was broken up
into a multitude of tongues at Babel, each one necessarily retaining
some particles of it, the one of עֵבֶר, Hebrew, being the most favored
among them, in that it had preserved more than the others some of
the elements of the Holy Tongue.[17]

It follows that, in order to unearth the authentic truth, the ἔτυμον, we have to gather as much material as possible from as many languages as possible to get at the real meaning of the words, the ἐτυμολογία or *veriloquium*, that fits the nature and essence of things and notions. This was a common conviction, as the semantic evolution of ἐτυμολογία demonstrates, and one which made Isidorus of Sevilla, as you know, call his encyclopaedia *Etymologiarum sive originum libri*. You are all more familiar than I with the philosophical writings dealing with these conceptions and with the *midrashim* based on them. But it was fascinating to discover their extensive application in biblical hermeneutics.

Let us now take up some of the data provided by Rashi's *glossa* and by the glossaries that illustrate the various modalities of metaphrasis in the order in which I have presented them. Limited by time and space, I can only cite two or three instances of each feature. This is rather frustrating. It is precisely the impact of the hundreds upon hundreds of occurrences that forced these conclusions upon my mind. I am also hindered by the fact that I have to make you accept without more ado the meaning and the phonetics of Old French vocables; consequently, too, the gallicized articulation of Hebrew by the French Jews, like nasalization, silencing of final consonants, the absence of gutturals and *shwa nâ*.

First then, interlingual paronomasia with Old French. Thus, as far as the *realia* are concerned, among the sixty or so noted,[18] let me just mention אָצִיל or אֲצִילָה glossed *èsèle* 'inner bend of the elbow' (Rashi Ezek. 13.8), בֹּטֶן *boton* 'haw of the white thorn' (Gen. 43.11), גֶּרֶם → *cran* 'notch' (Rashi 2 Kgs 9.13, אַלּוֹן → *chêne* 'oak' since its fruit is called *gland* 'acorn' (Rashi Hos. 4.13) and the *hapax* מֶשִׁי (Ezek. 16.10), curiously divided into מ 'from' → *de* and *seie* 'silk', the Old French form of *soie*. This designation has survived in Modern Hebrew.

With other vocables, when innovating, the translator-exegete mostly contents himself with the substitution of the Vulgate's term by a synonym, which has the advantage of being paronomastically closer to the biblical word. For example, *espletosement* 'briskly' replaces *an haste* 'hastily' rendering אָסְפַּרְנָא (Ezra 5.8; 6.8. etc.) in the Vulgate version; *ademer* 'estimate' for דִּמָּה (Judg. 20.5; Cant. 1.9) instead of traditional *cuyder*; the roots פצם, בצע, פתת, פצץ, פצץ, פצפץ, פרץ, נפץ, considered cognates, are all rendered by paronymous *depecer* 'break into pieces', doing away with former differentiations; פרץ is regularly glossed by *anforçer* 'strengthen', but also 'break through, violate'.[19]

The first two instances already show that we are not dealing with a mere substitution of a synonym. The improvement in the interpretive intention of the metaphrasis is even more vivid in such paronymous renditions as *ebahir* 'amaze, confound' for בהו (Gen. 1.2; Isa. 34.11; Jer. 4.23) and בהל (Gen. 45.2; Exod. 15.15 *et passim*) replacing *haster*. On the other hand, Rashi's explanation of בלהות (Ezek. 26.21) is based on the double paronymous equation with *balade* 'dancing' and *deables* 'devils'; he quotes indeed the פותרים 'glossators': מקום מרקד שעירים ומזיקים 'a dancing of devils and demons'. In the same way, גרה (Deut. 2.5, 19, 24; Jer. 1.24, etc.) loses its meaning of 'provoke' in favor of paronymous *geroyer* 'quarrel'. Or again פסח (Exod. 12.13, 23), first understood as חמל 'being kind, treat with understanding', through paronomasia with Greek πάσχειν, is understood by the French as 'pass over' thanks to *passer* and the cognation with פסע (Rashi 1 Kgs 18.26).[20]

The urge to corroborate the fundamental relationship between the two languages extends further to the Hebrew gloss, although here it cannot be ascertained what came first. Thus, Rashi adds לשון פיום everytime he proposes the phonetically close *la'az apaiement* 'appeasement, conciliation' for one of the derivatives of the roots רצה, ירט, רטה, *nine* times in all. The same objective dictates the presence of כובע 'hood' and כפה 'cap' in Rashi's explanations of מִצְנֶפֶת (Exod. 28.4) and of שְׂבָכָה (1 Kgs 7.17; 2 Kgs 25.17; Jer. 52.22; Job 18.8), glossed *coife*. The interpretation of קְשִׂיטָה (Gen. 33.19; Job 42.11) as מָעָה falls in with its translation as *maile* 'penny'. As Onkelos renders גֵּרָה (Lev. 27.25) by מעה, it, too, will be glossed *maile*. This is definitely not the only case of paronomasia with the Aramaic translations. Rashi's *fayséç* 'striped' as the *la'az* for ברודים (Gen. 31.10; Zech. 6.3) is inspired by Targum's פציחין. For כברה in Jacob's כברת ארץ (Gen. 25.16), the glossaries offer three translations, one of them being *charuée* 'acre', which does not exactly fit the context, but is echoed in Rashi's מידת ארץ 'a measure of land' and goes back to Aramaic כרובה. French *jeléde* 'rime' for כפור (Exod. 16.14; Ps. 147.16), too, is shaped after Targum's גלידה.

As to the metaphrastic elements in the other three columns of the glossaries, we already mentioned the frequent gallicisms of the Hebrew gloss. Thus, המתן 'wait' corresponds to Old French *atandre*, whose basic meaning is indeed 'wait', but had merged with *antandre* 'hear, understand, take care of', and therefore serves, strangely enough, to explain the roots שמע and שמר, even in Rashi (Gen. 37.11; Jer. 8.7 and elsewhere). To *sofrir* in the Vulgate version corresponds the Hebrew gloss לסבול, although in Hebrew it does not have the connotation of 'contain' or 'retain' like *sofrir* in French. The same is true of such Old French polysemic words like *conseil, mêler, parole* or *rayzon*, represented in the Hebrew commentary by their basic meaning עצה, ערבוב, דיבור, whatever the particular sense they might have in the translation.

This abuse should explain the incongruous presence, for instance, of מחשבה 'thinking' in Rashi's explanations of הנחם 'to think it over', when applied to God, or of אחז 'seize', when explaining the various forms of the root קנא 'to be zealous'. They are *calques* of the Vulgate version's *porpanser* 'think it over', taking *pansée* (מחשבה) as its radical, and of *anprandre* 'undertake zealously, burn, flare up',[21] a compound of *prandre* 'seize'. When מחשבה serves to explain מְזִמָּה 'scheme' (Jer. 23.20; Prov. 1.4, etc.), we have to remember that *pansée* in Old French is mostly used in a derogatory sense.

To this realm of slavish subordination to the vernacular belongs the recourse to binomials, where the commentator feels compelled to use two Hebrew words to render the French one, translating the biblical term. The first of the two refers to the primary sense of the French gloss, the second one to the special sense obtaining in that particular case. Thus, instead of לשון המתנה, just mentioned, we find the more accurate ממתין ומקוה or ממתין ומצפה, both 'waits and expects' (Rashi Gen. 37.11; Qoh. 11.4), also עמל וטורח 'toil and discomfort' corresponding to the two connotations of Old French *travail* (*Leipzig Glossary* Gen. 3.16; Prov. 5.10; 14.23) on עצב,[22] דילוג וקפיצה 'skip and jump' for *passer*, mentioned above, or שירות ועבדות for *service*, meaning both 'service' and 'servitude', translating כהן and שָׁרֵד (Exod. 28.41; 31.10).[23] As a matter of fact, there are several modalities of this procedure. The binomials (in some cases the commentator needs three and even four Hebrew words to circumscribe the French term or to suggest some case of paronomasia) constitute a key material not to be overlooked for the understanding of the semantics in the commentaries of the French school. It is impossible to get a full grasp of their significance by waving, as I do here, an instance here and an instance there. What has to be done, is to sit down with the texts in front of us: Bible, commentary and glossary.

How, for instance, can we understand the seemingly absurd text in
Rashi on כי שיח וכי שיג לו (1 Kgs 18.27), where שיג is explained as
משיג ורודף במלחמה, literally 'he overtakes (the enemy) and pursues
(him) in war'?[24] The clue is to be found in the glossaries, where שיג is
translated *atainemant*, embodying both Old French *ataindre* 'overtake'
(השג) and *atainer* 'harass'. Or what justifies RaShBaM's interpretation
of יוסיף (Qoh. 1.18) as מחשב ומעמיק 'ponders and scrutinizes', if not
the translation by *parsuivre*, whose basic meaning is indeed 'continue'
(הוסף), and that of ערום (Qoh. 5.14) as חסר ורש 'destitute and poor', if
not Old French *nu*?[25]

As to the quotations, the first observation is to be made is that it is
not always the same verse that is cited for the same biblical vocable,
but one where it has the same connotation as the French gloss. Thus,
for the corroboration of the various renderings of the root נשא, there
appear twenty-five different references, each one fitting the specific
compound of either *lever* 'lift' or *porter* 'carry', the basic meanings of
נשא. The root כרע is a common one, it should not, on the face of it,
require a comment at each reoccurrence. The quotations, which
regularly accompany its gloss, explain this insistence: it is either
ויכרע על ברכיו (2 Kgs 1.13), where כי לך תכרע כל ברך (Isa. 45.23) or
ברך 'knee', *genoil* in Old French, serves as an indicator both of the
cognation ברך/כרע and of its correlation in French, since כרע is
translated *genoilier*.

Here and there, the quotation concerns not the biblical term, but
the French gloss, like citing ותפל מעל הגמל (Gen. 24.64) for the sake
of וַתִּצְנַח (Josh. 15.18). This is not to say that וַתִּצְנַח there means 'she
fell off', but that, like ותפל in Genesis, it has to be translated *ecolorja*
'slipped down'. In the same way ארחות עקלקלות (Judg. 5.6) is quoted
with reference to הדורים (Isa. 45.2), both translated by derivatives of
tordre 'twist'. This practice leads to some curiosities, like summoning
ידבק (Jer. 13.11) to corroborate the translation of (עת) לחבוק (Qoh.
3.5). Both words are indeed translated by *acoler*, but in Qoheleth it
means 'embrace, hug' (from *col* 'neck'), while its homonym in
Jeremiah signifies 'glue, stick' (from *colle* 'glue'). At the same time, it
brings out the correlation between the two French verbs and the
Hebrew paronomasia חבק/דבק.

If we now go back to the interpretation itself of the biblical letter, we
notice that this procedure, namely the search for etymology, through
intralingual paronomasia by cognation of like-sounding roots, actually

is its mainspring. The old view, that the basic radical of a whole series
of roots may consist of only one consonant- and even that may get
lost-is still valid (Rashi Zeph. 3.18 on נוּגֵי). In the French school, we
find such arrays of paronomasia as מסר, נסר, סכסך, שיג, שגשג, משקה,
מזג, or כלא, אתל, כול, כלה, כלל and סמה, אפס אסף, אסף סוף beside such
cognations as מעון, עין, ענה, עניין in Qoh. 1.13 or אגפים and אפיקים in
Ezek. 12.14 and 17.21,[26] נרהם and נרדם in Jer. 14.9, נעתם and נתר in
Isa. 9.18.

The exegetes, however, did not stop at phonetics, but carried on
the principle of analogy to the semantic field, by substituting a
synonym for the traditional rendering. A synonym all right, but
possessing other connotations, one of which is then applied to the
biblical term.

If I translate קפץ, not by the current *saillir* 'jump', but by *tersaler*,
which beside being synonymous has the additional advantage of
being paronymous, I may attribute to קפץ the meaning of 'disappear',
as in Job 24.24.[27] Cognating רפא with רפה and rendering it by *lache*
instead of *faible*, the master is able to attribute to רְפָאִים (Prov. 2.18;
21.16; Job 26.5) the meaning of 'sluggards', 'sluggish in the fulfilment
of their religious duties', hence Rashi's רשעים 'impious ones', which
deserve גיהנום. *Mort* 'dead' also signifies 'weak' in Old French, which
makes it apt to gloss רְפָאִים in Isa. 26.14, retaining the primary sense
of 'dead' and accommodating it with parallel מֵתִים.

What made Rashi interpret יִתְרָה (Isa. 15.7; Jer. 48.36; Ps. 31.24) as
גאווה 'haughtiness, pride'? The glossaries write *outraje* as allogloss for
the traditional *sorplozemant* 'surplus'; it retains the basic meaning of
'more' (*outre*—יתר), but is mainly used in the sense of 'overbearing'.
Another synonym of *sorplozant*, *large*, appears as allogloss for יֶתֶר
(Prov. 12.26), but taken figuratively, *large* means 'generous'; it
underlies Rashi's interpretation there. His Hebrew gloss, וותרן, aims
at establishing the principle of paronomasia.

Like Hebrew paronomasia, the recourse to foreign languages in
the search for etymology did not originate with the French exegetical
school. Thus, the Midrash attributes to צָפִית (Isa. 21.5) the meaning
of 'lamp', on the basis of the testimony of a Rabbi, who had
overheard a conversation in an unnamed country, where a like-
sounding word was used to designate a lamp (*Bereshit Rabba* 43.19).
We also know of the Greek etymology of מְכֵרֹתֵיהֶם (Gen. 49.5):
μάχαιρα 'sword', and how neuter ἕν saved the life of the adulterer's

wife (*Sanhedrin* 76b on אֶתְחֶן in Lev. 20.14).

Beside the few overt cases of Greek metaphrasis, there are scores of unbetrayed Greek etymologies at the origin of the meaning attributed to biblical vocables. There, too, the various modalities exposed in the field of French were already applied.

Some are just amusing, like אֲבַטִּיחַ (Num. 11.5), which has come to designate a melon. The Greek word for melon is πέπον and is reminiscent of πέποιθα, translating בָּטַח in the old Greek versions. Others are more subtle.

Again, I feel so helpless. How can one, in a short space, unfurl the incredible rich web of interlacing paronomasia, synonyms and metaphrasis, involving two, three and sometimes four languages? I shall therefore limit myself to a few cases which I chanced upon in the last few weeks, just to show that I did not exhaust the material in my book.

I just mentioned the quotation of עֲקַלְקַלּוֹת to support the interpretation of הַדּוּרִים. The source lies in the paronymy of διαπρεπής 'eminent' rendering הָדוּר and διαπλοκή rendering עֲקַלְקַל, both in Aquila. More complex is the case of כְּסִיל. The root כסל has been interpreted as 'be stupid' (Rashi Jer. 10.8; Ps. 49.14: שַׁמּוֹת), the noun כֶּסֶל as 'thigh' or 'hip' (Lev. 3.4; Job 15.27), כְּסִיל as 'constellation' (Rashi Isa. 13.10: מֹזָל), hence 'destiny' and 'security, confidence', glossed מִבְטָח by Menahem ben Saruq (Ps. 38.7; Job 8.14). It is hard to believe that only by coincidence did the Greek say μωρός for 'stupid', μόρος for 'destiny', ὠρίων for 'constellation', μηρία for 'thigh' and that ἀμεριμνεῖν 'to be free of care' translated בטח. The French glossaries translate כְּסִיל in Isa. 13.10 by *ores*, phonetically reminiscent of the Greek word, but involving one more paronomasia, namely ὥρα 'hour', as confirmed by the Hebrew binomial gloss: לשון מזלות ושעות.

Atandre and *antandre*, which render, as already mentioned, שמע and שמר, also appear as paronymous translations of עתד. Thus, *etandemant* glosses עֲתִידֹת (Deut. 32.35) in the sense of 'what is to be expected', but, with its Old French pronunciation, *etanzemant*,[28] it is meant to remind us of *atanser*, formed on *temps* and meaning 'to be on time' or 'fix a date'. Aquila already cognated עתד with עת. On the one hand, we find עַתּוּד 'ram' called κρίος, and on the other hand καίριος 'the right time' translating עֲתִידוֹת as well as עִתִּי in Lev. 16.21, the latter indeed being glossed *atansé*. One wonders whether Rashi's מיום אתמול there does not reflect paronymous χθής.[29] A further paronomastic extension in the same class is the gloss *etance* 'position' for עתיד in Isa. 10.13, the basis of Rashi's binomial מעמד ומצב, where מעמד posits the primary meaning of *eter* 'to stand' and מצב the particular connotation applied here, namely 'position'.

The glossaries as well as Rashi refer to אכזר only when it denotes a somewhat atypical trait. In Deut. 32.33, Rashi says אויב, in Prov. 5.9 שר של גיהנום and in Job 41.2 גיבור ועריץ. The source of these interpretations lies in two paronymous translations of אכזר: ἐχθρός 'enemy', 'hostile' and ἰσχυρός 'strong', 'violent', with which Aquila glosses גיבור as well as עריץ. Rashi's שר של גיהנום is rather unexpected. In medieval literature *l'anemi* designates Satan.

Contrary to the Vulgate version, where סלף is rendered by *tortefinier* 'distort' (Rashi Prov. 11.3), Rashi interprets סֶלֶף further on as קלקול וכשלון (Prov. 13.6) and the verb as מקלקל ומשפיל (*ibid.*). These are the meanings of paronomastic φαῦλος 'worthless', 'bad' and φαυλίζειν 'disparage'. The Greek substratum of these interpretations becomes manifest by the fact that in the first comment he establishes his interpretation as a rule, referring clearly to the Greek words, which are of one and the same root, but differ semantically.

Another strange rule is stated in the same book (Prov. 11.25), where Rashi glosses בְּרָכָה—*foyzon* 'profusion', adding וכן כל לשון ברכה.[30] How should we understand this, when he himself defines בְּרָכָה elsewhere as 'gift' (Gen. 30.11; 2 Kgs 5.15; Isa. 36.16), 'greeting' (2 Kgs 18.31), 'generosity' (Prov. 11.25) and, of course, 'blessing' (*passim*)? The term implied in Rashi's rule here is εὐλογία. The rule again is a formal one: it refers to the term to be used in the translation and not to its meanings. And again the rule refers to the Greek source, since for the French translation he himself suggests two different terms: *salud* 'greeting' (Gen. 33.11; Isa. 36.16) and *foyzon*.[31]

In the traditional French version, too, the impact of the ancient Greek ones comes to light through the preservation of phonetic elements, independently of the semantic value of the term involved. Thus, the glossaries wrote *troyl*, *troel* or *trayl* to render חָרוּץ (Isa. 28.27; 41.15; Amos 1.3), which, according to Rashi, should designate a harrow. It derives from Greek τρίβολος 'caltrop', 'instrument of torture', beside 'harrow'. Aquila translated this חרוץ that way, preferring it to paronymous τροχός 'a torture wheel', because of the presence of דוש 'thresh' predicating חרוץ in these verses. In fact, τροχός survives as allogloss under the form of *troché*.

Blondheim has listed most of these relics in his *Parlers judéo-romans*,[32] but there are many more of them, and some curious ones. For instance, *dart* 'javelin', glossing חֲנִית; it echoes Aquila's δόρυ, establishing the double paronomasia חנית / חנן and δόρυ/δωρείσθα. Or *pièje* translating פַּח, reminiscent of paronymous πάγη 'trap'. And again גֵּיְא (Ps. 23.4), written as if by chance גֵּי in the Leipzig Glossary, is glossed *terre* 'earth' as if it were Greek γή. This interpretation is corroborated by Rashi's אֶרֶץ. Interesting, too, the vicissitudes of גִּלְבִּים (Ezek. 5.1). The Greek cognated it with גלח 'shave, clip', consequently translating it κουρέων 'barbers', which in the French version has become *couroyeurs* 'curriers, men who dress leather'. The anomaly stands out in Rashi's wording: רצענים, ולשון יווני הוא 'curriers. It is a Greek word'.[33]

The retranslation or metaphrasis into Latin for the Latin speaking communities adds more paronomastic innovations. The glossaries render דֵּרָאוֹן (Isa. 66.24; Dan. 12.2) by *despit* 'contempt, scorn', from Latin *despictum*. Like in the case of מֵשִׁי mentioned above. דֵּרָאוֹן was cut up into *de* (דְּ) and רָאוֹן, considered a derivative of ראה 'see'—*specere*. *Despicere* is also the basis for the interpretation of ראה as 'disparage' in 1 Sam. 6.19 and Cant. 1.6.

Various occurrences of the paretymological sequence מזג, מסך, etc., already mentioned, are explained in the glossaries by לשון ערבוב '(it has) the meaning of mixing'. It refers to the archaic *moytre*, attested in Jewish texts only, and is derived from paronymous *muscere*, a popular form of *miscere* contaminated by *mustum* 'must of grapes', and denoting foremost 'dilute wine'.[34]

Before tackling the question of metaphrasis as the foundation of exegesis *ad historiam* and *ad mores*, it is necessary to insist on the fact that the paretymological method applied to other languages than Hebrew, is not a matter of fancy or flight of extravagance. It is a deep anchored belief in the primordial unity of all languages. Only with this in mind may we justify the excessive practice of this interlingual paronomasia. An actual proof is found in Rashi's eagerness to add an illustration for his French etymology taken from German לשון אשכנז or even Czech (לשון כנען). The translation of ספן (1 Kgs 6.9) by *celer* was arrived at through a twofold paronomasia: ספן with צפן 'hide, cover' and *celer* 'hide' (from Latin *celare*) with *celer* 'cover with a roof' (from Latin *caelum* 'sky'). The latter etymology shows in Rashi's gallicism there: שמי קורה 'a sky (= ceiling) of timber', and he deems it necessary to bolster the argument by adding, that in German, too, *himmel* may designate a ceiling.

The two words לחם (Gen. 3.24) and להב (Judg. 3.22; Nah. 3.3) are regarded as cognates and made to designate the blade of a dagger, *alemele* or *lame* in Old French, 'because it glitters like burning fire' (*Leipzig Glossary* Judg. 3.22).[35] This note points to the proposed etymology of *alumer* or *flame* (wrong of course), which Rashi buttresses up with the example of German *brant*. In fact, *brant* was used in French, too, in the sense of 'blade of a sword', but Rashi brings out its German origin to prove his point of interlingual analogy.

While this belief or theory may only have been a kind of rationalization of a natural human bent, the application of the methods founded on it had real cultural value. It led the scholars to reason out, to philosophize about language. We already notice this in the remnants of Menaḥem ben Ḥelbo's teachings, but mainly in Rashi's. Whether all their ideas are original or not, whether they are correct or not from the point of view of modern linguistics is immaterial here. Whenever Rashi suggests a new *la'az*, he either gives a lengthy phonological or grammatical explanation, or else goes into a drawn out exposition of the semantic evolution, where all the details point to the various paronomastic elements involved. One should therefore carefully examine such elaborate descriptions as those of שְׂבָכָה (1 Kgs 7.17; 2 Kgs 1.2; Jer. 52.22; Job 18.8), קְיץ (Gen. 8.22; Isa. 16.9; Prov. 26.1), מַצָּב (1 Sam. 13.23), רגע (Isa. 51.15; Jer. 31.35; Job 7.5; 26.12) or בְּרוֹמִים (Ezek. 27.24), for example, compare them with the French translation, and unearth, beneath the Hebrew terms, these multilingual elements. In his commentary on the Talmud such descriptions are even more numerous and more elaborate, inasmuch as there the interest shifts from history and morals to daily life and its wherewithal.[36] The importance Rashi attaches to these explanations manifests itself by the very repetition of them, whenever the said term occurs. It is his way of bringing home the concordance between the appellations of things in the various languages and between them and their essence.

The historical lessons taught need no demonstration: they run through all the commentaries and the glossaries. I would like to elaborate only on two interpretations, that pinpoint a biblical scene and hereby enrich its dramatic value. In 1 Sam. 24.8, when Saul exposes himself dangerously to David's men in the region of En

Gedi, David's opposition to their wish of killing the King is expressed
by the verb שסע, which Rashi explains by the metaphrasis הבדיל ודחה.
This binomial reflects a word-play in French. The basic meaning of
שסע (Lev. 11.3) being 'split', *fendre* in French (from Latin *findere*), by
prefixing it and translating *defendre*, we get the sense of 'separate',
whence Rashi's הבדיל, but the French version's *defendre* points to a
different verb, one derived from Latin *defendere* 'forbid, put off', that
is דחה.

At the same time, we pick up here an example of the multifarious
exploitation of the system of prefixing, provided by the indo-
european languages, by all the translating exegetes, enabling them to
stay close to the primary signification of the Hebrew root, while
allowing the widest divergences. Its most effective use is that of the
antinomous prefix, *a-* in Greek, *dis-* in Latin, hence *de(s)-* in French.
Its justification lies in the *pi'el* of רשן (Exod. 27.3; Num. 4.13) and סעף
(Isa. 10.33), for instance, but is extensively used with all forms of the
verbs and even nouns and adjectives (עֲרִירִי Gen. 15.2).[37] Thus, to
explain the difficult וּמְסָרְפוֹ (Amos 6.10), they coin *desardre* 'stop
burning' from *ardre* 'burn', and the uncomfortable וַיִּשְׁכַּב of Reuben is
made innocuous by translating it *decocha* (*Ḥizkuni* Gen. 35.22) 'to lie
out of bed'.

Coming back to historical scenes, I would like to cite a luminous
example of the efficacy of metaphrasis. It concerns the account given
by Rashi, partly taken over by Menaḥem ben Ḥelbo, on Joab's visit at
תַּחְתִּים חָרְשִׁי (2 Sam. 24.6), during the ominous census ordered by
David. The glossaries translate it, as if it were no toponym, by *lieus
novos* 'new localities', as תחת is often used in the sense of 'in lieu of'.
This leads Rashi, conscious of the economic-political development of
his period, to comment as follows: 'it is a new settlement sparsely
populated, which might induce David to recall the census'. Rashi
expresses here the concern of the Lords of his time with the new
budding towns founded in the wave of the rebirth of the western
economy. In normal circumstances it would have been a numerous
population that might have moved the King to reconsider his
decree.

A last example, but an interesting one, should illustrate, beside the
finesse in the use of paronomasia, the real attitude of Rashi in his
conception of the relation between literal exegesis and the allegoric
one. The *hapax* כִּישׁוֹר (Prov. 31.19) should designate a part of the
spinning wheel like its parallel פֶּלֶךְ 'spindle', since in such cases, the

Jewish exegetes applied the principle of פתרונו לפי עניינו 'its translation should suit the context'.[38] The Vulgate version indeed glosses it *peson* 'balance (on the distaff)'. At the same time though, it was equated with ישר, כשר and כשרון.[39] As in most languages, 'right' (ישר) admits the connotations 'proper, efficient', so the Septuagint renders כישור by σύμγερον and Aquila by ανδρεία, corresponding to Latin *virtus*, *fortitudo*. The latter reappears in Jerome, but *virtus* made Rashi translate כישור in his literal exposition (לפי המליצה)[40] of this passage by paronymous *verteil*[41] 'ring attached to the spindle to have it turn more efficiently' (Rashi: המכשיר את הפלך לטוות). It is a typical comment on his part, conciliating the various interpretations known: *verteil*, paronomasia with *virtus* and מכשיר 'make efficient'. In what was supposed to be his allegorical interpretation (לפי המשל), he abides by the *historia*. The אשת חיל here is Deborah (v. 18) and בכישור is explained as בכשרון מעשיה 'through the efficiency of her deeds', still adhering to the *littera*.

Finally, a surprise for our German colleagues and those interested in the history of Yiddish. A few years after the completion of the glossary now at Leipzig, in the year 1306, its owner was expelled from Rouen together with all the Jews of France. Right across the border of the Kingdom, in Alsace, he was compelled to sell his precious possession. The new owner, who had no use for the French translation, had a scribe fill in the wide margins with Middle High German glosses taken from the German Jewish version. Beside the contribution to our knowledge of the Alemannic dialect of the period, these glosses have a great deal to tell about the tradition of biblical metaphrasis. On the one hand, they reveal the dominating impact of the Old Italian version, in its Lombardic dialect, providing at the same time an insight in the earlier Romance version; on the other hand, they make it clear that with the translation, the German Jews also learned the methods of paronomasia and applied them in order to enhance their own metaphrasis.[42]

The German version should also be of interest to Modern Hebrew semantics, since much of its vocabulary is used now in the sense attributed to it in the teachings of the *ḥeder* done in Yiddish.

NOTES

1. *Le Glossaire de Bâle*, Jerusalem (1972), *Introduction*, pp. xiv-xv.

2. The Romance glosses are called לעזים (*le'azim*), plural of לעז. More about it in *Te'udah* 5 (1986), p. 143.

3. Old French from *commentarius*. In the Hebrew texts: קונטרס.

4. A. Darmesteter, 'Glosses et glossaires hébreux-français du moyen âge', *Romania* I (1872), pp. 146-76; *idem, Les gloses françaises de Raschi dans la Bible*, Paris (1909); *idem* and D.S. Blondheim, *Les gloses françaises dans les Commentaires talmudiques de Raschi*, I, Paris (1929); II, D.S. Blondheim, Paris (1937); D.S. Blondheim, *Les parlers judéo-romans et la* Vetus Latina, Paris (1925).

5. Vollers' *Catalogue*, no. 1099; to be published under the title of *Le Glossaire de Leipzig* by the Israel Academy of Sciences and Humanities.

6. Cf. M. Banitt, *Rashi, Interpreter of the Biblical Letter*; Tel Aviv (1985), pp. 51-65.

7. Cf. W.A. Wright, *A Commentary on the Book of Job*, London (1905), and S.A. Poznanski, 'Un commentaire sur Job de la France septentrionale', *Revue des Etudes Juives* 52 (1906), pp. 51-70, 198-214.

8. Cf. M. Banitt, 'Les *Poterim*', *Revue des Etudes Juives* 125 (1966), pp. 21-33.

9. See below, note 40.

10. M. Banitt, 'Le renouvellement lexical de la *Version Vulgate* des Juifs de France', *Romania* 102 (1981), pp. 433-55.

11. *Id.*, 'L'étude des glossaires bibliques des Juifs de France au moyen âge', in *Proceedings of the Israel Academy of Sciences and Humanities*, II, Jerusalem (1967), pp. 188-210.

12. M. Liber, 'Compte rendu de la thèse d'A. Aron sur le Glossaire de Leipzig', *Revue des Etudes Juives* 55 (1908), p. 313.

13. On the eminence of the Jewish school of Rouen, see N. Golb, *Les Juifs de Rouen au moyen âge*, Rouen (1985).

14. Look over the list of *loazim* (*sic!*) on pp. 137-47 of A. Darmesteter's *Les gloses françaises de Raschi* (above, n. 4) and see how many times glosses like *apaiement, coife, desraisnier* and its derivatives, *destoldre* and its derivatives, *enprendre* and its derivatives, *fose* and *foséd, garantir* and its derivatives, *justice* and *justice, talant* and *trace* are repeated.

15. Cf. my *Rashi, Interpreter* (above, n. 6), p. 140.

16. *Midrash Haggadol, Pentateuch*, I *Genesis*, M. Margulies ed., Jerusalem (1974), p. 85.

17. Judah Halevy, *The Kuzari* translated by H. Hirschfeld, New York (1964), p. 124.

18. Listed in *Le Glossaire de Leipzig* (above, n. 5), §8.7.1

19. The root *force* reappears in the commentaries as לשון חוזק, whatever

the meaning of *anforcer*, even in Rashi: Gen. 28.14, 38.29, etc.

20. *Mekilta de Rabbi Ishmael*, J.Z. Lauterbach ed., Philadelphia (1933), I, pp. 56, 58, with Hebrew paronomasia, too: פסיחה/חיים.

21. The last two connotations of *anprandre* explain the presence of הבער 'burn' in the comments on קנא (Deut. 32.16, 21) and that of התחרה 'flare up' (Num. 25.11; Deut. 4.24).

22. Cf. Aquila: διαπόνημα.

23. Note the paronomasia שרד/שרת.

24. Cf. Exod. 15.9: ארדף אשיג.

25. S. Japhet and R.S. Salters, *The Commentary of R. Samuel ben Meir*, RASHBAM, *on Qoheleth*, Jerusalem (1985).

26. Rashi's שריו there corresponds to the glossaries' *ses forç* 'its noblemen', probably through paronomasia with Greek ἀγαθοί. This interpretation fits the context better than Targum's משריתיה 'camp' or כנפיו 'aisles' of Menahem ben Saruq. For אפיק—*fort*, see Rashi Gen. 43.31; Job 12.21, etc.

27. 'Disappear' is indeed the meaning of נקפצים in Rashi's comment there. As to *tersaler*, it underlies many other interpretations, especially that of דער; cf. *Rashi, Interpreter* (n. 6), p. 39.

28. Cf. *Glossaire de Bâle* (n. 1), *Introduction*, §7.21.22.

29. For Rashi's Greek antecedents, see *Rashi, Interpreter*, pp. 133 and 167.

30. Cf. Rashi in Josh. 15.19.

31. One wonders whether Rashi's insistence on referring to pigeons when interpreting בריכה (Cant. 7.5; *Beçah* 10a) is not due to paronomasia: περιστερά 'pigeon' and περισσεία 'abundance'.

32. See note 4.

33. Cf. Menahem ben Saruq and David Qimhi's commentary.

34. The interpretation goes back to Greek μίσγειν 'to mix', properly of liquids.

35. Cf. David Qimhi's comment there.

36. Cf. *Te'uda* IV (1986), pp. 161-66.

37. This practice is called לשון וחילופו.

38. Cf. W. Bacher, *Die exegetische Terminologie der jüdischen Traditionsliteratur*, 2 vols., Leipzig (1899-1905); reprint in one vol., Darmstadt (1965).

39. Cf. Menahem ben Saruq, *s.v.* כשר.

40. This is the meaning of מליצה and not as erroneously stated in my *Rashi, Interpreter*, p. 87. The meaning applied to מליצה rests on the paronomasia with μέλλησις 'an unfulfilled intention', in other words, the *letter*, as opposed to משל, which carries out the intent implied in it. Cf. Rashi Job 5.26 and Ibn Ezra Prov. 1.6.

41. From Latin *verticillus*. Cf. S. Mandelkern's *Concordance*.

42. The subject is fully treated in *Le Glossaire de Leipzig* (n. 5), *Introduction*, §10.9.

2

PHILO'S UNIQUENESS AND PARTICULARITY

Pin'has Carny

This communication is a résumé of my studies in Philonic exegesis, which led me to what I think could be a better understanding of Philo's intentions and methods as an interpreter of Scripture (most 'creative' and unique for his times).[1]

It seems that since the publication of Wolfson's monumental work[2] there remains little, if anything, to be said about Philo's philosophy in any field of interest. This statement cannot be applied to his exegesis, its techniques and methods, and mainly to his theoretical conception of allegory. We feel that his work as interpreter is based on a certain vision of the world, and that this vision is rooted again in his approach and attitude toward Scripture. The failure of modern scholars to grasp this interrelation has two main causes. First, Philo never gave a clear and succinct theoretical account of his position vis-à-vis allegory and the common allegorical theory of his day, just as he was reticent in other philosophical and methodical matters. Secondly, most modern scholars never depart from the view that Philo's use of allegory conformed with the common usage, as it was practised by Hesiod's and Homer's interpreters. In recent times some scholars became aware of the fact that the contemporary allegorical theory cannot explain Philo's statements and implicit attitudes toward the material he was working on. They recognized in Philo's interpretation a double understanding (and J. Pépin even a triple one)[3] of Moses' account of Creation and History. But this new view, although granting some value to the literal account and establishing some connection between it and the underlying, higher meaning, failed to recognize that the literal meaning as understood by Philo, actually represents *real facts* and cannot therefore be dismissed as a 'shadow' of the truth, as merely carrying the truth.[4]

In fact, the observer of Philonic studies in the last hundred years or so is able to distinguish between three major trends.

Generations of Jewish and Christian scholars (mainly German) have endeavoured to recognize the connection between Philo's exegetical method and Greek and Hellenistic allegory of myths.[5] They were bound to the view that Philo's large knowledge of Greek literature and philosophy, together with his presumed apologetic politics, must have conditioned his attitude to Scripture and its meaning.[6] Since on several occasions Philo himself mentions 'techniques and rules' of allegory, but only in most general terms without giving a detailed account of them,[7] the establishment of a full nomenclature of these became the main aim.[8] His special attitude towards the literal meaning has generally been dismissed. Scholars saw in him a split personality: the faithful and practising Jew attached to the letter of the Law, and the 'Greek' philosopher who tried to reach the real intentions of the lawgiver by means of the common use of allegorical methods. Between these two phenomena no connection has been recognized.

Another outcome was the emphasizing of the huge difference between Philonic and Rabbinic hermeneutics. I. Heinemann speaks about 'live, creative and organic' interpretation in the Midrash, while Siegfried deplores Philo's allegory as destroying the living sense and value of the biblical account.[9]

As a reation to this came the attempt of Wolfson[2] to discover the link between Philo and the Palestinian Midrash in order to fill the gap created by the Germans. Unfortunately, by levelling the obvious differences between them, he was led to disregard Philo's dependence on Hellenistic and Greek allegory.[10] He discarded contents and genres learned from a certain text and emphasized the method in itself.

> The main thing is that by the time of Philo the principle was already established in native Judaism that one is not bound to take every scriptural text literally.[11]

That there is an osmosis between Greek allegory and the Midrash has long been recognized and lately stressed. But my distinguished teacher, Professor Y. Amir, has shown in a series of articles the inadequacy of Wolfson's conceptions in the matter of Philo's theory of revelation, inspiration, authorship of the Torah and other crucial issues which are most important in trying to understand the whole picture. Moreover, Wolfson's stress on the similarity of methods between Philo and the Rabbis does not lead us to the real issues, namely, the understanding of the interrelation between Philo's conception of the world and his theory of allegorical interpretation.[12]

The third trend in the study of Philo's allegory has been achieved mainly by the French school.[13] These scholars applied the comparative method in order to understand the difference between Philo's allegory and the hermeneutics of the Church Fathers, just as the Germans did for the Rabbinic Midrash. Again, the similarity between Philo and Hellenistic allegory was stressed in opposition to what was now called the Christian typology. Jean Daniélou put it like this: 'What is characteristic for the Alexandrians (and he meant to include Philo) is not the typology, but the allegory'.[14] In other words, typology is strictly Christian and the common trend of Christian schools; allegory with all its abuses is strictly a heritage from Philo. H. de Lubac, while recognizing the huge influence of Philo on Origen, nevertheless showed that the latter understood Christian hermeneutics as opposed to Philo.[15] This distinction cannot be sustained when one thinks that in Philo's days, the interpreter learned from his sacred texts indistinctly by means of what was later called allegory, metaphorism, symbolism and so on, whatever seemed important to him in different fields: metaphysics, theology, cosmology, morality, spirituality, physics, and whatsoever. In those days there existed no distinction between the terms to designate methods: *Allegoria*, *Uponoia* and in St Paul even *Typos* were indistinctly considered as the means to reach the hidden meaning beyond the literal one. Philo certainly could not have known the later classification of the three- or fourfold approach towards a text (e.g. litera, allegoria, moralis, anagoge), but the evidence shows that he applied all of them in his work.—So, instead of being able to isolate Philo in his particularity by understanding the link between his concepts and his methods, we are bound to continue conceiving of him as a more or less 'Greek', or more or less 'rabbinic' interpreter, or a primitive pioneer of Christian hermeneutics.[16]

In order to escape this feeling of confusion and even frustration, I have tried to single out some points describing Philo's concepts and his work as an interpreter, and to understand him in his uniqueness, that is, to look at him and his work independently of any classification. The lack of time and space compels me to report only briefly the outcome of the steps by which I proceeded:

A. Philo's evaluation of what he thought to be the literal meaning of scripture, his attitude towards its essence and origin, along with modern views on the essence of myth and mythology, have led to a need to reconsider the issue from new angles. The common theory of allegory considers the myth to be interpreted as a fiction, the literal contents and sense of which are abolished when the interpreter has understood the spiritual meaning. Accordingly, allegorical interpretation is a de-mythologization ('Entmythologisierung') of language. What remains is its *contents*, its *meaning*. In this case, we are able to speak about compromise between myth and philosophy by means of rationalization. *Myth* has only a *relative value*, and even this is only in the measure that the human mind can detect its real value, which means that *human mind* is of *absolute value*. Now, considering Philo's attitude to Moses' law, its essence and origin, we are led to a revision of the former definition. He felt that the myth and its language, e.g. the Torah, has an everlasting and absolute standard. What is relative is human mind and science, which are of some value only if they are able to discover the intelligible value incorporated in the myth, and not only expressed by it. Scripture gives an account of actual facts in creation and the history of the Patriarchs, and these actual facts carry within them a hidden meaning. Since then, human mind is of relative, the Torah of absolute value. We cannot be sure whether Philo himself reflected on this immediate difference between his own procedures and the common theory of allegory as applied by Homer's interpreters. But a close reading of his statements and his use of metaphors, literal interpretations, and even his attempts to 'heal the myth' of Moses, have, in a few instances, led us to the conclusion that, in his view, the Law was written by Moses, a human author, who, nevertheless, was the best and greatest of all philosophers, divinely inspired, and that this law was not 'parachuted by Revelation', as Wolfson tried to put it. The biblical idea of Revelation, which is an intrusion of the transcendental into the immanent, created world, must have been remote in the view of Philo (cf. his effort to explain God's voice on the mount).[18] This leads to the next step.

B. Philo's idea of ideas. The question about what Plato conceived of by his theory of ideas has been discussed ever since Aristotle.[19] Philo's view, as learned directly from his own statements, and indirectly from his efforts in interpreting the scriptures, is as follows: (1) God created the ideas and they exist as ontological creatures besides him in the intelligible world (the voice on Mount Sinai).[20] (2) Ideas are intelligible types of earthly creatures. Nature performs its functions in concrete reality by means of these uncorporeal models. The creation of the intelligible world precedes the creation of the physical one as type and model.[20] (3) This 'precedence' should not be apprehended by the category of time. In Philo's conception there is an everlasting act of creation by God with ideas and powers for intercessors. The six days of creation are not mentioned chronologically. Moses established a hierarchy of values, not of time.[21]

C. A semantic examination of Philo's use of the term 'typos' points to the interesting phenomenon that it designates in his mind both the seal, the *model* after which another thing is created, and the *engravement* of the seal, that is what has been modelled. That means that creation is to be defined as 'type' of what preceded it and of what came after it. The interrelation between the intelligible uncreated and the different spheres of the concrete creation is bilateral. *Typos means both: 'Vorbild' and 'Abbild'*. This led us to the third step, which we call, only for the sake of inquiry, '*Philonic Typology*'.

To avoid any confusion we have to point out the difference between what, for centuries, has been considered the concept of Christian typology and Philo's typology.[22]

For Christian typology, both as a conception and as a hermeneutical device, the account in the New Testament is a *historical* fulfilment of the *Heilsgeschichte* narrated in the O.T. The relation between both is based on the real current of time. So, considering the signifying and the signified as two real historical events, Christian typology has been sharply distinguished from all allegoristic manners of dealing with Scripture. Christian (and Jewish) typology is based upon the idea that two events in God's activity are two poles upon the straight line of the stream of real time, while extremist allegory denies any historical value to events and persons in Scripture, using them only as representing spiritual values. One pole, the early archetype, is the account in the O.T., the *figurae*, which points to the second pole, the fulfilment in time of a prophecy. *Philonic typology* conceives hierarchy in cosmogony as static:[23] first comes God, the Father, the Creator. First in excellence, not in time. Then comes the Logos and the intelligible world with its ideas and powers, in the image of god, as a *type* of the former and as *archetype* of the next. And again: *former, next*, not in the sense of timely category, but in value. Lastly, there stands on the scale of values, the concrete world, the engravement of the ideal seal. This is what we call *Philo's typological synchronism*: Philo conceived the material world as created on the model of the intelligible one. But since each is the *type* of the other, one might say that each sphere is the image, the sign, the *chiffre* of the other (Abraham went one way, from the material towards the godly, Moses and Bezalel were led the other way, from God towards Creation).

According to Philo the composition of the Torah points to Moses' conception of the composition of the universe. The main part of Moses' book is the Law (for the happy Polis), but he gives two introductions: the account of the creation and the story of the Patriarchs. Creation is the source of the Law, because the world moves within the universal law which again is the archetype of Moses' perceptions of men living in the Polis in harmony with the universe. On the other hand, the real lives of the patriarchs are νόμοι ἔμψυχοι ('lived laws', *erlebte Gesetze*)[24] and serve as a model for Moses' written laws. So, Universe is conceived as a system of three structures: (i) The cosmological structure. Within this a 'typological' relation exists between God, the archetype of the Logos, also called the 'image of god', and man created in this image. The same relation exists between the ideas as archetypes and their earthly imitations. Every being points to another, up and down. The '*Sein*' and the '*Dasein*' each reveals itself in the other.[25] (ii) The historical structure. This includes the events from the Patriarchs down to the moment when the elected nation (Israel—*who sees God*') is about to enter the Promised Land. Persons and events in this cycle are conceived as 'living laws', which on the one hand symbolize the universal law and Moses' written law, and on the other hand prefigure the way of the sage to perfection. Thus, this structure also points both 'backwards' and 'forwards', and becomes timeless, although in itself there is time and movement. (iii) The actual Polis as conceived and foreseen by Moses as lawgiver and prophet. In this Polis, the sage lives in harmony with the creator and his universe by means of his understanding the structural system governing everything. The sage becomes a kind of incarnation of the model represented by the lives of the Patriarchs.

Within this system of three structures everything is an expression of something else, so that this 'typological' interrelation may have been conceived (and described) by Philo as 'allegorical'. Every being is a kind of language in which another being is signified 'allegorically'.[26]

It seems, therefore, that allegory, in Philo's view, is more than a kind of interpretation, which permits one to disregard the literal wording of a given text. The literal expression is part of a whole structure which must be apprehended integrally. Allegory is the language of signs (*Chiffresprache*)[27] by which one existent makes itself known in another existent to whoever is capable of 'reading' this language.

So Philo created by his conception of allegorical interpretation a whole structural vision of the universe, which in turn determined his work as an interpreter. This close interrelation is what makes him almost unique and his work quite particular in biblical exegesis.

NOTES

1. For a detailed account of the present thesis (with references and bibliography) cf. P. Carny, 'Philo's theory of allegory', in *DAAT, Journal of Jewish Philosophy and Kabbalah*, Bar-Ilan University (14) (Winter 1985), (Hebrew). See also my doctoral thesis on the subject (Hebrew), Tel-Aviv University (1978).

2. H.A. Wolfson, *Philo, Foundations of Religious Philosophy*, 1948.

3. J. Pépin, 'Remarques sur la théorie allégorique chez Philon', in *Colloques nationaux du C.H.R.S.*, Paris (1967), p. 131 *passim*.

4. On Philo's use of metaphors as 'the body and his shadow' or 'body and soul', see P. Carny, 'Rhetorical Figures in Philo's Allegory' (Hebrew), in *Te'uda* 3, Tel-Aviv University (1983), pp. 251-59.

5. E.g. I. Heinemann, L. Cohn, P. Wendland, S. Reiter, C. Siegfried.

6. Specially I. Heinemann, *Philon's griechische und jüdische Bildung*, Breslau (1932), pp. 511-28, 542-56 *et passim*; E.R. Goodenough, 'The Education of Philo', in *JR* 13 (1933), pp. 93-95.

7. *De somniis* I, 73; *De specialibus legibus* I, 287; *De Abrahamo*, 68.

8. Cf. Siegfried, *Philo von Alexandria als Ausleger des Alten Testaments*, Jena (1875), pp. 160-97.

9. I. Heinemann, *Darke Ha'aggada* (Hebrew), Jerusalem (1940), *passim*; for Siegfried, see n. 8.

10. For a detailed critique of Wolfson's attempt, see Y. Amir, 'Mose als Verfasser der Tora bei Philon', in *Die Hellenistische Gestalt des Judentums*, Neukirchen (1983), p. 77.

11. Wolfson (see n. 2), I, p. 134.

12. Y. Amir, 'Rabbinischer Midrasch und Philonische Allegorie', in *Die Hellenistische Gestalt u.s.w.* (see note 10), pp. 107-18.—Wolfson's tendency to level the differences between Rabbinic and Philonic approaches and methods raises also the question of the scientific value of such a comparison:

How can one compare a compilation of the work of hundreds of rabbis, using what we now call allegory, tropology, anagogy, typology, symbolism and so on, over a period of centuries, with the work of one single scholar working in a given period and a given context?

13. See different articles in the collection referred to in note 3.

14. J. Daniélou, *Philon d'Alexandrie*, Paris (1958).

15. H. de Lubac, 'Typologie et allégorisme', in *RSR* (1947), pp. 181ff.

16. See E.R. Goodenough, *An Introduction to Philo*, New Haven (1940), p. 124.

17. Cf. n. 1.

18. P. Carny, 'A story about the origin of language' (Hebrew) in *Reflections on the Bible* II (1976), pp. 223-32.

19. See P. Natorp, *Plato's Ideenlehre*, Hamburg (1961²), pp. 419-56; J.A. Stewart, *Plato's Doctrine of Ideas*, New York (1964²), pp. 107-18.

20. For evidence see n. 1, *DAAT*, pp. 8-9.

21. See n. 20, pp. 10-11.

22. On this possible confusion, see n. 15. On the whole see L. Goppelt, *Typos—die typologische Darstellung des A.T. im Neuen*, Darmstadt (1966), *passim*.

23. Th. Boman, *Das Hebräische Denken im Vergleich mit dem Griechischen*, Göttingen (1959³), p. 107.

24. For evidence see n. 20, pp. 13-14.

25. See n. 27.

26. Cf. E. Cassirer, *Die Philosophie der symbolischen Formen*, III, Berlin (1925), p. 51: 'Das Bild stellt die Sache nicht dar, es ist die Sache .... es wirkt gleich ihr ... es ersetzt sie in ihrer unmittelbaren Gegenwart'.

27. In the sense of K. Jaspers, *Philosophie*, III (1956), p. 128: 'Das Lesen der Chiffresprache', *et passim*.

3

MYSTICAL AND REALISTIC ELEMENTS IN THE EXEGESIS AND HERMENEUTICS OF THOMAS AQUINAS

M. Dubois

St Thomas Aquinas is considered in the Catholic theological tradition as the theologian par excellence of the four senses of the Scriptures, *quadruplex modus exponendi Scripturam*. He determines its statute, in his clear and concise manner, from the first question of the *Summa Theologica*, in the exposé of the method characteristic of the Sacra Pagina. Let us read this text that admirably resumes the whole problem:

> That God is the author of Holy Scripture should be acknowledged, and he has the power, not only of adapting words to convey meanings (which men also can do), but also of adapting things themselves. In every branch of knowledge words have meaning, but what is special here is that the things meant by words also themselves mean something. That first meaning whereby the words signify things belongs to the sense first mentioned, namely the historical or literal. That meaning, however, whereby the things signified by the words in their turn also signify other things, is called the spiritual sense; it is based on and presupposes the literal sense. Now this spiritual sense is divided into three. For, as St Paul says, 'The Old Law is the figure of the New' (Heb. 7.19) and the New Law itself, as Dionysius says, 'is the figure of the glory to come'. Then again, under the New Law the deeds wrought by our Head are signs also of what we ourselves ought to do.
>
> Well then, the allegorical sense is brought into play when the things of the Old Law signify the things of the New Law; the moral sense when the things done in Christ and in those who prefigured him are signs of what we should carry out; and the anagogical sense when the things that lie ahead in eternal glory are signified.
>
> Now because the literal sense is that which the author intends, and the author of holy Scripture is God who comprehends

everything all at once in his understanding, it comes not amiss, as
St Augustine observes, if many meanings are present even in the
literal sense of one passage of Scripture (*Sum. theol.*, Ia, q.1, a.10).

In this article of the Summa (1268), Thomas takes up again the
elements of a debate to which he returned several times, first in the
Quodlibet VII, between 1255 and 1257, then in the commentary on
the Epistle to the Galatians, probably in 1266-1267. Whatever the
context of these different exposés may be, Thomas' thesis is, both
here and there, the same. To the question: 'Do the Holy Scriptures
under a single letter have several meanings', the answer is clear.
According to St Gregory, whom Thomas quotes in the *sed contra*,
and who is for him an authority in this field: 'telling a fact, in a single
discourse, the Holy Scriptures confide a mystery'. Thus, the holy
books contain, at one and the same time, according to a fundamental
distinction, a primary meaning and a secondary meaning, a literal
sense and a spiritual or mystical sense. As to the latter, it unfolds
itself in three directions or according to three levels: the allegoric,
according to which the New Testament is prefigured in the Old; the
moral, according to which the word of the Scriptures is a rule of life;
and finally the anagogical, by which the Scriptures signify the eternal
realities of the glory or the Kingdom to come.

St Thomas does nothing here but synthesize, according to a clear
and systematic order, a traditional doctrine. Moreover he has no
pretentions of innovating since he cites his authorities: Augustine,
Gregory, Denys, Bede, and we know that closer to him, Hugh of St
Victor had already assembled the elements of this synthesis. His
exposé was to become a basic text for the later hermeneutics and
theology. The famous distich of another Dominican, who was more
or less contemporary with Thomas, Augustine of Denmark, only
resumes in four expressions the doctrine of the article that we have
read: 'Littera gesta docet, qui credas, allegoria, moralis quid agas,
quo tendas anagogia'. This formula has crossed the centuries. Father
de Lubac made history of it.

I will not enter here into the double debate that Thomas' text
provoked, on the one hand in the history of medieval exegesis, and on
the other hand in the elaboration of biblical theology. The former
concerns the innovation and the originality of St Thomas in the
discussion and the solution of these problems and also in the manner
according to which he carried out his doctrine in his own exegetical
works. The latter concerns more precisely what he says of the literal

sense. The file on these two questions is considerable. I will content myself with recalling briefly the principal lines of this double problem since our reflections today are developed in this general framework.

Let us look first at what is said of the literal sense, since it is this insistence that struck the most, and sometimes divided, the contemporaries of St Thomas and his commentators. The text that we have read suggests three remarks. First, St Thomas affirms that the spiritual senses and the theological argumentation must be founded on the letter. The literal sense comes first. In second place, Thomas connects the metaphor to the literal sense, distinguishing it from the allegorical sense. The allegory recovers for him what the patristic and medieval tradition concealed in the spiritual or mystical sense. Finally, the third fact worthy of note, a sentence of St Thomas seems to suggest the possibility of a plurality of literal sense. As I have just said, it is not in my intention to review here the debate raised by this text among the interpreters of St Thomas, even among his disciples inside the School. What is important, is precisely the insistence, novel for its clarity, that all noticed, namely, the importance attached to the literal sense as the foundation of the others. It is not, strictly speaking, an innovation, since Thomas cites Augustine to support his synthesis. It is certain, however, that he proposed, on this base, once affirmed, a new equilibrium, or at least a new way of organizing it.

Concerning more precisely the originality of the hermeneutics proposed here by St Thomas, many recent studies have shown that, in the line of literal exegesis as well as that of spiritual exegesis, the points where St Thomas really appears as an original thinker must be examined more carefully.

There was a time when historians of medieval exegesis, in particular authorities such as Father Spicq[1] or Miss Beryl Smalley,[2] emphasized the quasi-revolutionary character of his insistence on the literal sense and on the historic truth of the *realia* of the Old Testament. In his great work on medieval exegesis. Father de Lubac showed that it was necessary to attenuate somewhat the sharpness of the distinction between the scriptural interpretation of the high Middle Ages in the twelfth century,[3] that had practised an allegorizing reading without rule or measure, and that of the thirteenth century that could be characterized by a more objective exegesis, more rational and more scientific because of the new mentality and the new instruments that it could utilize; the works of Aristotle, a better knowledge of Maimonides and of the Jewish writings, *hebraica veritas*. In the preface to the third edition of her book, *The Study of the Bible in the Middle Ages*, with a modesty, sense of humour and objectivity that do her honour, Beryl Smalley recently corrected,[4] or rather improved upon, her presentation of the medieval exegesis at the turning point of the twelfth and thirteenth centuries. It must be recalled, moreover, that it is she who first revealed the importance of the work of Andrew of St Victor in the literal reading of the Old Testament. In her recent preface, she revises in particular the boldness of the positions in her preceding editions, on the 'decline of the spiritual exposition' as well as on the radical originality of St Thomas' literal exegesis. Still more precisely, in an important article, written on the occason of the seventh centenary of St Thomas,[5] on the medieval interpretations of ancient law, she showed that one of Thomas' predecessors, William of Auvergne, not only a well-known theologian, but also Archbishop of Paris, showed himself much more audacious than him in his *'Tractatus de lege'*. William had read Maimonides and he had been struck by the rationalization of the law proposed by the Jewish philosopher in his 'Guide for the Perplexed'. Taking it as a model, he did not hesitate to consider ancient law according to its literal meaning, according to the intention of the law-giver. He saw the legal precepts as no more a veil for the spiritual senses, but as having moral reason and purpose. This discovery led William to question the validity of exposition according to the four senses. So, a respected doctor and Archbishop of Paris had planted a bomb in the Paris schools! John of La Rochelle hurried to defuse it in his *De legibus*. He argued against William for the traditional interpretation of Old Testament precepts and ceremonies while allowing that some of them *could* have a rational and moral purpose according to their literal sense. It is striking that Thomas adopted John's argument; he set it out in a clearer, more orderly way in the section on the Old Law in his *Summa Theologiae*. Miss Smalley corrects her former position, showing that, as a matter of fact, William was the *radical*, more so than Andrew of St Victor, and Thomas the *enlightened conservative* on the four senses.[6] We shall have to balance our judgment, measuring to what extent Thomas was at the same time a witness of traditional spiritual interpretation and a theoretician of literal sense.

In short it is certain that before Thomas, Andrew of St Victor and

William of Auvergne had already discovered the necessity of a return to the literality of the text, to the *hebraica veritas*, and, the importance of Maimonides. If it is certain that in the line of spiritual interpretation, Thomas shows the necessity of basing the interpretation he calls allegoric on a reading as rigorous as possible of the letter of the text, he remained faithful to the traditional categories of patristic exegesis. Even more, his practice follows this direction in a spontaneous way.

Thus, as Father Congar writes with humour: 'No more here than elsewhere, should one make of St. Thomas a solitary phenomenon or an absolute beginning, a sort of Melchisedech of theology'.[7] His originality consists of a more penetrating vision and a more orderly presentation. In an article on 'the ties between the two Testaments according to the theology of St. Thomas', Dom Gribomont wrote quite rightly: 'He synthesizes a long tradition that he improves upon by endowing it with a strong intellectual structure'.[3] This is what another of my Dominican masters, Father Spicq, confirms for his part in his *History of Latin Exegesis in the Middle Ages*: 'What distinguishes St. Thomas from his contemporaries or from his predecessors, is much more the quality of his mind than the originality of his method or of his formulae'.[9] However, it is the same author who invites us to discover, in the properly exegetical work of St Thomas, the clearly marked distinctions between the *ratio litteralis* and the *ratio mystica*: ['The richness of the tradition is conserved, but all things are clarified, each interpretation being specified with a qualification of its own nature: ratio litteralis mystica'].

Indeed, the thought of St Thomas, in its most systematic expression, was hardly open to what we call the sense of history, nevertheless he recognizes the value of history in the divine scheme of salvation. Biblical history, that of the people of God and of the Church, is a history of salvation. It studies the events of the Old Testament and the mysteries of the life of Christ in their 'concrete unfolding' (Karl Rahner's expression).

It is striking in this respect that the *Summa Theologica*, at the very heart of its theoretical and synthetic construction, contains three parts of direct evaluation of the Holy Scriptures: *Genesis*, in the treatise of the creation (Hexameron, Ia, q.66-74); the legislative books of ancient law in the treatise of the law (1-2, 98-105); finally, the Gospel in the contemplation of the events of the life of Christ, in the treatise on the Incarnation. Contrary to the more recent theologies, biblical theology, as a reading of the history of salvation, remains present in the speculative theology. The *Theologia* is still confounded with the *Sacra Pagina*.

Of course, in this reading of history as history of salvation, Thomas is the heir to the vision of the Fathers of the Church, that of St Augustine in particular. In this history, he discerns clearly the two great stages and the end: from the old covenant to the new, then from the new covenant in the Church to the celestial consummation of the Kingdom. The second stage is prefigured by the first and the end by the second. Thus it marks both its double character of continuity and of discontinuity, in the same manner as did the ancient tripartite division: *umbra, imago, veritas*. According to the Christian tradition, he shows that the two last members are more closely welded than the second is to the first, because the New Testament, that ends in the *Patria*, began here below. But one can discern in his teachings a similar relationship of preparation and anticipation in the ties between the Old and the New Testament. For him, as for his predecessors, all the people of Israel were a 'prophetic and figurative' people (et ideo oportuit totum illius popule statum esse propheticum et figuralem', 1a-2ae q.104, a.2, 2um). The allegorical sense of things, namely, the *res*, wished for by the Author who is God himself, is essentially the sense of the history of Israel. Taking up an old image, he sees in the new law the fruit born by the branch of the old law: 'Sic igitur est lex nova in lege veteri sicut fructus in spica'.

In this view of things, which is that of traditional allegory, St Thomas affirms with all the Fathers who preceded him, and whose commentaries he abundantly quotes, the equivalence between two dualities, the *fundamental duality* of the scriptural senses and that of the successive testaments. Such a duality creates the risk of dualism, that would tend to belittle the literal sense that the texts had for contemporary readers and their strict historical significance.

The situation of the people of Israel before Christ was completely 'figural', and Thomas supports the Pauline principle 'omnia in figura'. He is in all this the disciple of Augustine. He bases himself in particular on the *Contra Faustum*—a book whose purpose was, however, to justify the value of the Old Testament against the Manicheans—to give this principle a universal value. This is the case in questions 102 and 104 of the 2a-2ae. It concerns the text of the second Epistle of Paul to the Corinthians in which the veil that covered the face of Moses is spoken of: 'Velamen evacuatur, id est tollitur per Christum, scilicet implendum in Veritate quod Moises tradidit in figura: quia omnia in figura contingebant illis', 'The veil is taken away, i.e. suppressed by Christ, namely by fulfilling, according to truth what Moses expressed through figures, since everything happened to them in figures' (in II Cor., III, Vivès, XXI, 80). Elsewhere it refers again to Paul, in the manner of Augustine, and it sets one against the other, the Old and the New Testament, as the testimony of the letter to that of the Spirit. 'Non littera sed spiritu'. Elsewhere again, it says that the Spirit had been sent into the heart of the believer: 'Ut intelligerent spiritualiter quod Judaei carnaliter intelligunt' (1a-2ae, q.102, a.2). Figure and reality, letter and spirit, flesh and spirit. One could cite, concerning Thomas, the remarks often made on the subject of the Platonic duality that marked the thought of the Fathers, in particular that of Augustine. How can we interpret, according to this black and white opposition, the values attached to the letter of the Law and to the historical reality of events in the history of the Jewish people in the Bible?

In more precise terms, taking up again the very terms that St Thomas proposed in the text of the *Summa*, how did Thomas consider the literal sense of the *verba* written and lived by the Jewish people in its piety and its faithful existence. How did ͜e read the texts that the Jews read according to the *hebraica veritas*? What meaning did he accord to the *res* of biblical history if their literal sense opened directly onto an allegorical or mystical sense? By posing these questions, we are posing in reality a more general question, that which is at the centre of our reflections in this essay; what is the stature of the *ratio litteralis* under or inside the *ratio mystica*, if one admits like Thomas that *this one* is based on *that one*, if the realia of the Old Testament are its figuration and the *inchoatio*, in the perspective of the history of salvation?

It is my conviction that Thomas answered these questions and that—even if its application does not appear often in his exegesis, very dependent on that of the Fathers, as we have seen—he supplies the principles and the elements of response. To surmount the risk of a dual opposition, according to which the Old Testament appears only in a negative manner, it is important to restore to the holy history that the Bible recounts, the continuity of the plan of God and the realism of the *realia* that it contains. There is a text of St Thomas that could serve as a key in the elucidation of this problem. In the commentary on the Gospel of St John, in Chapter 6, Thomas explains the meaning he gives to the word *verus* in the expression *panis verus* by which Jesus designates himself, and designates also the eucharist. Was not the manna a real bread? 'Si accipiatur verum secundum quod dividitur contra falsum, sic panis ille verus fuit, non enim falsum erat miraculum de manna: si autem accipiatur verum, prout veritas dividitur contra figuram, sic panis ille non fuit verus, sed figura panis spiritualis, scilicet Domini Nostri Jesu Christi, quem ipsum manna significat, ut dicit apostolus, I Cor. X,8: Omnes eadam escam spiritualem manducaverunt'. 'If the word *true* is understood as opposed to *false*, then this bread was a true one, since the miracle of manna was not false, but if true is understood as *truth* is opposed to *figure* then this bread was not true but the figure of spiritual bread, i.e. of the Lord Jesus Christ, whom the manna signified, as Paul says in 1 Cor. 10.8: All of them ate the same spiritual food'. It is not a matter of opposing the manna to the eucharist or to Christ himself, as the false to the true, but as the figure to the truth, involving the whole dynamism of the annunciation and of the anticipation that what is destined to be accomplished in reality allows.

Reading in this light, the treatise of the Old Law, that Thomas, as I have recalled, inserted into the *Summa Theologica*, is an example of exegesis that respects the realities of the Old Testament, both in their consistency—imperfect, inchoative, certainly, but real—and their value as figure and as preparation. In analysing the Old Law, Thomas, citing the text of Deuteronomy, divides its precepts into three categories: *moralia, caeremonalia, judicialia*. He shows the value that the judician precepts had in the legal and communal system of the Jewish People, he insists on the permanence of the moralia for the regulation of human behaviour. As for the ceremonial precepts, the commentators too often consider them as objects of pure allegory, since they were the principles of a cult henceforth vanished. An attentive analysis shows that St Thomas tries to measure their real value, for the sanctification of the Jewish People, sometimes, having recourse to Maimoides in order to seize the sense more adequately and to better establish the allegorical value. In this respect, the treatise of the Old Law furnishes precious elements for a response to the question we were posing. We obviously do not have the time to read here all the texts; I will content myself with reviewing the most important elements. I recalled above that, according to Thomas, the history of salvation is divided into three stages, of which each one leads towards the following one, that is found in relation with it in the very precise relationship of the perfect to the imperfect (in a sense more ontological than moral). Under the Law, the precepts 'in letters engraved on stones' deserved terrestial rewards, thus the promise to Abraham of a posterity and of a land. The ritual purifications regulated a carnal justice and an exterior cult: the kingdom of God was political and its instauration among men *had* a geographical sense; such was at least the *letter*. All this exterior order was 'good, just and holy' in the measure that, like a pedagogue, it prepared the childhood of humanity for the coming of Grace. Let us recall that an analogous relationship subsists between our present state and the eschatology. Thus the 'imperfect' is necessarily figure and sign, because it is the outline of the perfect in its kind, since it is the participation in this that gives it its very form.

Thus the ritual purification prepared the souls for an interior purification, by making them aware of their state of impurity: the presence of the *shekhinah* on the cherubs, the pilgrimages 'to see the face of God', the overflowing joy of the festivals in the Temple orientated piety towards a more real and more immediate meeting.

All the religious worth of the 'imperfect' comes to it from this participation, from this typical anticipation of the 'perfect'. St Thomas, after St Paul, recognized in the figurative rites, in the ancient sacraments, a great importance, as 'protestatio fidei, *inquantum* erant figura Christi'. Because of this typological worth, the worshippers who used it could, penetrating and vivifying the Letter (*Kavanah*) be of the New in the Old. (It is obviously a Christian who is speaking.) Even more, in each faithful Israelite (that is to say, believing in the religious worth of the covenant) St Thomas recognizes (in accordance with his principles) an 'implicit knowledge' of the spiritual sense, by which he explains the 'implicit faith', that allowed going beyond the Letter and of 'being of the New in the Old'. Only the figurative rites could make possible these 'acts of implicit faith', realizing this paradox of a knowledge radically incapable of expressing itself to itself and nevertheless orientating, in all reality, life. The worshipper who considered the realities of the law, *realia*, for their religious worth (all stemming from the Promises to the Seed of Abraham, to the posterity of David) reached without knowing it the promised realities, *in quantum imago*. 'Aliquid continetur in alio dupliciter: uno modo in actu, sicut locatum in loco; alio modo virtute, sicut effectus in causa, vel completum in incompleto' (1-2, 107, 3).

It is interesting to note that Thomas proposed in the *Treatise of the Sacraments*, in the third part of the *Summa Theologica*, a theoretical and systematic presentation of the exegesis of which we have just observed the application in the treatise of the Old Law. In this respect the Treatise of the Sacraments is an excellent treatise of hermeneutics. One understands it all the better since Thomas carried out on this point a radical about-face. At the beginning of his career, in his commentaries on the book of the Sentences, he insisted on the transcendency of the Christian sacraments in that they are the efficient causes of grace. A prolonged reflection on the symbolic nature of human knowledge and on the role of the sign in all relationships of man with God, especially if it is a matter of the community, led him to pass, in the *Summa Theologica*, from a definition by the cause to a definition by the sign: 'signum rei sacrae'. This widening of the definition by an insistence on the signification permits him to integrate all the religious signs, in particular those of the old covenant, under a simple analogical notion, and in a single historical perspective. The law of nature, Old Law, New Law, the Celestial Kingdom are the four stages of a unique history 'totum mysterium salutis nostrae', history that is realized by successive systems, of which each one is separated from the preceding one by a decisive threshold, but that are reunited nevertheless in a single continuity; continuity of the plan of God for the salvation of man; continuity of the faith by which man adheres to it, continuity of the sacrament in its very structure, as sign of holy reality and act of cult. Continuity of the sacraments of the Old and of the New Law in the affirmation of the unique God.

These diverse reflections help us to understand the manner according to which Thomas understood the ties between the literal sense and the spiritual sense. One can say that for him, if the spiritual sense was that towards which the intention of the hagiography leaned, one must seek it in the authentic prolongation of the literal sense, in these realities that correspond to a deeper plan, to religious values of the Letter in accomplishing them.

Thus the allegorical sense, even in its most mystical amplification, implies first realism, a realism already open to the spiritual of the *realia*, a history of which God is the author and the master.

Among the disciples of St Thomas in our time, the one who no doubt best understood this incarnation of the spiritual sense in the realism of a history, is one of my masters, a great historian of medieval theology. I am happy to quote him here.[10] He insists in his books devoted to this question, on the 'efficacious worth, preliminary to all figure' of the historical reality, that of biblical history. He finds examples of this in St Thomas and willingly quotes, to support his thesis, a text of the treatise of the Old Law: 'Had the ceremonial precepts any literal cause, or only a figurative one?' He answers: 'The end of the ceremonial precepts was two-fold: they were ordained for the worship of God at that time, and for prefiguring Christ; just as the words of the prophets had regard to the present, yet were also figurative of what was to come, as Jerome says. In the same way, then, the reasons for the ceremonial precepts of the Old Law may be taken in two ways. First, in relation to the divine worship to be observed at the time. In this aspect, they are literal, whether they concern the avoidance of idolatry, or the commemoration of particular divine benefits, or point to the divine excellence, or else indicate the frame of mind required of the worshippers of God. Secondly, their reasons may be assigned according to their purpose in prefiguring Christ. In this aspect, their reasons are figurative and mystical . . . ' Father Chenu refers to this text and to other texts of the same kind to find there an argument against the absolute allegorism that claimed to empty of all value the ritual of the Old Testament, reduced to a role only of 'figure' without efficacious historical content. His conviction was in effect that 'it is the reality of history that establishes, by means of symbols, the truth according to the spirit'. In speaking thus, he expresses, in perfect fidelity to St Thomas, what the latter meant, when he affirmed in the *Summa*, that the literal sense is not only in the *verba* of the text, but in the *res*, the realities of which the supreme author of the Bible, God himself, saw all the signification in its future development.

What has been the practical application of these principles in the exegetical works of Thomas? Within the dimensions of this paper I cannot do more than to ask the question and give some examples of the way in which Thomas has used the resources of a literal exegesis. It would be very interesting to analyse his works according to the criteria which we have mentioned, namely the *hebraica veritas* and the reference to Jewish commentaries.

As far as the *hebraica veritas* is concerned, it is rather astonishing, as Miss B. Smalley has pointed out that Thomas not does quote

Andrew of St Victor. Nevertheless, he pays attention to the original meaning of hebrew words, especially in his commentaries on the Gospels, trying to explain the etymology according to the roots. But his method is far from being scientific and his intention is generally to achieve a spiritual interpretation (for instance Hebrew names of persons and places as meaning a vocation or a destiny).

Many things could be said about his reading of Maimonides and it would be fruitful to analyse the development of his references to the *Guide for the Perplexed*, especially in his interpretation of the Old Law. But, as we have already seen, in spite of his insistence on the priority of the literal sense, Thomas remains in a great part dependent on the traditional interpretation of the Church Fathers according to the spiritual meaning of Scripture.

This gives more significance to the cases in which he presents an objective and literary approach to the text. Let us give some typical examples. For instance, when Thomas comes to the prohibition against boiling in milk, according to the precept of the Law 'Thou shalt not boil a kid in the milk of his dam' (Exod. 23.9), he states the objection that the literal sense is absurd, and gives an answer which is partly suggested by Maimonides: 'Although the kid that is slain has no perception of the manner in which its flesh is cooked, yet would savour of heartlessness if the dam's milk which was intended for the nourishment of her offspring, were served up on the same dish . . . it might also be said that the Gentiles in celebrating the feats of their idols prepared the flesh of kids in this manner'. In other words, prohibitions of this kind were not irrational at the time. The Law took man as he was, a compound of reason and feeling: it worked on his pity for animals in order to increase his kindness to his fellow men. As Miss Smalley comments: 'Modern study of primitive law has shown that the purpose of these precepts was more complicated than Maimonides and St Thomas thought. But this is a very minor point. St Thomas had brought Christian exegesis to a stage where the Old Testament precepts could be made a subject of scientific study. At the same time, he was giving content to the teaching of the Fathers, that the Old Testament was a history of religious education'.

Another example: in one of his prologues, the introduction to his commentary on the Psalter, he declares his intention, beginning by quoting a text in a traditional way, but using it to open and justify a literal approach: 'In all his works he gave thanks to the Holy One and the Most High, with words of glory' (Ecclus 47.9). This is said of

David, *in a literal sense*, and may be taken to show the cause of his work'.

But the most striking and the most beautiful example of this literal method is his commentary on the book of Job. This work impressed by its novelty and rapidly gained its author great influence. William of Tocco, one of the first historians of St Thomas, wrote: 'Thomas scripsit ... super Job ad litteram, quem nullus doctor litteraliter tentavit exponere propter profunditatem sensus litterae, ad quem nullus potuit pervenere', 'Thomas wrote on the text of Job, what no other doctor attempted to explain because of the depth of the literal sense, to which none of them was able to reach'. This particular work could be used as a typical example of the renewal of his approach and a measure of the distance between Thomas and his predecessors. One of his former commentators, an anonymous canon of St Victor, allowed no 'useful' literal significance to Job: 'Let it be read forthwith of Christ and his Church'. The whole tradition read the book of Job according to St Gregory's *Moralia*. Thomas does not ignore that and he respects this tradition but he wants to comment on the *letter* as such in order to understand the wisdom of Job according to its literary meaning. He exposes with forcefulness his purpose in the *proemium*: 'As in things produced in the course of nature, gradually through the imperfect the perfect is reached, so it happens to man in his understanding of truth ... ' Surely, one could ask, the traditional Gregorian view of the book will be recognized somewhere? Reading through the prologue one waits with some excitement to see what treatment it will get. St Thomas leaves it to the last sentence. He proposes 'to expound this book compendiously according to the literal sense, for blessed Pope Gregory has opened its mysteries to us so subtly and discretely, that it seems nothing more need be added'. There is no irony, no bitter humour, in these lines. Only the affirmation of a clear distinction between different levels of reading and interpretation.

In the introduction to the most recent edition of the *Expositio super Job ad litteram* in the leonine collection, Father Antoine Dondaine has beautifully explained the extraordinary originality of Thomas' approach and the decisive influence of his commentary on medieval exegesis.[11] In particular, he shows how it would be interesting to compare, as he does, the *Guide for the Perplexed* and the commentary of Thomas. As a matter of fact, Thomas does not quote the text of the *Guide* a great deal. Certainly less than his master Albertus Magnus will do after him. But it is clear that he has assimilated and made it his own. He takes his own position, within the framework proposed by Maimonides, and his approach is quite original. Maimonides considered the book of Job as a philosophical discussion on Providence and human suffering. The book shows us that the sufferings of the righteous will end in consolation, and are necessary to teach them wisdom in this life. It exhorts to patience. For Thomas, the aim of the book of Job is first of all to show 'by probable reasons that human affairs are governed by divine Providence'. Patience is not even mentioned. Job is not considered as a sinner. Thomas finds in the book of Job a kind of divine philosophy, a revealed wisdom about Providence and about the presence of God to human action. But what is more striking is the fact that he does that through a very objective analysis of literal sense, word by word, sentence by sentence. Therefore, this commentary appeared as witness to a new exegesis. Father Dondaine wrote in his introduction to the new edition: 'S. Thomas est resté fidèle au genre littéraire qu'il avoit reconnu dans le livre de Job, il a expliqué le sens littéral par des raisons probables. Mais il l'a fait avec une maîtrise et une sûreté qui font de l'*Expositio super Job* le sommet de l'exégèse médiévale . . .' And he goes on: 'Quand on lit les commentaries scripturaires de S. Thomas dans le perspective de l'exégèse moderne, on s'étonne naturellement de leur caractère médiéval; mais si on les aborde à partir du XIIème et du XIIIème siècle, on s'étonne davantage encore de leur modernité'.[12] Such was also the opinion of Miss Smalley: 'Reading these against a background of modern exegesis, one naturally finds the medieval element in them startling; approaching them from the twelfth and thirteenth centuries, one is more startled by their modernity'.[13] It is certain that, in the development which begins at this time towards a new way of approaching the texts, the *Expositio super Job* is one of the most important documents. Teachers and preachers adopted, or tried to adopt, the principles and the method applied in this work by Thomas Aquinas. From this point of view, the commentary on Job has had a considerable influence and should be considered as one of his most inspired works.

So it can be said that, in spite of limitations due to his time and his dependence on tradition, Thomas is one of the protagonists of a return to the *hebraica veritas* of the Scripture which appears in his care for the literal sense.

But it seems to me that, in this direction, we have to pay attention to another dimension of his approach which I would call a subjective one, more precisely a way of sharing the Jewish subjectivity before God and his word. Thomas has emphasized the similarity between the Jewish and the Christian dependence on the gift of a revealing God, and on the way of receiving the Revelation. We find in his treatise on the Old Law a very interesting remark about this similarity. He asks the question: 'Why was the Law given to the Jewish people and not to another?' (Ia-IIae,q.98,a.4). His answer explains the rule of our common dependence to the Word of God. He says: 'It clearly appears that the Fathers have received the Promise and that their descendants have received the Law only in virtue of a gratuitous choice. We read in the book of *Deuteronomy*: 'You heard Him speaking out of fire. For love of your fathers he chose their descendants after them' (4.36)'. This is the biblical and traditional answer, but Thomas goes on, and what he says then is very important for our present reflection: 'If one insists and asks why God has chosen His people and not another to give birth to Christ, we have to answer with Augustine: 'Why does he attract this one and not that one, dont try to judge and decide if you dont want to mistake'. So, Thomas uses what Augustine says about the gift of grace to explain the singular privilege of the gift of the Law. This means that, listening to the Word of God as a gift, Jews and Christians are depending on the initiative of God. And so, there must be a similarity in our attitude and in our way of listening to the word of God. In other words, the Jewish people have given us the Word, which they have heard and which has called them to life; but they have also shown us how to be attentive, to listen, to receive, to keep and to live according to this message. *Shema Israel*. Listen, Hear Israel. We have inherited from the people of the Covenant this invitation and the relation with God which it implies. Without any doubt, this is the deepest way, for a Christian, in his approach to the Bible, to share the *hebraica veritas*.

NOTES

1. C. Spicq, *Esquisse d'une histoire de l'exégèse latine au moyen âge* (Bibliothèque Thomiste 26), Paris (1944).

2. Beryl Smalley, *The Study of the Bible in the Middle Ages*, Oxford (1952) (3rd edn, 1983).

3. H. de Lubac, *Exégèse médiévale, Les quatre sens de l'Ecriture*, Vol. IV: ch. IX, §2, *La 'nouveauté de saint Thomas'* (pp. 285-302), Paris (1964).

4. B. Smalley, *op. cit.*, 3rd edn (1983), Preface, pp. vii-xviii.

5. B. Smalley, 'William of Auvergne, John of La Rochelle and St Thomas Aquinas on the Old Law', in *St Thomas Aquinas, 1274-1974, Commemorative Studies*, Vol. II, Toronto (1974), pp. 11-72.

6. *Ibid.*, p. 68.

7. Y.M.J. Congar, in Festgabe Lortz (1957), pp. 91-96.

8. J. Gribomont, 'Le lien des deux Testaments selon la Théologie de S. Thomas', *Eph. Theol. Lov.* 22 (1946), pp. 80-83.

9. *Op. cit.* p. 315.

10. M.D. Chenu, 'Le sens de l'économie salutaire dans la théologie de S. Thomas', in Festgabe Lortz (1957), p. 71; *idem, Théologie au XIIème siècle*, Paris (1957), p. 208; *idem*, 'La théologie de la loi ancienne selon S. Thomas', in *Revue Thomiste* 61 (1961) pp. 485-97.

11. *Sancti Thomae de Aquino, opera omnia, tom. XXVI, Expositio super Job ad litteram*, A. Dondaine, Praefatio, pp. 420-30.

12. *Ibid.* p. 300.

13. B. Smalley, *op. cit.*, p. 301.

4

'TODAY IF YOU WILL LISTEN TO HIS VOICE' CREATIVE JEWISH EXEGESIS IN HEBREWS 3-4

David Flusser

Before speaking about the special object of my study, I want to put before my readers some common theses about the Jewish Midrashim and their function in the New Testament epistles. Both the Jewish and Christian Midrashim are the fruit of a creative understanding of the Old Testament texts. At least, biblical verses are so very decisive for the making of midrashim because of the reciprocal ties between the text of Scripture and the religious inclination and tendency of their authors and inventors. The Old Testament is the serious point of departure, and the search for truth from the text of scripture was more decisive than in most modern ideologies. Also it should be known that Jewish, as well as the subsequent Christian ancient midrashic homilies are collective enterprises. Being built through the ages, in their complex origin they resemble medieval cathedrals. The reader should know that the midrashic units, both Jewish and those which appear in the New Testament epistles and the Apostolic Fathers, are real homilies whose small particles are interwoven together. Moreover, not only is this development evident, but one must also understand that the extant homilies are but a part, which was created *ad hoc*, from a larger varying system. Because of this specific situation, it became inevitable that the readers, and even the authors of these homilies and midrashim, more often are not able to grasp fully the meaning of all the items which they inherited from their forerunners. The best explanation for the nature of midrashic homilies appears in the *Encyclopaedia Britannica*[1] and describes the complex nature of fungi:

> The body of fungus is underground and consists of a tremendous network of hyphae—the mycelium—spread over a very large area, often several metres (yards) in diameter. This mycelium . . . grows

outward, just below the surface, in a circular fashion. In certain species the hyphal branches at the edge of the mycelium become organized at intervals into elaborate tissues that develop above ground into mushrooms ... The ring marks the periphery of an enormous fungus colony, which, if undisturbed continues to produce even wider rings year after year.

The task of the present study is to exemplify the 'tremendous network of hyphae' of midrashic homilies, both Jewish and Christian.

The main case and the point of departure of the homily in Hebrews 3–4 is Ps. 95.7-11. This passage from Psalms is quoted fully in Heb. 3.7-11, but here we want to start from the two following verses, 'Take care, brethren, lest there be in any of you an evil, unbelieving heart, leading you to fall from the living God. But exhort one another every day, as long as it is called 'today', that none of you may be hardened by the deceitfulness of sin' (Heb. 3.12-13). The command to reprove one another, stems from Lev. 19.17 and it is, among other things, first part (Mt. 18.15-17) of a Matthean passage (Mt. 18.15-20), which, in its present form, is a secondary formulation.[2] The obligation to reprove one's neighbour is already expressed in Ben Sira 19.13-17. Josephus (*Bell.* 2.141), moreover, mentions that the Essenes are obliged 'to be forever lovers of truth and to reprove and expose liars'.[3] So it is no wonder that this obligation appears not only in sources which are near to Essenism[4] but also in the Essene scriptures themselves.[5]

In Heb. 3.13 the command from Lev. 19.17 of reproving one another is connected with the word 'today' from Ps. 95.7. This creative combination of the two biblical verses was made possible because of the name of the place Meribah (as also the following name Massah, Ps. 95.8). It was interpreted according to its proper meaning[6] here in Hebrews, as it was understood in the Greek Old Testament as meaning 'rebellion', and in the Aramaic translations as 'quarrel'. You have to reprove your neighbour today, and not to harden your hearts so as to prolong the quarrel. 'Exhort one another every day, as long as it is called "today"'. Otherwise you will, 'harden your hearts' and also the heart of the one being reproved.

Our interpretation is not a mere hypothesis, as it is closely related to passages from the Dead Sea Scrolls. According to the Damascus Document the members of the Sectarian new covenant are obliged, 'to reprove each man his brother according to the commandment and not to bear rancour from one day to the next' (CD 7.2-3). According to CD 9.2-8, moreover, 'every man of the members of the covenant'—has to reprove his neighbour before witnesses. It is forbidden to abstain from reproving him and to keep silence from one day to the next and to react in anger.[7] But the most important passage is that in the Essene Manual of Discipline 5.25-6.1, each man has, 'to reprove his fellow in truth and humility and loving mercy towards him. He shall not address him in anger or with grumbling or with a stiff neck ... and he shall not hate him ... in his heart; but on the same day he shall reprove him and not heap iniquity upon him. No man shall bring against his fellow a matter before the many which has not been subjected to reproof before witnesses'.[8] The first duty is to rebuke a transgressor oneself, 5.25f. and Mt. 18.15; if this is unsuccessful, take witnesses, 6.1 and Mt. 18.16; if this is also unsuccessful, report it to the assembly, 6.1 and Mt. 18.17.[9]

There is no doubt that the same halakhic midrash is behind Heb. 3.13, and Mt. 18.15-17 and the passages from the Dead Sea Scrolls, even if in Matthew the link with Ps. 95.7 ('today') does not appear. Thus here an Essene origin is probable, but the creative handling of biblical verses is the same as in the rabbinic world. In this case, therefore, the Essene exegesis and the rabbinic midrash do not represent two different worlds—both belong together. This can be seen from Hebrews, chapter 3–4, where most of the motifs are attested in rabbinic literature. All who read this New Testament passage in the light of pertinent rabbinic parallels will easily recognize the connection. Unfortunately, until now, insufficient attention has been paid to the Jewish background of this ancient Christian homily.

In Heb. 3.15, Ps. 95.7b-8 is quoted: 'Today, if you will listen to his voice, do not harden your hearts as in rebellion', and the author asks: 'Who were they that heard and yet were rebellious? Was it not all those who left Egypt under the leadership of Moses?' (Heb. 3.16). This was the wicked 'generation of the wilderness', those who were disobedient and therefore unable to enter because of disbelief. God swore that they would never enter into his rest and so their bodies fell in the wilderness (Heb. 3.17-19). Though they died in the wilderness, is it so certain that they will not inherit the world to come? The opinions are divided.[10] In the debate about this issue the word 'today' and Psalm 95 play a significant role.[11] According to the first view, the generation of the wilderness will not inherit the world to come, because it is written: 'As I swore in my wrath, They shall not enter my rest' (Ps. 95.11). According to the second opinion, the generation of the wilderness will inherit the world to come, but the same biblical verse must be interpreted as follows: In my *wrath* I swore, but I changed my mind, because I am no longer angry. There was also a similar debate concerning the question of whether the ten tribes disappeared forever or whether they will return again in future. Those who held the view that they will not return, based their argument upon Deut. 29.28: 'And the Lord uprooted them from their land in anger and fury and great wrath, and cast them into another land, as at this day'. The opposite opinion has found support in the last word of the same biblical verse: It is said, 'as at this day', i.e. only if their deeds are the same as they were on 'that day'. If so then they will not come, however if they changed their ways—they will come. According to an even more optimistc view the ten tribes will come in any case, as it is written: 'And *in that day* a great trumpet will be blown, and those who were lost in the land of Assyria and those who were driven out to the land of Egypt will come and worship the Lord on the holy mountain at Jerusalem' (Isa. 27.13). So we could see how important were the various meanings of the word 'Today' for the discussion about the future of the generation of the wilderness and of the ten tribes. The same small word 'today' is also the key-word of Hebrews 3–4.

It is important for the interpretation of the passage in Hebrews that according to rabbinic dialectics, the generation of the desert will indeed enter God's rest in the age to come if he will abandon his wrath. In addition, the ten tribes will not return if their deeds will be as wicked as they were on that 'day', but if their deeds will then be good, they will come, 'And to whom did he swear that they should never enter his rest, but to those who were disobedient? So we see that they were unable to enter because of unbelief' (Heb. 3.17-18). Or, in other words, both according to the rabbinic view and to the Epistle to the Hebrews, the future bliss depends upon the condition, expressed in Ps. 95.7-8: 'Today, if you will listen to his voice, do not harden your hearts as in the rebellion' (see Heb. 3.14-15).[12] If you will listen to God's voice today,[13] you will receive God's bliss today (see Heb. 3.13b). There is an eschatological aspect in the biblical 'today' both according to the Epistle to the Hebrews and in the rabbinic sources.

According to a famous legend[14] Rabbi Joshua ben Levi asked the Messiah: 'When will you come?' and the Messiah answered:

'Today'—but he did not come that day. Then the prophet Elijah explained to the rabbi the meaning of the word 'today' in the mouth of the Messiah, 'Today—if you listen to His voice' (Ps. 95.7). According to Rabbi Johanan[15] the salvation is preordained but it will come earlier if repentance will be performed even during one day, as it is written: 'Today, if you will listen to His voice'. The same idea with reference to Ps. 95.7 is also expressed by other Jewish sages.[16] Rabbi Levi connects the idea with the day of the Sabbath,[17] but quotes another biblical verse other than Ps. 95.7. The Messiah will come if all Israel will observe one Sabbath completely, as it is written: 'Today is the sabbath to the Lord' (Exod. 16.25). Here the connection between 'today' and the sabbath is clear enough, but Rabbi Levi also quotes on this occasion Isa. 30.15: 'in returning and rest you shall be saved'.[18] So in rabbinic Judaism the concept of 'today'—or 'one day'—as in Ps. 95.7 is tied with the efficacy of repentance—'today if you will listen to His voice'. It is also connected with the Sabbath, both in the verbal sense and according to eschatological typology. The whole complex could be developed from the very words of Psalm 95. The day of Ps. 95.7 was identified with the Sabbath not only because the sabbath is one day of the week, but also because it is a day of rest, about which we read in the same Psalm (95.11): 'As I swore in my wrath, if[19] they will enter my rest' (see Heb. 4.3). For it is said about the seventh day: 'And God *rested* on the seventh day from all his works' (Gen. 2.2), and in the same Bible it is also written: 'If[20] they will enter my *rest*'. This is the way of creative exegesis in Heb. 4.1-5 and it fits also the method and the spirit of rabbinic Judaism. Moreover, the author of the epistle continues to develop his creative work, 'Since therefore it remains for some to enter it (i.e. the rest), and those who formerly received the good news failed to enter because of disobedience, again he sets a certain day, 'Today', saying through David so long afterward, in the words already quoted, 'Today if you will listen to His voice, do not harden your hearts' ... So then, there remains a sabbath rest for the people of God; for whoever enters God's rest also ceases from his labors as God did from his' (Heb. 4.6-10).

If one knows the rabbinc parallels, the passage from the epistle becomes more meaningful. We were also able to discover the 'mycelium', i.e. the network of exegetical tissues from which both the pertinent rabbinic sayings and the exegetical material in chapters 3-4 of the epistle to the Hebrews became visible. The eschatological—

soteriological—aspect is present both in the rabbinic sphere as well as in the passage of the epistle. It stems, among other things, from the typological interpretation of the Sabbath as the age of future salvation.[21] As we have seen, this eschatological expectation caused—somewhat like a flashback—the connection between the final salvation and the observance of at least one sabbath.[22] As might be expected, though the eschatological dimension is preserved in the New Testament epistle, the obligation to observe the sabbath is omitted. On the other hand the Christian author stresses the Christian faith of his community: 'For we share in Christ, if only we hold our first confidence firm to the end' (Heb. 3.14). Furthermore he acknowledges the difference between the Christians and the non-Christian Jews who died in the wilderness because of unbelief, 'The good news came to us just as to them; but the message which they heard did not benefit them, because it did not meet with faith in the hearers' (Heb. 4.2). The generation of the wilderness was annihilated; they did not enter God's rest. 'For if Joshua had given them rest, God would not speak later of another day. So then, there remains a sabbath rest for the people of God' (Heb. 4.8-9). I venture that the people of God are here those who believe in Christ. Not only here, but in the whole epistle to the Hebrews there is no contrast between Israel and Christianity, but an essential gradation. It seems that as a consequence of this approach, the futuristic aspect of the hope of salvation is somehow weakened, when we compare our passage with its Jewish parallels, but it is not easy to come to firm conclusions on this point.

The aim of the present study was to help the reader to better understand two chapters of the epistle to the Hebrews. This aim could be achieved only with the help of the parallel Jewish texts, both Essene and rabbinic. It is a pity that this work has not been done fully until now, as the two communities, both the church and the synagogue, have co-existed side by side for such a long time. Jewish sources have shown again, that there are motifs which at first are thought to be genuinely Christian, but in reality they are common both to ancient Judaism and Christianity. Jewish studies also have a great deal to gain from such comparative research as has been accomplished in this essay. In our case, I hope that it has helped to clarify the age, the form and the method of ancient Jewish midrashim from a period during which Jewish witnesses are extremely rare. We tried also to show, with the help of one example, that single midrashim once belonged to much larger homiletic systems, similar to those in later collections of homiletic midrashim or to a mycelium of fungi. This fact can be clearly demonstrated not only from the Dead Sea Scrolls but also from the New Testament epistles.

NOTES

The present study is closely connected to my work, 'Messianology and Christology in the Epistle to the Hebrews' which will appear in my new book which will contain a collection of my papers along with a number of new studies, *Judaism and the Origins of Christianity* (Jerusalem, in press).

1. *Macropaedia XII*, Chicago (1979), p. 758, 'Mycota'.

2. See my study 'I am in the Midst of Them', in my *Judaism and the Origins of Christianity* (Jerusalem, in press).

3. 'elenchein proballesthai'. The text is difficult. The first Greek verb means 'to reprove' and it appears in both the Greek translation of Lev. 19.17 and in Mt. 18.15.

4. *Test. Gad* 6.3-6, The Jewish source of the *Didache* 2.7; 4.3 (and in the Christian part, *Didache* 15.3).

5. CD 7.2-3; 9.6-8, cf. 8.5-6 and 9.2-4; and especially 1 QS 5.25–6.2.

6. See P. Billerbeck, *Kommentar zum Neuen Testament*, III, München (1926), p. 684. See also *A Greek-English Lexicon of the New Testament*, W.F. Arndt and F.W. Gingrich, Chicago (1979), p. 621.

7. The passage is probably somehow corrupt, but even so it is pertinent both to Mt. 18.15-17 and to Heb. 3.13.

8. The translation is taken (with corrections) from A.R.C. Leaney, *The Rule of Qumran and its Meaning*, London (1966), p. 176. See also especially the commentary in J. Licht, *The Rule Scroll*, Jerusalem (1965), pp. 136-37 (Hebrew).

9. Leaney, p. 180 and see CD 9:2-4 quoted above.

10. See L. Ginzberg, *The Legends of the Jews*, Philadelphia (1946), vol. I, p. 22, vol. III, pp. 79, 313, vol. V, p. 31, vol. VI, pp. 30, 109.

11. The main passage about the generation of the wilderness and also about the ten tribes is—*Tosefta Sanhedrin* 13.10-12. The text is also quoted in *b. Sanh.* 110b and cf. also *m. Sanh.* 10.3 and ARN, pp. 107-108.

12. According to Heb. 3.7 and 15, the end of Ps. 95.7 ('Today, if you will listen to his voice') belongs to the following verse. However, there is no indication in Jewish sources that such a Jewish tradition existed, though the possibility cannot be excluded.

13. J.H. Bengel, *Gnomon* to Heb. 3.13b is right, when he explains 'donec: quamdiu. Non erit hoc *hodie* perpetuum'.

14. See L. Ginzberg, *op. cit.* above n. 10, vol. IV, p. 22 and vol. VI, p. 333 and W. Bacher, *Die Agada der Palästinensischen Amoräer*, Strassburg (1892), vol. I, p. 190. The passage is in *b. Sanh.* 98a. See also M. Zobel, *Gottes Gesalbter*, Berlin (1938), p. 79.

15. W. Bacher, *ibid.*, p. 33, *Exodus Rabba* 25.15.

16. W. Bacher, *op. cit.*, vol. II, p. 429 (R. Levi) and vol. III, p. 638 (R. Ranhum ben Hayya).

17. W. Bacher, *op. cit.*, vol. II, pp. 314-15.

18. *Ibid.*, n. 8.

19. The meaning is, 'They will never enter my rest', but the first Hebrew participle can be understood as meaning 'if'. This is the way it was translated in the Greek Bible as well as in Heb. 3.11-4.3 and 5. This conditional phrase, 'if they will enter my rest' is important for the right understanding of the midrash in the Epistle to the Hebrews and most probably also for the parallel Jewish midrashim.

20. See the preceding note.

21. See M. Zobel, *op. cit.* above, pp. 69-71 and P. Voltz, *Die Eschatologie der jüdischen Gemeinde*, Tübingen (1934), p. 434, 'Weltsabbat'.

22. See above, n. 18. See also the saying of Rabbi Eliezer in *Mechilta d' Rabbi Ismael*, ed. H.S. Horovitz and I.A. Rabin, Jerusalem (1960), p. 169, lines 10-12 and p. 170, lines 13-15.

5

THE FUNCTION OF THE BIBLE
IN RECENT PROTESTANT ETHICS

Christofer Frey

1. H.G. Gadamer, German philosopher and adept in hermeneutics has restored the meaning of 'prejudice' (*Vorurteil*). According to him *understanding* (*Verstehen*) is not the empathetic process of re-enactment (as propagated by Dilthey), but the *ontological condition of subjectivity itself*. Not in a formal continuum, but in the involvement in the process of life and understanding lies the possibility of understanding itself.[1] Critics of Gadamer have remarked, that the so-called 'fusion' (combination) of the horizons of a text and its exegete presupposes a framework of certain social conditions (Habermas: language in the context of work and interaction;[2] Apel: the apriori of corporate being).[3]

This debate leads to the conclusion that our own *interest* forms a frame of reference in every exegesis. No one can be entirely devoted to the meaning of a text without profound reflection upon his present state in the social world; indeed, the critical impact of the meaning of a text on our present life presupposes critical knowledge of and critical distance from it.[4] *Ethics*—as a science not only of norms, but of the normative patterns of the reality of life—is a contribution to our actual self-enlightenment, and it could also affect the tendencies of contemporary exegesis.[5]

2. Whoever investigates the conditions of *contemporary Protestant Theology*, will find that ethics as a scientific discipline is not very well integrated. One major problem is its relation to dogmatics as a combination and reflection of the institutionalized doctrine of the religious body to which it is related. Dogmaticians frequently regard ethics as a system of moral dicta derived from dogmatic guidelines; and it could be that the majority of exegetes follow this line; they expound as ethics what they discover as moral advice in the

scriptures upon which they concentrate.[6] In contrast to this, an alternative theory has developed which claims ethics to be a 'Wirklichkeitswissenschaft' (a science of the reality of life), a theory of reality either entirely independent of institutionalized dogmatic doctrine or transcending a system of moral dicta, but remaining inside the theological dispute.[7]

The following arguments rely neither on the deductive view nor on the theory of complete independence. As the religious doctrine must respond to the junctures of actual life, it relies on the kind of analysis which is developed by social ethics; as ethics has to debate the groundwork of human life, it will consider the perspectives which religious belief reveals.[8]

3. In recent decades the *theory of ethics* evolved considerably. The impact of moral philosophy on religious ethics cannot be neglected.

3.1 The so called *analytical moral philosophy* emphasizes the independence of the logic of norms. The most general norm, however, the 'moral point of view' (*Baier*)[9] or the most general imperative (*Hare*)[10] produces a reflective equilibrium within a given set of norms;[11] it is not a productive principle in itself. Philosophers therefore tend to rely on certain historical configurations of normative behaviour (*Lebensformen*) which includes a certain perspective of meaningful human life.[12]

3.2 The idea of meaning is closely associated with hermeneutics. Recent elaborations of different scientific methods prove that a basic framework of meaning is not only implied in the process of 'understanding', but also in social sciences, as well as in the paradigms (Kuhn) of the natural sciences.[13] Key concepts as well as basic structures of scientific thought reveal a network of common convictions which count for more than merely subjective opinions, but which are at a notable distance from immovable metaphysical truths. Therefore hermeneutics is not compelled to claim a realm of its own—of 'Verstehen'—beyond explanation ('Erklären').[14] It is compelled, however, to free itself of individualistic tendencies, for it is not the ingenious mind of an exegete but the common sense of his scholarly community which projects itself into a text and participates in the universe of possible meaning which the system of language contains.

3.3 The following passages presuppose that ethics is devoted to the normative implications of such *basic orientations*. What kind of effects could be expected when ethics is integrated into the exegesis of the Bible?

4.1 Quite commonly Protestant ethics accentuate theological programmes and tend to select key words from the scriptures. This is especially evident in the so-called 'Theorie des neuzeitlichen Christentums' (theory of secular Christianity) which claims to propound modern freedom and civil religion on the basis of the New Testament concept of freedom granted by God. All the eschatological contents of the New Testament message are converted to mere symbolism; exegesis is submitted to the special interest of a theory developed to legitimize Christian convictions in a secular world.[15]

4.2 A true dialogue with exegetical endeavours evolves where theological key-concepts are discussed. The so-called *Sermon on the Mount* (Matthew 5-7) is a splendid example of such a possibility.[16]

4.2.1 As long as the *distinction between Law and Gospel* prevailed and ethics was subordinated to the theological ideas of the law, the Sermon on the Mount was generally considered as the proof that man is incapable of obeying the commandments of God by his own power.[17] Law as a theological category could even develop into a substitute for natural theology, a preparation for the revelation of God. The preacher of the Sermon on the Mount was regarded as subordinate to the sphere of divine promise, not to the final self-revelation of God. Jewish belief and ethics, together with it, fell into this more or less negative preparatory stage.

It was D. Bonhoeffer, one of the rare examples of theologically motivated *political* resistance in Protestantism during the Nazi Period, who overthrew this theology in his book *Nachfolge* (Following Christ).[18] The Sermon on the Mount is a breviary of serious possibilities of orientation towards the world.

Two examples may illustrate what he intended. The City on a Hill, visible to everybody (Mt. 5.14), has a political character; this is part of the sanctification of the congregation; and sanctification means that the world has to remain world, and the congregation congregation. But exactly this tension between these two realms should be seen as a testimony to God's claim on the *whole world*.[19]

Most exegetes today will consent to this explanation as consonant with what the Judeo-Christian author Matthew may be assumed to have believed. But the type of exegesis represented by Bonhoeffer resulted from the concrete experience of how Christians neglected the political implications of their reading of the Scriptures.

4.2.2 Another and even more illuminating example is the *commandment of love towards one's enemy*. Bonhoeffer fights against a type of Protestantism which subordinates the love of Christ to patriotism. Pursuing his actual motives he discovers the realistic sense of this commandment: The hearers of the Sermon on the Mount are urged to do the περισσόν, the extraordinary. There is no reciprocity in enmity; though there can be numbers of enemies hostile to those addressed by Jesus, the disciples of Jesus have none.[20] And this is not a matter of purely inner conviction (*Gesinnung*), but a distinction with real consequences.[21]

4.2.3 Insofar as Bonhoeffer insists on real consequences, his ideas are not very distant from those of P. Lapide, a Jewish New Testament scholar, very popular in Germany, who emphasizes the serious intentions of the commandments propounded by the Rabbi of Nazareth. He developed the striking word 'Entfeindung' (de-enemization). All normative statements within the Sermon on the Mount can be compared with radical rabbinical teaching.[22]

But there is, however, a striking difference which turns up in the light of the recent developed understanding of ethics as 'Wirklich-keitswissenschaft'. Normative statements cannot be any longer regarded as mere imperatives, but should be recognized as speech-acts in a much wider sense.[23] Evidently the Rabbi of Nazareth used *hyperbolic phrases*; and in doing so his illocutionary intention was not commanding but disclosing the very being of man. By prohibiting the writing of a bill of divorce he revealed the relation of men to women; by stating 'Ye have heard that it has been said: Thou shalt love thy neighbour, and hate thy enemy'[24] he pointed to a type of common sense he encountered, but certainly not to the Hebrew Bible. Discovering the stratum of social meaning already condensed in the background rules of everyday life implies activating people. But what is his deeper aim?

If his teaching transcends the catalogue of directly intended moral dicta (in which Lapide, for example, is interested) does he then reveal the wicked state of man, as a modern version of Lutheranism thinks? According to Bonheoffer and a number of recent specialists in ethics, Jesus intends to release people from their closed world of a more or less fixed morality; they are encouraged to discover new possibilities of common life. Or, in other terms: He tries to transfer us from the antithesis between the ethics of conviction and the ethics of responsibility, as Weber expressed it, to an ethics of responsibility, of a higher order: to discover responsibility for the fixations of our everyday life (by moral norms and attempts at legitimation) and to overcome their consequences which are so harmful to life. The idea of revelation takes on a very concrete meaning: to reveal new, hitherto hidden or lost possibilities of common, that is, communal life.

These intentions could lead to a new appreciation of Gunkel's 'Sitz in Leben' (the original life-setting of literary statements).[25] The 'Formgeschichte' (historical explanation of literary forms) after Gunkel frequently neglected this original intention. Behind the composition of the Sermon on the Mount we presume a weak and almost expelled community following the Nazarene; perhaps it is still an internal Jewish struggle. The only power of those who are weak is the *reformulation of the conditions* under which the contest is to be interpreted. 'If men define situations as real, they are real in their consequences'.[26]

4.3　The basic question of ethics is not only: 'What should we do?' but 'Who are we?' (the question of identity), 'What is our common world?' and 'From what perspective shall we arrive at a common future?' The last question transcends the bias towards law and gospel in a certain Lutheran tradition; the question of identity overrules the point of view proposed, e.g. by Lapide, who concentrates more or less on single moral statements.

The question of identity is indirectly stressed by a rather neglected study of Karl Elliger: *Das Gesetz Leviticus 18*.[27] The first stratum of this law regulates the sexual order of a large semi-nomadic family; it could be interpreted in a utilitarian way. A second stage (by addition of vv. 17b-23) develops a strict moral taboo, which is supported by the authority of the Lord (. . . I am the Lord). A third stratum (vv. 24-30) aims at ceremonial cleanliness or pollution; it emphasizes the difference from other populations. Norms serve different interests. They reside in the search for identity over against (the case of Leviticus) or together with other people (the case of the Sermon on the Mount).

5.　Hermeneutics includes a frame of reference. Our contemporary social identity (or identities) represents one necessary element of understanding texts from earlier periods. What aspect could be of more than purely historical interest? A basic question of modern social thought is the *identity of collective bodies* as well as the *identity of individuals* in a given set of socially enacted forms of life. It is joined, however, by the question of transformation inside and even beyond a frame of presupposed norms, too.

If we adopt this point of view, the *transformation of socially acquired norms and forms of life* could be regarded as a major theme of biblical writings. This embraces at least two levels: the collection and interpretation of normative statements as ethics in a narrower and more traditional sense, and the regulation by more *general rules*—'norms for norms'—as well as by statements concerning individual and collective identity as the very groundwork of ethics. Part of the latter could be the *commandment of love* and the *Golden Rule*; but certainly it includes statements which clarify the situation of man before God and his fellow man.

Arguing in this way it is no longer possible to maintain an unsophisticated interpretation of law and gospel as a series of normative statements on the one hand (which cannot be fulfilled), and reestablishing statements on the other hand. Some rather crude ideas about Jewish religion spread among Protestants lose their basis.

Hermeneutics has to enlarge its frame of presuppositions of understanding: No longer does the existential scheme guide interpretation, nor is language only the basic condition of subjectivity in the changing and modified horizons of understanding. Language is a universe of possible meaning, which is reflected by man as a social being in active search for and passive experience of identity in all the forms of life and their transformation.

NOTES

The present study is closely connected to my work, 'Messianology and Christology in the Epistle to the Hebrews' which will appear in my new book which will contain a collection of my papers along with a number of new studies, *Judaism and the Origins of Christianity* (Jerusalem, in press).

1. *Macropaedia XII*, Chicago (1979), p. 758, 'Mycota'.

2. See my study 'I am in the Midst of Them', in my *Judaism and the Origins of Christianity* (Jerusalem, in press).

3. 'elenchein proballesthai'. The text is difficult. The first Greek verb means 'to reprove' and it appears in both the Greek translation of Lev. 19.17 and in Mt. 18.15.

4. *Test. Gad* 6.3-6, The Jewish source of the *Didache* 2.7; 4.3 (and in the Christian part, *Didache* 15.3).

5. CD 7.2-3; 9.6-8, cf. 8.5-6 and 9.2-4; and especially 1 QS 5.25–6.2.

6. See P. Billerbeck, *Kommentar zum Neuen Testament*, III, München (1926), p. 684. See also *A Greek-English Lexicon of the New Testament*, W.F. Arndt and F.W. Gingrich, Chicago (1979), p. 621.

7. The passage is probably somehow corrupt, but even so it is pertinent both to Mt. 18.15-17 and to Heb. 3.13.

8. The translation is taken (with corrections) from A.R.C. Leaney, *The Rule of Qumran and its Meaning*, London (1966), p. 176. See also especially the commentary in J. Licht, *The Rule Scroll*, Jerusalem (1965), pp. 136-37 (Hebrew).

9. Leaney, p. 180 and see CD 9:2-4 quoted above.

10. See L. Ginzberg, *The Legends of the Jews*, Philadelphia (1946), vol. I, p. 22, vol. III, pp. 79, 313, vol. V, p. 31, vol. VI, pp. 30, 109.

11. The main passage about the generation of the wilderness and also about the ten tribes is—*Tosefta Sanhedrin* 13.10-12. The text is also quoted in *b. Sanh.* 110b and cf. also *m. Sanh.* 10.3 and ARN, pp. 107-108.

12. According to Heb. 3.7 and 15, the end of Ps. 95.7 ('Today, if you will listen to his voice') belongs to the following verse. However, there is no indication in Jewish sources that such a Jewish tradition existed, though the possibility cannot be excluded.

13. J.H. Bengel, *Gnomon* to Heb. 3.13b is right, when he explains 'donec: quamdiu. Non erit hoc *hodie* perpetuum'.

14. See L. Ginzberg, *op. cit.* above n. 10, vol. IV, p. 22 and vol. VI, p. 333 and W. Bacher, *Die Agada der Palästinensischen Amoräer*, Strassburg (1892), vol. I, p. 190. The passage is in *b. Sanh.* 98a. See also M. Zobel, *Gottes Gesalbter*, Berlin (1938), p. 79.

15. W. Bacher, *ibid.*, p. 33, *Exodus Rabba* 25.15.

16. W. Bacher, *op. cit.*, vol. II, p. 429 (R. Levi) and vol. III, p. 638 (R. Ranhum ben Hayya).

17. W. Bacher, *op. cit.*, vol. II, pp. 314-15.

18. *Ibid.*, n. 8.

19. The meaning is, 'They will never enter my rest', but the first Hebrew participle can be understood as meaning 'if'. This is the way it was translated in the Greek Bible as well as in Heb. 3.11–4.3 and 5. This conditional phrase, 'if they will enter my rest' is important for the right understanding of the midrash in the Epistle to the Hebrews and most probably also for the parallel Jewish midrashim.

20. See the preceding note.

21. See M. Zobel, *op. cit.* above, pp. 69-71 and P. Voltz, *Die Eschatologie der jüdischen Gemeinde*, Tübingen (1934), p. 434, 'Weltsabbat'.

22. See above, n. 18. See also the saying of Rabbi Eliezer in *Mechilta d' Rabbi Ismael*, ed. H.S. Horovitz and I.A. Rabin, Jerusalem (1960), p. 169, lines 10-12 and p. 170, lines 13-15.

23. Cf. the studies of J.L. Austin, *How to Do Things With Words*, Oxford (1962); J.R. Searle, *Speech Acts*, Cambridge (1969).

24. Matthew 5.43.

25. H. Gunkel: 'Die israelitische Literatur', in *Kultur der Gegenwart*, reprint of the second edition (1925): Darmstadt (1963).

26. W.J. and D.S. Thomas, *Person und Sozialverhalten*, ed. E.H. Volkart, Neuwied (1965), p. 114.

27. In *ZAW* 67 (1965), pp. 1-25.

6

THE TECHNIQUE OF QUOTATION AND CITATION
AS AN INTERPRETIVE DEVICE

Yair Hoffman

I

'Creative Exegesis' seems to be both logically and methodologically a self contradiction, a paradox, if not an absurdity. Apparently creativeness stands in opposition to the humility and even submissiveness towards a given text, which is demanded from an exegete. In its very essence exegesis is a serving genre, its end being the correct understanding of a text. Without an important text—in our case a sacred one, the Bible—there is no exegesis as a literary genre. Theoretically, then, it should be the aim of all interpreters to reach the same conclusion, namely, the correct meaning of the text. Accordingly the different philosophical, religious or social views of the exegete should not be reflected in his work, let alone determine his exegetical conclusions. Exegesis is therefore a genre which forces the exegete to give up his own ideas, restricting himself to revealing the ideas of the text, even if he himself does not share them at all. It is therefore an *uncreative* genre.

However, this short description is only correct providing two premises are accepted:

(a) That any given text has only one correct meaning, namely, it is subject to the law of contradiction. This philosophical dilemma will not be dealt with here.[1]

(b) That exegesis is defined as 'a literary genre, which aims at interpreting correctly a given text' (or any other similar definition), and not, e.g. as 'a literary genre which is built around a given text, using it as a hanger for expressing original ideas' or, another possible phrasing—'a conventional disguise for ascribing the exegete's own ideas to a given text'.

These latter two optional 'definitions' would suit the term 'creative exegesis'.[2] Of course, both types of exegesis are legitimate, providing a strict theoretical border is drawn between them; providing one understands that semantically two different meanings are applied here to the same term—exegesis.

A religious believer, facing a sacred text, would obviously approve the superiority of the first kind of interpretation, namely, he would always prefer to rely on the 'real' meaning of the text. Therefore one should not be surprised to realize that sometimes an exegete of a holy text tries to disguise the fact that his exegesis is a 'creative' one. In other cases, one's zeal to find one's own ideas in the sacred text, blurs subconsciously the border between those two different types of exegesis. In both cases such a creative exegete would use in his work the same terminology and the same techniques which are used by non-creative exegetes. One of these techniques which aims at convincing the reader that the expressed idea is based upon the sacred text and not upon the exegete's personal views is *the use of quotations* from the holy scriptures.

It is my purpose in this short paper to raise some points regarding the two major appearances of this technique: The *explicit quotation*, which uses a quotation formula, such as καθὼς γέγραπται; לאמור; כאמור; שנאמר etc. before or after the quoted phrase; and the citation, which is, in a sense, an *implicit quotation*, which does not use any quoting formula.[3] A similar though mentally and formally opposite technique will not be discussed here, namely, the systematic exegesis of a quoted text, such as the *Pesharim* Literature.[4] The whole research is intended to be comprised of two parts, but only outlines of the first one are introduced here, which deals with some post-biblical material; while the *second* part would deal with the material of the Hebrew Bible (HB). This chronologically unexpected order is based upon the methodological idea, that the late sources reveal much more clearly than the HB some poetic features and generic exigencies of the technique of quotation. These characteristics could be very useful while coming to expose the use of the same technique by the HB. Some aspects of this phenomenon in post-biblical sources have been illuminated in different works dealing with quoting formulas within the NT and the Mishna;[5] they were compared with each other as well as with the Dead Sea Scrolls.[6] However, I would like to concentrate here on some other aspects.

II

Here are three post-biblical sources which are chronologically close to each other:

(a) 'From what time in the evening may the "*Shema*" be recited?—
    The School of Shammai say: In the evening all should recline when
    they recite, but in the morning they should stand up *for it is written*
    "and when thou liest down and when thou risest up" (Deut. 6.7).
    But the School of Hillel say: They may recite it every one in his
    own way, *for it is written* "and when thou liest down" etc.? It
    means the time when men usually lie down and the time when men
    usually rise up' (Mishna *Berachot* [Benedictions] I, 3. Trans. by
    Danby).[7]

(b) 'The beginning of the gospel of Jesus Christ (the son of God) *as it is
    written in the prophets* "behold I send my messenger before thy face
    who shall prepare the way. The voice of one crying in the
    wilderness, make ye ready the way of the Lord, make his paths
    straight": John did baptize in the wilderness and preach the
    baptism' (Mark 1.1-3).[8]

(c) 'But he (Satan) saith to me: "Art thou Eve?" and I said to him: "I
    am". "What art thou doing in Paradise?" And I said to him: "God
    set us to guard and to eat of it". The Devil answered through the
    mouth of the Serpent: "Ye do well but ye do not eat of every plant"
    and I said: "Yea, we eat of all save one only, which is in the midst of
    Paradise, concerning which God charged us not to eat of it. For he
    said to us: on the day on which ye eat of it ye shall die the death"'
    (*Adam and Eve* 17).[9]

In these three passages quotations from the scriptures are used, yet
the difference is clear: The Mishna and the NT use explicit
quotations, whereas the book of *Adam and Eve*, while citing Gen.
2.17 and 3.2, does not use any introductory formula. Can these
examples be regarded as representative of the Mishna, the NT and
the Apocrypha as far as the technique of quotation is concerned? A
positive answer can surely be given regarding the Mishna and the
NT: their use of HB explicit quotations is well-known. It is suggested
that such a use might be a consequence of the *polemic* character of
these two sources. But how about the example from the Apocrypha?
Is it a typical representative one? Here is another example from
Jubilees 3.3-4:

> And on these five days Adam saw all these, male and female,
> according to every kind that was on the earth, but he was alone and

> found no helpmate for him. And Lord said unto us: It is not good
> that the man should be alone: let us make a helpmate for him.

Once again, just as in *Adam and Eve* the book of Genesis is quoted
with no introducing formula. In *Jubilees* 14 a great portion of
Genesis 15 is quoted similarly. Many other examples of this
technique from *Jubilees* can easily be shown, which justifies the
generalization that this is the poetic norm of *Jubilees*. The same
holds true for the *Assumption of Moses*; *The Testament of the Twelve
Patriarchs*; *The Epistle of Jeremiah*; *Prayer of Manasses*; Baruch; *2
Baruch*; *Enoch* and many other apocrypha: none of them uses a
quotation formula while quoting the HB.[10] I suggest that The
tendency of the major bulk of the Apocrypha not to make use of
explicit quotations is to be explained as a *generic exigency*. In some of
the above mentioned books an explicit quotation even from the
Pentateuch was logically impossible, since they are Pseudepigraphs,
which pretended to have been composed *before* the Peutateuch—
Adam and Eve; *Enoch*; *Jubilees* etc. Hence, the genre dictated the
absence of the quoting formulas while citing the Pentateuch.[11]
Nevertheless, these books were well aware of the need to derive their
teaching from holy scriptures, and therefore they make use of
implicit quotations—namely, citations. In other cases they apply a
different method, using a quotation formula and yet managing to
avoid the trap of anachronism. A good example would be passages
such as *Jub.* 50.13:

> The man who does any of these things on the *Shabbat* shall
> die.... *as it is written* in the tablets which He gave into my
> hands...

Here, instead of mentioning the still 'non-existent' Book of Moses,
the author uses a quotation formula which refers to mysterious
'Tablets of Heaven'. This tactic, namely quoting explicitly non-
existent sources, is an evidence of the author's feeling that his
argument should be rather based upon explicit scriptures.This
recognition, at least once, caused him an acute error, when, while
using an excited polemic style, the author forgets his pseudepigraphic
identity and puts into God's angel's mouth the following human
words:

> For I know and from henceforth will I declare it unto thee, *and it is
> not of my own devising*; for the book lies written before me, and on
> the heavenly tablets the division of the day is ordained (6.35).

The suggested explanation for the absence of explicit biblical quotations in the pseudepigraphs as a generic exigency does not explain the fact that the same literary method is also shared by pseudepigraphs which could have quoted the Pentateuch explicitly since their hero was supposed to have lived *after the Torah* had already been written by Moses, e.g. *The Epistle of Jeremiah*; Baruch; *The Apocalypse of Ezra* etc. Why, then, in spite of their awareness of the importance of explicit quotations do they not quote explicitly? Two possible—not necessarily alternative—answers can be proposed:

(a) Those pseudepigraphs whose heroes are the most ancient personalities—*Adam and Eve, Enoch* etc.—established a literary convention of implicit citations, which determined the character of the other pseudepigraphs.

(b) The quotation formula sharpens the distinction between two kinds of texts of different importance: the canonical quoted text and the non-canonical text. Since some pseudepigraphs claimed to have been holy books, it was their prime interest to avoid such a distinction and therefore they preferred not to use quoting formulas. This ambition to be regarded holy scripture while a sealed canon had already been in existence is well attested in the final passage of the *Ezra Apocalpyse*, which claims to be one of the seventy hidden holy scriptures which were allowed by God only to the wise people. However, there is still the other side of the coin: Since by being explicitly quoted a book is gaining importance and perhaps even a holy status, some pseudepigraphs used explicit quotations in order to advance their own sectarian views and religious standing. Hence the book of *Enoch* is quoted explicitly in some pseudepigraphs, e.g.: 'For the house which the Lord shall choose shall be called Jerusalem, as is *contained in the Book of Enoch* the righteous' (*Testament of Levi* 10.5). I have *found it written in the Books of my forefathers and in the words of Enoch* and in the words of Noah (*Jubilees* 21.10). Then things I say unto you, my children, for I have read in the *writings of Enoch* that you yourselves also shall depart from the Lord (*Testament of Naphtali* 4.1).

The absence of explicit biblical quotations in Apocrypha such as Sirach; *The Words of Job*; Wisdom of Solomon; *Psalms of Solomon* and others calls for a different explanation. They simply follow the biblical generic convention of the Wisdom and Psalms Literature of avoiding explicit quotations. Here is one example of a citation in Sirach and one in Ecclesiastes. After praising the Wisdom in a style very similar to Proverbs 8 Sirach writes:

> All these things are the book of the covenant of God Most High, the Law which Moses commanded to us an heritage for the assemblies of Jacob (a citation from Deut. 33.4).

In Eccl. 5.4 another verse from Deuteronomy is cited implicitly and interpreted.

> When thou vowest a vow unto God defer not to pay it. For he hath no pleasure in fools: pay that which thou hast vowed' (referring to Deut. 23.22).

I will not elaborate here on the DSS, yet they should not be completely overlooked. These sectarians recognized the two techniques of quoting and were well aware both of their literary advantages and limitations. The advantages as an exegetical device are clear; one of the disadvantages has been pointed out above. Another one is the difficulty in finding an appropriate quotation for every new, original idea. Still another limitation is of a literary character. The repetition of quoting formulas disturbs the fluency of the composition. I suggest that these two limitations explain the absence of quotations and citations in the major part of the War Scroll, which uses quotations only in two consecutive pages (10-11) of the 19 pages of the whole scroll, when the priest is quoting explicitly (a) the laws of the war from Deuteronomy 20; and (b) the perhaps most frequently cited biblical phrase of that period's literature—Num. 24.17, 'there shall come a star from Jacob'.

The technique of explicit quotation is widely used in the Damascus Scroll, while citation is the very essence of the Temple Scroll. This unique pseudepigraph is composed, as is well known, of two elements: an original composition about the future temple, the holy city, etc., and a mosaic work of successive, continuous citations from the Pentateuch.[12] This construction[13] was probably determined at least partly by two reasons: (a) The necessity and wish to be based upon the holy scriptures. (b) The awareness of the two above mentioned limitations of the explicit quotation, with the addition of another shortcoming of this technique: The quoting formula stresses the separation between the quoted sacred text and its suggested

exegesis, triggers the attention of the reader, and thus might evoke a
critical and suspicious reaction. This undesired possible response is
avoided in the Temple Scroll by the rearrangement of the pentateuchal
passages, without using any external phrases. Here is one example:
In 52.6 it is written:

ושור ושה אותו ואת בנו לא תזבח ביום אחד

ולא תכה אם על בנים

Two verses have been modified and combined here: Lev. 22.28—
ושור או שה אותו ואת בנו לא תשחטו ביום אחד ('and an ox or a lamb ye
shall not slaughter it and its young in one day') is interpreted by a
mixed citation of Gen. 32.12 —פן יבוא והכני אם על בנים ('lest he will
come and smite me, the mother with the children') and Deut. 22.6—
לא תקח האם על הבנים ('thou shall not take the mother with the
sons').

By this the author expresses his mind in a legal controversy, which
is dealt with in the Talmud[14] and is partly reflected in the Onkelos
Targum and in the Septuagint. By changing לא תשחטו (thou shall not
slaughter) to לא תזבח (thou shall not sacrifice) he makes clear, that
the prohibition refers only to a sanctified slaughtering, and not to a
profane one. By the addition of ולא תכה אם על בנים not only does he
give a moral explanation to the law, but suggests that שור או שה
(male ox or sheep) should be interpreted as females—namely cow
and ewe. The same legal interpretation is expressed by Onkelos, who
translated Lev. 22.28 ותורתא או שיתא לה ולברה לא תכסון ביומא חד, and
the same translation is found in the LXX—καὶ μόσχον ἢ πρόβατον
αὐτὴν καὶ τὰ παιδία αὐτῆς οὐ σφάξεις ἐν ἡμέρᾳ μίᾳ.[15]

So much for the delineation of some characteristics of the
technique of quotations in the post-biblical literature. I believe that
our conclusions could serve as *working hypotheses* for the study of the
use of biblical and non-biblical quotations. Let me outline briefly
such possible working hypotheses.
(1) The use of quotations in the HB is evidence for a polemic
style.[16]
(2) Sometimes a quoting formula is used, referring to non-existent
sources.[17]
(3) The Deuteronomic school was the first to make a sophisticated
use of biblical quotations:

   (a)   It uses implicitly previous biblical sources (e.g. J; E).
   (b)   It uses explicit quotations while referring to *deuteronomic*

> sources, e.g. Deut. 24.16 is quoted explicitly in 1 Kgs 14.6;
> Deuteronomy 27 is quoted in Josh. 8.31.[18]

(4) Sometimes biblical sources are referred to only implicitly since
they were not yet recognized as holy, let alone canonical.
(5) Some biblical genres—the Wisdom and Psalmodic literature—do
not use explicit quotations following an international literary
tradition.

NOTES

1. See I. Heinemann, *Darchey Ha'aggada*, 2nd edn, Jerusalem (1974),
pp. 7-13 (Heb.).
2. Heinemann coined the term 'organic thinking' to express the mentality
behind this kind of exegesis. See *op. cit.*, pp. 8-10.
3. The term 'explicit quotation' is taken from J.A. Fitzmyer, 'The Use of
Explicit O.T. Quotations in Qumran Literature and in the N.T.', *NTS* 7
(1960), pp. 297-333.
4. A recent study of this genre is B. Nitzan, *Pesher Habakkuk* (1QpHab),
Jerusalem (1986), (Heb.). The methods and techniques of this exegetical
genre are discussed on pp. 29-80.
5. B.M. Metzger, 'The Formulas Introducing Quotations of Scriptures in
the N.T. and the Mishna', *JBL* 70 (1951), pp. 297-307.
6. See: J.A. Fitzmyer, *op. cit.* n. 3; M. Burrows, 'The Meaning of
in DSH', *VT* 2 (1952) pp. 255-60.
7. H. Danby, *The Mishnah*, translated from the Hebrew, London
(1938).
8. This version is quoted here, and not the one which mentions Isaiah, in
order to avoid the problem of citing Malachi first, and only later Isaiah.
9. R.H. Charles, *The Apocrypha and Pseudepigrapha of the O.T.*, I-II,
Oxford (1913). All the passages from the Apocrypha and Pseudepigrapha in
this paper are taken from Charles's edition.
10. This is not the case in *Aristeas* 155, which uses a quoting formula while
referring to Deut. 7.18-19. A. Kahana, *Hasefarim Hahizonim II* (Heb.), Tel
Aviv (1959), p. 49, regards this as the first time in the Jewish post HB
literature in which this method of quotation is applied. One quoting formula
is found in 1 Macc. 3.56 (referring to Deut. 20.5); one in 2 Macc. 10.26
(referring to Exod. 23.22) and few quotations in *4 Macc.* I shall not elaborate
here on these cases. It is possible that the use of explicit quotations here is
due to the Hellenistic influence in these books.
11. Some exigencies of the Pseudepigraphic genre are revealed and

discussed in Y. Hoffman, 'Exigencies of Genre in Deuteronomy' (Heb.), *Shenaton, an Annual for Biblical and Ancient Near Eastern Studies*, ed. M. Weinfeld, vols. V-VI, Jerusalem (1978-79), pp. 41-54.

12. A thorough discussion of this scroll with the complete and interpreted text is Y. Yadin, *The Temple Scroll*, Jerusalem (1977).

13. In a way, this construction is similar to the construction of Deuteronomy, which makes use of many citations from the JE documents. See S.R. Driver, *Deuteronomy*, 3rd edn, ICC, Edinburgh (1902), pp. iii-xix.

14. 'What is this dispute between Hananiah and the Rabbis? It was taught: The law of It and its young applies to the female parent only and not to the male. Hananiah says it applies both to the male and female parent. What is the reason of the Rabbis? It was taught: I might have said that the law of 'It and its young' applies to both male and female parents; there is, however, an argument against this' etc. (*Hulin*, 78b-79a; *The Babylonian Talmud*, trans. by Rabbi I. Epstein, London [1948]).

15. A similar translation is preferred also by the AKJV—'And whether it be cow or ewe ye shall not kill it and her young both in one day'.

16. See e.g. Ezek. 11.15; 18.2.

17. E.g. 2 Chron. 12.15; 13.22. The assumption that at least some of the sources mentioned by the Chronicler are 'non-existent' sources is raised by E.L. Curtis, *The Book of Chronicles*, ICC, Edinburgh (1910), p. 24. He is quoting Torrey saying—'It is time that scholars were done with this phantom 'source' of which the internal evidence is absolutely lacking'.

18. The only exact explicit quotation of a prophecy is found in the deuteronomistic story in Jer. 26.18, referring to Mic. 3.12.

7

MAIMONIDES' EXEGESIS OF THE BOOK OF JOB

J.S. Levinger

Unlike Nachmanides or Gersonides, Moses Maimonides, the great philosopher and codifier of Jewish law of the twelfth century, did not write a special commentary on the book of Job, but merely devoted to it two chapters in his *Guide for the Perplexed*: chs. 22 and 23 of the third part. In these two chapters, however, he claims to have truly encompassed and explained the entire book. Chapter 22 is mainly devoted to the 'framework story' contained in the first two chapters of the book of Job, which could also be called the prologue to the book, whereas ch. 23 is devoted to the discussion between Job and his friends: Eliphaz the Temanite, Bildad the Shuhite and Zophar the Nàamite, to the long speech of Elihu the son of Barachel the Buzite, and finally to the revelation of God to Job in chs. 38-41.

In order to understand Maimonides' exegesis of the 'framework story' it is vital to realize that, according to Maimonides, true perfection does not consist of moral virtue but rather of rational and intellectual excellence. It is more important to be wise than to be just. This intrinsic principle is basic to his philosophy. Genuine perfection consists of the conception of intelligibles, which teach us true opinions concerning divine matters.

In light of this, let us now turn to the first verse of the book of Job:

אִישׁ הָיָה בְאֶרֶץ עוּץ אִיּוֹב שְׁמוֹ וְהָיָה הָאִישׁ הַהוּא תָּם וְיָשָׁר יְרֵא אֱלֹהִים וְסָר מֵרָע

> There was a man in the land of Uz whose name was Job; and that man was blameless and upright, one who feared God and eschewed evil.

Seemingly, a quite remarkable person! But indeed only a fool would think so, for a wise person would seek in this verse that which is not mentioned, namely that he was wise, intelligent and learned.

Indeed, the main perfection of a human being does not appear in this verse, so if it is now read as it ought to be, one can understand that Job was not really perfect at all, because he was lacking in wisdom. This lack of wisdom constitutes a privation (στέρησις, *privatio*) and this privation was Satan. According to Maimonides, Satan symbolizes the absence of intellect in Job's personality.

Hints of this identification of Satan with privation are given in verses 6 and 7 of the first chapter. In v. 6, it is written:

ויהי היום ויבאו בני האלהים להתיצב על ה' ויבא גם השטן בתוכם

One day the sons of God came to present themselves before the Lord and Satan came among them.

Maimonides emphasizes that it is not written that the sons of the Lord *and Satan* came to present themselves before the Lord, but that the sons of God came to present themselves before the Lord and *Satan came among them*. This expression 'came among them' is used because Satan is not a positive element that can appear by itself but rather something negative that can only appear among other elements. In other words, it is an absence of something, a privation.

The other allusion to the identification of Satan with privation is given in the following verse, v. 7. There it is written:

ויאמר ה' אל השטן מאין תבא, ויען השטן את ה' ויאמר משוט בארץ ומהתהלך בה.

The Lord said to Satan; whence have you come and Satan answered the Lord, from going to and fro on the earth and from walking up and down on it.

Satan walks 'on the earth' because only on earth is there privation. In the spheres, where everything is already perfect, there is no privation, and no absence of anything.

Furthermore, if Job were wise, there would be no Satan, for wisdom and Satan are contraries. Moreover Job would not have suffered. The wise know that happiness is included in intellectual perfection, so nothing could harm Job's happiness; neither the loss of his propery nor the loss of his children, nor his health. Something might perhaps injure him but he would never really suffer.

Turning now to Mamonides' exegesis of the main part of the book of Job, namely the discussion between Job and his friends. According to chapter 23, we see that previously in chapter 17, Maimonides presented five opinions on providence. It is crucial to understand these opinions in order to understand the opinions held by the people in the book of Job.

The first opinion is that of Epicurus, according to whom there is neither providence nor laws of nature. Everything is generated by pure chance.

The second opinion is that of Aristotle. In his opinion, insofar as there are laws of nature there is also providence. Everything outside of the earth, the spheres and whatever is contained in them, is regulated by absolute laws of nature and hence by the providence of God. But on earth, providence pertains only to the species and not to any particular thing—neither to particular animals nor to particular men. The species of man does have providence but no individual man does.

The third opinion is that of the Islamic sect, the Ash'ariyya. According to them, nothing is regulated by laws of nature; instead, everything is regulated only by providence and everything, even the behaviour of man, has been everlastingly decreed. Accordingly there is also no reward or punishment by God, the latter making everything arbitrary without being subjected to or constrained by any laws.

The fourth opinion is held by the Mu'tazila, another Islamic sect. Their opinion is very similar to that of the Ash'ariyya. They, too, deny the existence of the laws of nature and believe that every particular thing is regulated by providence. however, according to them, God regulates everything with wisdom. It is therefore possible that somebody might suffer throughout his life without having committed any sins but this man will get his compensation in the next world, in the world to come. This is true not only for mankind but also for animals; a mouse that suffers because a cat is constantly chasing it will get its reward in the world to come.

The fifth opinion is the generally accepted opinion of Judaism. According to Maimonides' interpretation, this opinion is very similar to that of Aristotle, but in it, providence is combined with the laws of nature. Thus on earth only the species and not particular things are regulated by providence with the sole exception of mankind. In the case of mankind it is not only the species that has providence but also the individual person. Providence is regulated by the principle of justice; hence everything that happens to main is either reward or punishment for his preceding behaviour. This generally accepted opinion is not, however, identical to the personal opinions of

Maimonides himself, which are very subtly alluded to and hinted at in chs. 18 and 51 of the third part, thus enabling only the very learned to discern them. In Maimonides' own opinion providence follows the intellect, and therefore only the wise will enjoy providence. Indeed, there are levels of providence and only men with high degrees of intellect will have high degrees of providence. Only the man who is totally concentrated on intellectual topics can have absolute providence. Only during those moments in which he is totally concentrated on intellectual topics will he suffer no harm. This is apparently no miracle but a pure psychological fact: He will enjoy his study so much that he will not feel any harm. However, see the letter of Samuel Ibn Tibbon in *HUCA* 11 (1936), pp. 353-62.

Five opinions are also represented in the book of Job, but these opinions are not the same five as found in ch. 17. The opinion of Epicurus is not represented at all, possibly because, as Maimonides remarks in ch. 17, 'Aristotle has already demonstrated that this opinion is inadmissible'.

Job represents the opinion of Aristotle, which, according to Maimonides, is the highest opinion that can be represented by somebody who is suffering so much and knows that he has done no evil. Eliphaz represents the common opinion of Judaism, and he is therefore convinced that Job has committed great sins. Bildad represents the opinion of Mu'tazila, namely that of compensation, which is expressed by him in the verse (Job 8.7):

והיה ראשיתך מצער ואחריתך ישגה מאד

> And though your beginning is small your future will be very great.

Zophar represents the opinion of Ash'ariyya, although unlike the case of Bildad, Maimonides was unable to find in Zophar's speeches any convincing verse to represent the opinion as given in his exegesis.

However, ch. 32 of the book of Job suddenly produces a 'deus ex machina', a new figure in the person of Elihu the son of Barachel the Buzite, a heretofore unmentioned visitor to Job. In the beginning of his lengthy speech, which fills an entire chapter, he claims that the three old men, Eliphaz, Bildad and Zophar, are foolish, and only he, the young man, is wise. He then continues to speak incomprehensibly of many things. But according to Maimonides, this is precisely the person who secretly represents the opinion of Maimonides himself.

Elihu deliberately speaks profusely so that only very few will be able to ascertain his true opinion, which is contained in two verses. First in Job 33.23:

אם יש עליו מלאך מליץ אחד מני אלף להגיד לאדם ישרו, ויחננו ויאמר פדעהו מרדת שחת מצאתי כפר

> If there be for him an angel, a mediator, one of a thousand, to declare to man what is right for him: Then he will be gracious to him and will say deliver him from going down to the pit: I have found a ransom.

and secondly, in the same chapter, v. 29:

הן כל אלה יפעל אל פעמים שלש עם גבר

> Behold God does all things twice or three times with a man.

Maimonides does not explain the hint given in these verses. But it is very clear. At the end of the previous chapter (22), he has already explained that in the same way as Satan (who is the evil inclination in man) is called an angel, so too is the good inclination in man's soul called an angel. According to Maimonides, however, the good inclination in the soul is the intellect. Thus Elihu is saying: Only the intellect may save you, but this relief will not endure forever but only 'twice or three times with a man' that is in those certain moments in which man is so concentrated on high intellectual topics that he is not able to feel his suffering at all.

The final solution to the problem of Job the man is to be found, according to Maimonides, in the revelation of God in chs. 38-41 of the book of Job. These chapters contain descriptions of natural phenomena which symbolize the true answer to his problem. Job began to study science, physics and biology, which are, in the view of both Maimonides the Aristotelian philosophers, the gates to wisdom. Job has become wise and so now responds with the words (Job 42.5):

לשמע אזן שמעתיך ועתה עיני ראתך, על כן אמאס ונחמתי על עפר ואפר

> I had heard of thee by the hearing of the ear, but now my eyes see thee. Therefore I despise myself and repent in dust and ashes.

Maimonides interprets this to mean: Before I studied science I had only heard of you by tradition, but now I recognize you scientifically; therefore I am happy in spite of my sitting in dust and ashes. I no longer suffer despite all that happened to me with the loss of my property, my children and my health.

The last chapter of Job is not explained by Maimonides but his opinion of it is quite clear. He infers that this chapter constitutes merely a kind of 'happy-end' for the masses who need some form of compensation and do not understand that to a wise person, as Job has now become, such material goods no longer command any relevance or importance. According to several commentators on Maimonides, that this chapter was written only for foolish people is alluded to in the following verse (Job 42.15):

ולא נמצא נשים יפות כבנות איוב בכל הארץ

And in the whole of the world there were no women so beautiful as the daughters of Job.

Surely only simple folk could be satisfied with the notion of daughters travelling around the world as beauty queens, but certainly not men of the calibre of Job after his studying and subsequent philosophical recognition of God.

Our sole intention in the previous discourse was to present a very general overview on Maimonides' exegesis of the book of Job without going into excess detail, much less into all the problems this interpretation leaves open. At this conference, intended not for the professional scholar in Maimonidean research, I wish to limit myself to one of the problematic issues which may be of interest to those present.

Maimonides interprets the essence of Satan as privation, but refrains totally from explaining the term בני אלהים (sons of God), who according to the 'framework story' of the book of Job came together with Satan to present themselves before the Lord. Indeed, from the words of Maimonides it may be understood that contrary to Satan, who is nothing more than privation, the sons of God are positive objects, apparently emanating from godliness; however Maimonides does not explain their essence and does not refer at all to the term 'sons of God' as used by the author. Moreover, the first chapters of the first part of the *Guide for the Perplexed* are devoted to the different denotations of words used by the Bible to refer to God or to the connection with God. In the seventh chapter he promises to devote a special discussion to the various denotations of the word בן (son). Such a discussion might have shed some light on the exact meaning of the expression 'sons of God' as it appears in the 'framework story' of Job, but unfortunately, Maimonides did not keep his promise and of all the semantic discussions in the first part of the *Guide for the Perplexed*, not one deals with the word 'son'. Indeed, this is the only promise in the entire *Guide for the Perplexed* that Maimonides fails to keep, and this might quite possibly be far from coincidental. We may assume that Maimonides refrains from explaining the term 'son' because he did not wish to pave the way to a philosophical interpretation of the central tenet of Christianity, namely Jesus as the son of God. We may assume that instead of the chapter which deals with the equivocal term 'son' Maimonides wrote the short chapter 14 which deals with the word אדם (man), since most of the verses in it refer to the word בן (son) or the word בני (the sons of). The last two verses even refer to the term בני האלהים (sons of God) of Gen. 6.2 and the term בני עליון (sons of the Most High) in Ps. 82.6 (the expression which comes before the verse אכן כאדם תמותון 'nevertheless you will die like men', which is mentioned explicitly but without an explanation of the term 'sons of the Most High' in the former verse, the meaning given by Maimonides to the term 'men' in the latter verse could not be understood). This chapter, appearing instead of the chapter dealing with the term 'son' also explains its strange position between chapter 13, which deals with the term עמידה (standing) and chapter 15, which deals with the roots יצב and נצב (to stand or to present oneself). The explanation for this phenomenon is that in the 'framework story' of the book of Job a term formed from the root יצב or נצב always follows the term בני האלהים (sons of God):

ויבאו בני האלהים להתיצב על הי

The sons of God came to present themselves before the Lord (Job 1.6 and 2.1)

BIBLIOGRAPHY

L. Strauss, 'Der Ort der Vorsehungslehre nach der Ansicht Maimonides' *MGWJ* 81 (1936), pp. 93-105; *ibid.*, *Persecution and the Art of Writing*, Glencoe (1952), pp. 63-64; Z. Diesendruck, 'Samuel and Moses Ibn Tibbon on Maimonides' Theory of Providence', *HUCA* 11 (1936), pp. 341-66; L.S. Kravitz, 'Maimonides and Job', *HUCA* 38 (1967), pp. 149-58; A.J. Reines,

'Maimonides' Concept of Providence and Theodicy', *HUCA* 43 (1972), pp. 169-206; M.D. Yaffe, 'Providence in Medieval Aristotelianism; Moses Maimonides and Thomas Aquinas on the Book of Job', *HST* 20-21 (1979-80), pp. 62-74; H. Kahser, 'Job's Image and Opinions in Maimonides' (Hebrew), *Da'at* 15 (1985), pp. 81-87.

8

LITERARY INDIVIDUALITY AS A PROBLEM OF HERMENEUTICS IN THE HEBREW BIBLE

Rüdiger Liwak

In dealing with that which is 'many and various' (Heb. 1.1), it would be asking too much of a single rubric fully to define the subject in question. However, such a rubric may prove useful as a preliminary aid to orientation and understanding.

'Book religion'[1] is one such rubric, and it has often been employed in an attempt to characterize Israelite religion. Nor are these efforts inaccurate, at least to the extent that Israel's literary heritage provided, if not throughout her history, then for at least much of it, both the preconditions and essential possibilities of Israelite religious life.

Of course, our rubric finds its limitations already, when we consider the structure of the Hebrew Bible, since this work resembles less a book than an entire library in which some determinative chronological and factual criteria have governed the order and arrangement of its parts. Furthermore, the various sections are only partially supplied with the names of their (even putative) authors, and they practically never contain references to their being 'revised editions'.

The problem of the successive and often complicated developmental history of these books was first recognised by critical research.[2] As is well known, this discovery has led to a variety of conclusions in connection with the prophetic books. Here the distinction between the 'ipsissima verba' of the prophet whose name designates a given book and the words of unknown additional authors has been highly significant.

Where the earlier literary criticism divided the contents of a prophetic book into 'authentic' and 'inauthentic' sections, the more recent disciplines of form and tradition history have devoted their attention to the supra-individual constant factors, and to their appropriation and evaluation. Most recently, criticism has tended to study the compositional and redactional history of the structure of individual books and parts of books, a procedure which has given special exegetical weight to the final form of the text.

During the first-mentioned phase of biblical criticism, the developmental history of a given book was primarily understood as the result of individual contributions.[3] The latest phase, however, has regarded this history as the product of a common or group enterprise.[4] Form, Gattungs, and tradition history play a rôle in both of the previously mentioned positions, in that they acknowledge in the search for text types and typical texts a reciprocal relation between the collective and the individual aspects of the text.[5] Thus the hermeneutical contradictions are relativized, although this does not do away with the literary and theological tensions contained within many of the prophetic books.

In his *Contra Apionem* the Jewish historian Flavius Josephus maintains that during the period between Moses and Artaxerxes (I) the prophets had written down the events of their own times.[6] This sharply asserts the notion of literary individuality, a notion which Josephus naturally associated with divine inspiration of the prophets, and which he defended against misrepresentation by means of the repeated injunction not to add anything to or take away anything from their works.[7] The question is whether this understanding of the matter had established itself already in the time of the prophets.

The concept of literary individuality naturally presupposes a generalized concept of individuality as such. In order to understand and explain these features, one ought not to employ the individualizing simplifications of the Western traditions of Idealism and Romanticism. Nor, for that matter, should one adopt the postulate of a collective interpretation, in which some sort of 'greater I/ego' speaks for the organisms of the family, clan or tribe.

In the Hebrew Bible, about 1400 names are mentioned and approximately 2400 individuals of whom often not much more than their names is known. Their names, however, refer only rarely to some larger social unit; as a rule, both the name-giver and the name-bearer are individuals.[8] This experience of individuality is further reflected in the region of religious structures, since theophoric names, individual laments, and the religion of the patriarchs point to a 'persönliche Frömmigkeit' or 'personal religion'[9] which contrasts the religious institutions of the people with the official religion. It is additionally questionable whether the patriarchal narratives attempt to relate a personalized history of the Israelite tribes or folk. Considered as a historical model, the genealogy attempts to represent and legitimate the origins of the people's history via the use of ancestors who themselves possessed the only personal history deserving of the name.[10] However, this does not mean that in such genealogies we are confronted by a personal history which runs an individual course. Rather, we have always to do with the family or clan whose fortunes are invariably interwoven with the doings of the individual and via whom the borderlines of social solidarity are demarcated. Although the concept of Corporate Personality implies this, this does not signify any priority of the community as acting subject.

The notion of Corporate Personality may be traced back to ethnological theories which attempted to describe the mentality of 'pre-logical' thought. This concept is not adequate to describe Israelite experience.[11] In Israel the individual stood in a relation to a society which protected him and punished him and furnished him with elbowroom for his enterprises. And these enterprises had consequences for society, just as they in turn were regulated by it. Fundamental to this is the concept that a connection existed between the activities of the individual and the fate of his surroundings.[12]

During the time in which the prophets were active, the general forces governing the small-farming, small business and soil-exploitation of the society lost their power and the inhabitants of Israel and Judah suffered a collective catastrophe. During this period, a new perspective arose which freed the individual from the collective guilt relation which was thought to embrace numerous generations. The relationship between act and consequence became individualized after the disintegration of the old social ideal. This idea is expressed in the book of Ezekiel, and also in the book of Jeremiah,[13] in which the heightened sense of individuality is particularly prominent in the 'confessions'[14] of Jeremiah.

In both works, this individualism becomes limited, or, perhaps better, relativized by society, the fate of which was shared by both prophets, but which they also desired to change. Nevertheless, the so-called 'exclusive I'[15] of the prophets, which is first detectable in the works of Amos, is a sign of the new experience.

It should be noted that it was not only in ancient Israel at this time that this discovery was made. Additionally, the dialectic of new individual development and restoration of tradition which is particularly characteristic of the tangibly Israelite traditions in Deuteronomy,[16] was shared by Israel in the time of Jeremiah with her Near Eastern environment.

Thus, for example, in then-contemporary Egypt (i.e. the 25th Dynasty) in the field of visual art we find both the copying of ancient memorials, using archaizing tendencies, together with quite new productions of a previously unknown individual type of portrait modelling.[17] In Assyria, we find in addition to the collection of ancient cuneiform texts a more creative literary process which bears just as many indications of individual tendencies as does the visual art which decorated the palaces of Sennacherib and Asshurbanipal, and which no longer attempted to represent the stereotypical idealization of monarchy, but rather an individual understanding of the various details.[18]

But above all the new consciousness of individuality was burgeoning in ancient Greece.[19] If, within the confines of epic literature, Hesiod had emphasized personal features, then the lyrical poets in particular followed him closely in this. Even more revolutionary was the practice of Theognis and other makers of homilies and poems in using their own names in connection with their works. At this time potters, painters, and sculptors also began to sign their works. All of these characteristics are clear signs of the experience of a spiritual sense of self which has often been denied to antiquity.

Both in Egypt and in Mesopotamia, some references to authors had been made even in earlier times. However, these were not typical cases, for the literature of both cultures was by and large anonymous. It is unlikely to be coincidental that a fragmentary cuneiform catalogue which lists a considerable number of texts together with their authors was produced in the years just prior to the reign of Asshurbanipal, in whose library the catalogue was discovered. Although these authorial references are often of little historical value, the significance of the catalogue is occasioned by its understanding of literary individuality at this time.[20]

As in the case of the ancient Near East at large, so, too, the literary works contained in the Hebrew Bible are mainly anonymous. Three areas might seem at first sight to provide us with some exceptions to this rule: the Psalter, the Wisdom literature, and the prophetic books. The superscriptive notice לדוד, which occurs frequently in the

Psalms, is not unambiguous (3.1, etc). It is possible to regard it as a sort of registration siglum, as, for example, in *lbʿl* at Ugarit. However, by reason of the frequently following description of the situation in question, it would be more reasonable to regard the ל as a ל of possession or authorship (ל-auctoris). The tradition about David also makes this conclusion inviting.[21] It is typical of the tradition to derive a text retrospectively from the one who was assumed to be the best known exponent of the literary Gattung in question. In precisely the same way the Homeric hymns and epics, the fables of Aesop and the medical treatises of Hippocrates accumulated around these figures.[22]

Like David in the Psalter, so, too, Solomon has been turned into an author in the Wisdom literature,[23] since, according to the tradition, he was the very incarnation of Wisdom.[24]

The prophetic books distinguish themselves sharply from the mainly anonymous literature of the Hebrew Bible in that they are supplied with the names of authors.[25] However, the questions as to when and by whom these writings were supplied with such author superscriptions can be answered only vaguely. The only thing of which we can be sure is that the prophets in question are not to be suspected, since such superscriptions invariably make use of the 3rd pers. masc. sing. In some cases, as, for example, in that of Amos, this procedure may have been undertaken already a short time after the appearance of the prophet in question. Nevertheless, even for some pre-exilic prophetic books we shall have to reckon with the exilic-post-exilic period as the time when this occurred; this applies above all to the Deuteronomistic redaction which is detectable in some of the superscriptions.[26]

The practice of making a more or less 'bibliographical' notice which corresponds to some extent with the super- and subscriptions of Egyptian and Assyro-Babylonian texts has occasioned a variety of responses among scholars. Some have regarded this custom as a scribal device intended to aid the cataloguing and future use of the work in question.[27] But if this were the case, why do the superscriptions differ so very much, and why are they confined to the prophetic books alone? Other scholars have pointed to the theological problem of authority and revelation as the cause;[28] but to this end other means already existed within the various books themselves in the form of such things as call narratives, the so-called messenger formula, and the so-called word-event formula.[29] The information contained in the superscriptions is simply too varied to represent any fundamental reflection over the contents of the works.

Another explanation is more likely: in the Peshitta, the Syriac translation of the Hebrew Bible, we read in Isaiah 38 at the end of v. 8 the addition 'Isaiah ends'; this is quite plain and unmistakable, while the following verse continues with the notice 'passage of Hezekiah'. In other words, Isaiah's own contribution is thus delimited. Nor is the remark in Jer. 51.64 to be understood differently, where we find the end of the work established by ירמיהו ער־הנה דברי. We have to do with a way of ascertaining the contents of a collection similar to that which we encounter in Egyptian and above all in Hittite and Assyro-Babylonian texts.[30] In ancient times, if one desired to protect a corpus against alteration or falsification, there were also other—and on occasion, better—defensive measures,[31] like the contingent curse, the simple association of the author's identity by means of a seal or an acrostic, or the warning neither to omit anything from nor to add anything to the work, which is, of course, also present in the book of Deuteronomy.[32] Thus, in Jeremiah, too, we find an attempt being made to respect the individual contributions and so to proclaim the end of their extension.

The fact that in the Hebrew Bible it is specifically and only in the book of Jeremiah that the beginning and end of an individual and conscious collection of prophetic words is designated as described above is quite significant, particularly so when we consider that according to the general view the work contains not only words of Jeremiah, but also such foreign materials as narratives about the prophet and sermons in Deuteronomistic language. No matter what rôle was played by the scribe Baruch in the course of the development of the narratives or of the entire work,[33] the problem remains of the Deuteronomistic theology which propounds its intentions in the guise of the 'I' of Jeremiah. The case is not remarkably different in the matter of those prophetic books in which Deuteronomistic influence is also noticeable and particularly in the superscriptions, in which the individuality of the prophetic witnesses is emphasized. We must ask ourselves whether it is not above all in the prophetic literature in which problems arise which may be characterized by the terms orthonymity, anonymity, and pseudonymity.

Now, the poetical words of Jeremiah are orthonymous, the narratives about him are anonymous, while the Deuteronomistic sermons are pseudonymous, since the ostensible relationship between the author and the last-mentioned parts of the work is not correct. To put the matter sharply, the Deuteronomistic texts move across the grey borderline between literary fiction and literary imposture or falsification,[34] that is, in the event that the principle of individual performance and spiritual property was both acknowledged and expressed at the time in question. Since the Jeremianic predictions had come true, the Deuteronomistic circles utilized his name in order to establish new guidelines for the people during the changed situation of the Exile. Their motives were religiously founded; their intentions were paedogogical; both were in good faith. Literary individuality was usurped, since the authority of the individual promised success for the project in hand, and also because a tendency towards individualization had been in progress since the days of Amos with which such a collective and anonymous movement as the Deuteronomistic one was forced to come to terms. The previously adumbrated sociological and spiritual-historical aspects recur in the literary and theological tensions present in the book of Jeremiah. Thus, the prophet Jeremiah bears traces of an individuality whose radicality affects society, and vice versa.[35] Jeremiah's historical and theological orientation is not merely directed towards that which is new and previously unheard-of, for his re-emphasis on the traditions of the Exodus, Covenant, and Settlement represents an ancient stage in the national history.[36] The name of Jeremiah, which was inserted in the superscription and in the subscription of his work, designates the spiritual property of this prophet. However, the process of tradition was not content to rest with the sayings of Jeremiah, as both narratives and reflections were added which both developed and added wholly new accents to the proclamation of the individual. Thus, for example, where the fate of the individual is vivid in the narratives about Jeremiah, the Deuteronomistic sermons are preoccupied with the lot of the community. At some point the closing notice in Jer. 51.64 was added, thus both separating off the historical section Jeremiah 52 as non-Jeremianic and attempting to prevent the further extension of the literary production. Perhaps one ought to go even further and hypothesize that the super- and subscriptive notices represent a remarkable and possibly even critical feeling towards literary individuality. For both of these framing notices contain a

formulation which is quite unusual in superscriptions, namely דברי +
PN. This is not necessarily to be rendered 'words of Jeremiah' or
equivalent terms, as it may be simply understood in a more general
way: 'the affairs of Jeremiah', that is, that which pertains to him.[37] If
this sense is correct, then no comment on Jeremiah's authorship is
actually being made. In this event, the theological tensions between
the various parts of the book do not disappear, but it was possible for
the exilic or post-exilic community to tolerate them.

What conclusions are we to draw from all this? Earlier exegetical
efforts have pursued a correct and historically orientated approach in
their attempts to discover the so-called 'authentic' and individual in
the prophetic books. Unfortunately, earlier scholars were exclusively
interested in the question of authenticity, and so negatively evaluated
everything which they found to be 'inauthentic'. More recent
exegetical efforts have tended—correctly, on my view—to concentrate
more on the previously ignored final form of the great compositions
and whole books, and on the historical contexts in which they were
appropriated. But the process of book-making was only understood
as prehistory, the function of which was solely regarded as of interest
for illuminating the final form.

The prophetic and other literatures require investigation of both
viewpoints, that is, of the origin and the end. And yet, exegesis ought
not to limit itself to these parameters. At the beginning were the
words of an individual figure; at the end we find a complex book
which transcends this figure. There were not only recipients in the
situation of the final book during the exilic or post-exilic periods.
There were also recipients when Jeremiah proclaimed his words, just
as there were some along the pathway from the prophet Jeremiah to
the book of Jeremiah.

Unfortunately, we have no way of knowing who it was who had
'charge' of the texts, and it would be inappropriate to reckon with the
existence of archives or libraries, at least at the beginning. As long as
the process of tradition was creative, it did not take place within the
limits of a chancellery or registry. It has recently been suggested that
the entire tradition of the Hebrew Bible is to be assigned to school
traditions,[38] that is, that there were schools in which one not only
learnt to write, but also how to preserve and transmit texts.
According to this view, the texts were repeatedly copied and
eventually arrived at the status of authoritative and solely applicable
texts. However, in view of the wide variety of texts, not all of which

could possibly have served didactic purposes, and also because of the very complicated history of the canon, this view seems very improbable.[39]

Nevertheless, it would be appropriate to think of a sort of 'school' tradition of the prophetic texts in an extended sense, that is, one in which personal or topical interests occupied the foreground. As in the case of other prophetic books, so also in the case of the book of Jeremiah at least a part of the texts seems to have arisen from the personal connection between the prophet and his 'pupil', while another part has arisen from the topical association with a tradition which was passed on and which had 'scholastic' aspects. Baruch would seem to represent the former case, while the Deuteronomistic circles would seem to represent the second case.[40]

If the question of theology and history is to be made vital and relevant, it is unavoidable that the literary and theological interweavings and connections between the individual and the collective should be studied. This should be done in both the synchronic and the diachronic directions, and with reference to both the personal and the factual perspectives.

It is only with some reservations that we may use the concept of a 'book religion' relevantly with respect to the time of Jeremiah, even when ch. 36 signifies the beginning of a process which led from the words of Jeremiah to the final book of Jeremiah. This pathway was more or less creatively directed. The process of re-discovering the text requires a creative exegesis which admits of a multi-dimensional concept of task and methodology, if the complex state of the texts and their history is to be satisfactorily studied.

NOTES

1. The Egyptologist S. Morenz brought this insight into play in his book *Gott und Mensch im alten Ägypten* (1964), 2nd edn, Zürich/München (1984), pp. 21ff., see already J. Leipoldt und S. Morenz, *Heilige Schriften*, Leipzig (1953), *passim*. According to S. Morenz, the real beginning of the 'book religion' is to be sought in the latter part of the Judaean monarchy, when Deuteronomy reduced the cultic radius of action; see already S. Morenz, 'Entstehung und Wesen der Buchreligion', *ThLZ* 75 (1950), pp. 709-16, esp. pp. 711ff.

2. See further H.-J. Kraus, *Geschichte der historisch-kritischen Erforschung des Alten Testaments*, 3rd edn, Neukirchen (1982). A review of the critical study of the prophets is to be found in J. Blenkinsopp, *A History of Prophecy in Israel*, London (1984), pp. 26ff.

3. The pathfinder here was B. Duhm, *Das Buch Jesaja* (HK 3/1), Göttingen (1892), 5th edn, 1968); *idem*, *Das Buch Jeremia* (KHC 11), Tübingen/Leipzig (1901).

4. See, e.g. R. Rendtorff, 'Zur Komposition des Buches Jesaja', *VT* 34 (1984), pp. 295-320. R. Rendtorff expresses his opinion in his essay: 'Zur Bedeutung des Kanons für eine Theologie des Alten Testaments', in *'Wenn nicht jetzt, wann dann?'*, Aufsätze für H.-J. Kraus zum 65. Geb., ed. H.G. Geyer *et al.*, Neukirchen (1983), pp. 3-11.

5. This was first fundamentally developed by H. Gunkel, 'Die Propheten als Schriftsteller und Dichter', in H. Schmidt, *Die großen Propheten* (SAT 2/2), Göttingen (1923), pp. xxxiv-lxx.

6. I.37-41; I.40: τὰ κατ᾽ αὐτοὺς πραχθέντα συνέγραψαν (*Josephus*. With an English Translation by H.St.J. Thackery, Vol. I [Loeb], London/Cambridge, Mass. [1926], reprints).

7. *Antiquitates* I.17; IV.196 (*Josephus*. With an English Translation by H.St.J. Thackery, Vol. IV, Loeb, London/Cambridge, Mass. [1930], reprints); X.218 (*Josephus*. With an English Translation by R. Marcus, Vol. VI, Loeb, London/Cambridge, Mass. [1937], reprints).

8. Cf. M. Noth, *Die israelitischen Personennamen im Rahmen der gemeinsemitischen Namengebung* (BWANT 4/10, 3rd series), Stuttgart (1928), reprint Hildesheim (1966), pp. 217f.

9. Demonstrated by R. Albertz, *Persönliche Frömmigkeit und offizielle Religion. Religionsinterner Pluralismus in Israel und Babylon* (CThM A,9), Stuttgart (1978); cf. H. Vorländer, *Mein Gott. Die Vorstellung vom persönlichen Gott im Alten Orient und im Alten Testament* (AOAT 23), Neukirchen (1975).

10. Cf. E. Blum, *Die Komposition der Vätergeschichte* (WMANT 57), Neukirchen (1984), p. 482.

11. This has been countered by J.W. Rogerson, 'The Hebrew Conception of Corporate Personality: A Re-Examination', *JThS* 21 (1970), pp. 1-16.

12. Cf. G.E. Mendenhall, 'The Relation of the Individual to Political Society in Ancient Israel', in *Biblical Studies in Memory of H.C. Alleman*, ed. by J.M. Myers, O. Reimherr, H.N. Bream; New York (1960), pp. 89-108; Mendenhall criticizes the concept of Corporate Personality.

13. Jer. 31.29; Ezek. 18.2; cf. Lam. 5.7 and Deut. 24.16.

14. N. Ittmann, *Die Konfessionen Jeremias. Ihre Bedeutung für die Verkündigung des Propheten* (WMANT 54), Neukirchen (1981). The individualizing understanding has not always been advocated in the history of research; see the survey of N. Ittmann, *op. cit.*, pp. 4-18. T. Polk (*The Prophetic Persona. Jeremiah and the Language of the Self*, JSOT Suppl.

Series 32, Sheffield [1984]) has shown that the 'I' of Jeremiah is also an exemplary 'I'.

15. G. von Rad, *Theologie des Alten Testaments*, II; 7th edn, München (1980), p. 62, cf. pp. 86f.

16. Cf. S. Herrmann, 'Die konstruktive Restauration', *Das Deuteronomium als Mitte biblischer Theologie*, G. *von Rad zum 70. Geb.*, ed. H.W. Wolff, München (1971), pp. 155-70, esp. pp. 169f.

17. W. Wolf, *Die Kunst Ägyptens. Gestalt und Geschichte*, Stuttgart (1957), pp. 612ff. On the simultaneity of restoration and innovation in the Egyptian Late Period see E. Otto, 'Die Endsituation der ägyptischen Kultur', *Die Welt als Geschichte* 11 (1951), pp. 203-13, esp. pp. 211f.

18. S. Smith, in *The Cambridge Ancient History*, ed. J.B. Bury etc., III: *The Assyrian Empire*, Cambridge (1965), pp. 75ff. and 109ff. In particular on the literary materials, see W. von Soden, 'Das Problem der zeitlichen Einordnung akkadischer Literaturwerke', *Mitteilungen der Deutschen Orientgesellschaft zu Berlin* 85 (1953), pp. 14-26, esp. 24f. On the reliefs, see R.D. Barnett, *Assyrian Palace Reliefs*, London (1960).

19. For what follows, see U. Wilcken, *Griechische Geschichte im Rahmen der Altertumsgeschichte*, 9th edn, München (1962), pp. 118ff. and 126ff.

20. W.G. Lambert, 'A Catalogue of Texts and Authors', *JCS* 16 (1962) pp. 59-77, cf. *idem*, 'Ancestors, Authors and Canonicity', *JCS* 11 (1957), pp. 1-14, 112.

21. See 1 Sam. 16.17ff.; 2 Sam. 1.17ff. and elsewhere, cf. H.-J. Kraus, *Psalmen* (BK 15/1), 5th edn, Neukirchen (1978), pp. 15ff.

22. Cf. A. Gudeman, 'Literary Frauds among the Greeks', in *Classical Studies in Honor of H. Drisler*, New York (1894), p. 70.

23. Prov. 1.1; 10.1; 25.1; Cant. 1.1; cf. Qoh. 1.1; in the Apocrypha, see the Wisdom of Solomon. Like David, Solomon, too, was thought to have written some psalms, see Psalms 72 and 127; in the Pseudepigrapha, see the *Psalms of Solomon*.

24. See 1 Kgs 3.4-15, 16-28; 5.9-14; 10.1-10, 23-24.

25. The superscriptions do not expressly speak of authorship; but at least the mention of the names suggests origins. On the superscriptions cf. G.M. Tucker, 'Prophetic Superscriptions and the Growth of a Canon', in *Canon and Authority. Essays in Old Testament Religion and Theology*, ed. G.W. Coats and B.O. Long, Philadelphia (1977), pp. 56-70.

26. On Amos see W.H. Schmidt, 'Die deuteronomistische Redaktion des Amosbuches', *ZAW* 77 (1965), pp. 169ff.; H.W. Wolff, *Dodekapropheton 2. Joel und Amos* (BK 14/2), 2nd edn, Neukirchen (1975), pp. 146ff.; on Hosea see H.W. Wolff, *Dodekapropheton 1. Hosea* (BK 14/1), 3rd edn, Neukirchen (1976), pp. 1f.; on Micah see H.W. Wolff, *Dodekapropheton 4. Micha* (BK 14/4), Neukirchen (1982), pp. 1ff. In connection with the superscription in the book of Jeremiah, W. Thiel (*Die deuteronomistische Redaktion von Jeremia 1-25*, WMANT 41, Neukirchen [1973], pp. 49ff.) holds that we have to do

16279

with Deuteronomistic reworking. On Deuteronomistic reworking of the superscription in the book of Ezekiel see R. Liwak, 'Überlieferungsgeschichtliche Probleme des Ezechielbuches. Eine Studie zu postezechielischen Interpretationen und Kompositionen', Diss. Bochum (1976), pp. 44ff.

27. G.M. Tucker, 'Prophetic Superscriptions' (cf. n. 25), p. 67; cf. H.M.I. Gevaryahu, 'Biblical Colophons: A Source for the 'Biography' of Authors, Texts and Books', *VTS* 28 (Congress Volume Edinburgh 1974), Leiden (1975), pp. 42-59.

28. H. Wildberger, *Jesaja 1-12* (BK 10/1), 2nd edn, Neukirchen (1980), p. 6.

29. The call narrative may legitimize either the prophet himself (1 Kgs 19.19ff.) or his message (Isaiah 6; Jer. 1.4ff.; Ezek. 1.1ff.). On the legitimizing function of the messenger formula (כה אמר יהוה) and the word-event formula (ויהי דבר־יהוה אל־) see K. Koch, *Was ist Formgeschichte? Methoden der Bibelexegese*, 4th edn, Neukirchen (1982), *passim*.

30. On the colophons, see C. Wendel, *Die griechisch-römische Buchbeschreibung verglichen mit der des Vorderen Orients*, Halle (1949); E. Leichty, 'The Colophon', *Studies presented to A.L. Oppenheim*, Chicago (1964), pp. 147-54; H. Hunger, *Babylonische und assyrische Kolophone* (AOAT 2), Neukirchen (1968); cf. H.M.I. Gevaryahu, 'Biblical Colophons' (cf. n. 27).

31. On these and other precautions, see W. Speyer, *Die literarische Fälschung im heidnischen und christlichen Altertum. Ein Versuch ihrer Deutung* (Handbuch der Altertumswissenschaften 1/2), München (1971), p. 93.

32. Deut. 4.2; 13.1; cf. Jer. 26.2; Prov. 30.6; Qoh. 3.14. On the generality of the usage of the 'canonical formula', see H. Cancik, *Mythische und historische Wahrheit* (Stuttg. Bibelstudien 48), Stuttgart (1970), pp. 88ff., 99ff., and pp. 26f. n. 11.

33. S. Herrmann reviews the history of research in this area in 'Forschung am Jeremiabuch. Probleme und Tendenzen ihrer neuen Entwicklung', *ThLZ* 102 (1977), pp. 481-90.

34. In connection with the prophetic literature, the problem has especially to do with falsification via addition, elimination, or change of the existing materials. In connection with the Hebrew Bible, the relationship between orthonymity, anonymity and pseudonymity has not yet been sufficiently evaluated; but to date, see esp. L.H. Brockington, 'The Problem of Pseudonymity', *JThS* 4 (1953) pp. 15-22, which appeared under the title 'Das Problem der Pseudonymität' in *Pseudepigraphie in der heidnischen und jüdisch-christlichen Antike*, ed. N. Brox (Wege der Forschung 484), Darmstadt (1977), pp. 185-94; M. Smith, 'Pseudepigraphy on the Israelite Literary Tradition', in *Pseudepigrapha I. Pseudopythagorica—Lettres de Platon. Littérature pseudépigraphique juive* (Fondation Hardt, Entretiens sur l'antiquité classique, 18), Vandœuvres/Genève (1972), pp. 189-215. It is debatable to what extent the 'echte religiöse Pseudepigraphie' is a problem in

its own right, see W. Speyer, 'Religiöse Pseudepigraphie und literarische Fälschung im Altertum', *JAC* 8/9 (1965/66) pp. 88-125; *idem, Die literarische Fälschung* (cf. n. 31), pp. 150ff.; *idem,* 'Fälschung, pseudepigraphische freie Erfindung und "echte religiöse Pseudepigraphie"', in *Pseudepigrapha I,* pp. 33-366.

35. In addition to the 'confessions', see e.g. Jer. 16.1-13.

36. G. von Rad, *Theologie des Alten Testaments,* II (cf. n. 15), pp. 199ff.

37. See, in detail, R. Liwak, *Der Prophet und die Geschichte. Eine literar-historische Untersuchung zum Jeremiabuch* (BWANT 121), Stuttgart (1987), pp. 78ff.

38. A. Lemaire, *Les Écoles et la formation de la Bible dans l'Ancien Testament* (OBO 39), Fribourg/Göttingen (1981).

39. Cf. the review of H.-P. Müller, in *WO* 13 (1982), pp. 172-74; S. Herrmann, in *OLZ* 80 (1985), pp. 255-58.

40. On the former G. Wanke, *Untersuchungen zur sogenannten Baruch-schrift* (BZAW 122), Berlin (1971), esp. pp. 144f.; K. Baltzer, *Die Biographie der Propheten,* Neukirchen (1975), p. 128; on the latter W. Thiel, *Die deuteronomistische Redaktion von Jeremia 1-25* (cf. n. 26); *idem, Die deuteronomistische Redaktion von Jeremia 26-45* (WMANT 52), Neukirchen (1981).

9

A NEW READING OF THE BIBLE?
ECUMENICAL PERSPECTIVES FROM
LATIN AMERICA AND ASIA

Konrad Raiser

I

There should be nothing extraordinary about the emergence of a new reading of the Bible in our generation. The Bible itself is full of examples which show that and how later generations have read the ancient stories of the encounter between God and human life with new eyes. Even the teachings of Jesus and the early Christian writings emerged from a new reading of the Hebrew Bible and were influenced in part by Rabbinic biblical interpretation.

There should be nothing extraordinary...I said! Yet any new reading regularly meets with opposition by the guardians of tradition, for it carries with it a changed perspective on the present life of the human community. Historically, at least, the emergence of a new reading of the biblical story, the return to the Bible itself with fresh eyes, was nearly always coupled with the experience that the traditional order of life could not be taken for granted any more. Limiting myself to the history of the Christian community, I believe that this was true at the time of the Church Fathers, especially John Chrysostom and Augustine, for the medieval reform movements, e.g. the Waldensians and the Franciscan order, and particularly for the Reformation in the sixteenth century. The same could be said for the modern ecumenical movement emerging, as it did, from a new reading of the Bible at a time when the old Christendom synthesis in Western Christianity was beginning to crumble.

All this has been analysed and interpreted many times. We understand better today than earlier generations that the different forms of Christian as well as Jewish community life have been shaped by different readings of the same Bible and the relationships between them. Yet, traditional theology, with all its sharpened historical consciousness of the fact that the meaning of the Bible is only in the reading, which is itself conditioned by the experience of present reality, has difficulties in responding to the challenges coming from a new reading of the Bible which is taking shape among Christian communities in Asia, Africa and Latin America. For generations—and in the case of Latin America for centuries—indigenous Christians knew of the Bible only as a sacred book in the hands of those who had transmitted the faith to them and who had maintained the leadership of their communities. The translation of the Bible into a growing number of vernacular languages, coupled with the spread of literacy programs, has placed the Bible into the hands of the ordinary people themselves who are now beginning to appropriate the faith in their own terms. They explore the Bible with their own eyes and what they discover is different from what they had been taught.

In this brief talk I propose to look at some examples of such new readings of the Bible, particularly from communities in Latin America and Asia. Latin American liberation theology is being discussed widely and *minjung* theology from Korea as well as theological developments in China are beginning to draw some attention. What is less known and acknowledged is the fact that these tentative theological formulations are rooted in a new reading of the Bible which is coupled with a provocative perspective on the place of the Christian community in contemporary history.

My primary interest, therefore, is not in new exegetical findings or new methods of interpretation, nor will I enter the highly sophisticated and specialized hermeneutical debate. My concern is rather: How does a new reading, in the sense of an encounter between the biblical story and the life story of people today, come about? For, what is being read, particularly by the Christian communities in Latin America, is not so much a 'text' which calls for translation, analysis and interpretation, but rather an account of human experience with God. Reading, in the sense of entering into dialogue with the Bible, is in itself an encounter of life with life. Our conversation about different readings of the Bible can thus become a paradigm for the ecumenical dialogue of cultures which encounter one another today across differences of time and place.

II

Let me present to you some examples of the new readings of the Bible which come to us from Latin America and from Asia.

1. My first example is from an interpretation of the songs of the suffering servant in the book by Carlos Mesters, *The Message of the Suffering People*.[1] In the introduction to his book Mesters talks about a conversation with an old priest who had been suffering for days from terrible pain in his back. He said: 'During these days I have thought a lot about suffering. What kind of meaning am I to give to this suffering which I cannot escape and for which I cannot discover any reason? . . I tell you, here in Brazil there are many people like me, people who suffer continuously with no reason . . . This makes me think of the suffering of the servant of God of whom the prophet Isaiah talks . . . I think our poor and suffering people is called to be this servant of God today who brings justice and liberation to all people through his suffering'. After a pause he continued: 'Your face tells me that you haven't understood what I tried to say. You do not suffer what I suffer and even less what the people suffer. You only have thoughts *about* suffering but not the experience of suffering itself. What I just said will probably sound like folly and appear like a stumbling-block, just like the cross of Christ was folly and a stumbling-block. But suffering must have an inner meaning: . . . Therefore, read again those four songs of the prophet Isaiah which speak of the suffering servant. Meditate on them in depth and then come and tell me what you have found. Who knows, perhaps the Word of God will bring us some light to clarify the question about the suffering of the people. But be careful! Never go alone into the world of the Bible. You would only lose your way and wouldn't find anything. Take with you the memory of the suffering of the people to whom you belong'.[2]

2. The second example is taken from a popular catechism which comes from the catholic diocese of Bambamarca located high up in the Peruvian Andes. This catechism 'Vamos caminando!'[3] (Let's walk together) starts from the elementary, everyday experiences of the Indian campesinos and tries to weave together their story and the biblical stories. The section about the birth of Jesus, entitled 'Jesus lives with us—just as poor as we are', begins with the arrival of

Joseph and Mary in Bethlehem. But instead of starting from the account in Luke 2.1-7, the catechism first presents the story of a young campesino couple, José Blanco and his wife Maria. It is structured like a role-play to be read by different voices. A narrator begins by explaining the situation: The president of Peru had issued a decree that everybody in Peru had to have a birth certificate. Without this certificate the farmworkers were threatened with losing their jobs. So José and Maria walk to the next town. Maria was about to give birth to a child. They arrive too late at the office and have to look for a place to stay overnight. Then follow two dialogues with people from the town, a man and a woman. Both reject their plea for a place of rest. The whole story evokes the long memory of the campesinos of being rejected by the white folk of European descent in the cities, an experience which is shared by all Indians and Mestizos. The dialogue breaks off open-endendly and the text of the catechism reproduces Luke 2.1-7. And, as a comment on this seemingly hopeless situation, the catechism adds a paraphrase of 1 Cor. 1.26-29: 'God has chosen those who are being considered stupid and useless by "cultured people". This will shame the educated and powerful! God has chosen the Indios and Mestizos who are being counted as nothings in order to overthrow those who consider themselves very important. And so there is no place for human pride in the presence of God'.[4]

In a comment on this passage, Hugo Echegaray, one of the theological advisers of the pastoral team of Bambamarca, admits that the paraphrase might appear to twist the Pauline text. But, he continues, 'the decisive thing is to understand the lasting character of God's love, which is being expressed here. Thus, we recognize that the son of Mary and Joseph will be the son of God, God-with-us as was foretold by Isaiah. Even Jesus has been marked by the rejection which hits all those who belong to the class of the common people. But for this very reason he is the Son, the source of great joy for the whole people. No doubt this is narrative and kerygmatic theology which is concerned about praxis, about doing. It wants to bring us closer to what the persons in the story are doing and to invite us to participate. The word of Scripture is like a commentary on this primary concern, opening up its spiritual and communal depth but also serving as its critical corrective'.[5]

3. My third example which is of a very different character is taken

from the Korean discussion about 'theology of *minjung*'. *Minjung*, translated literally, means 'mass of the people' or simply 'the people'. David Suh explains the background of this theology in the following way: 'Minjung theology is a Korean theology. 'Minjung' is a term which grew out of the Christian experience in the political struggle for justice over the last ten years. Theology of minjung is a creation of those Christians who were forced to reflect upon their Christian discipleship in basement interrogation rooms, in trials, facing court-martial tribunals, hearing the allegations of prosecutors, and in making their own final defence . . . Theology of minjung is a socio-political biography of Korean Christians in the 1970s. This is the way in which Korean Christians have lived and acted, prayed and participated in the Lord's supper'.[6]

A new reading of the history of Christianity in Korea through the eyes of Korean Christians shows that Christianity in Korea from the beginning has been a vital centre of the politics of nationalism against Japanese oppression. From the moment that the Bible was translated into the language of the common, oppressed people, it became a subversive document. The Japanese authorities even banned the books of Exodus and Daniel from the churches. 'Korean Christians understood the story of Moses not only as a *literal* event in the history of Israel but also as a literal event in the history of the oppressed people of *Korea*. This identification, evident in the development of the language of the Christian church in Korea, led to the subsequent resistance against the Japanese.'[7]

The essential paradigm of minjung theology comes out of the social biography of the Korean people. This has led biblical scholars like Ahn Byung Mu into a new reading of the Bible with eyes sharpened by contemporary social experience. Ahn begins his famous article about 'Jesus and the Minjung in the Gospel of Mark'[8] with the following sentences: 'Although New Testament scholarship has focussed a great deal of attention on the people who were the audience and the object of Jesus' teaching, not much attention has been paid to the social character of his audience. Consequently the words and deeds of Jesus have been desocialized'. Ahn, to my knowledge, is the first to have discovered the critical importance of the term *ochlos* which Mark uses to describe those whom Jesus addressed. In his essay, Ahn probes into the meaning of this term for Mark using as a key his understanding of the situation of the Korean minjung.

His meticulous analysis cannot be reproduced here; I will instead quote some sentences from his summary.

1. Mark deliberately avoided the term *laos* and used the term *ochlos* to indicate the *minjung*. This is different from the people of God ... It is also different from the laos in *Luke* which refers to those who repent and become the new people of God. The *minjung* do not belong to either group, nor are they the baptized crowd. They belong to a class of society which has been marginalized and abandoned.

2. However, the term *ochlos* is not consolidated into a concept but is defined in a relational way, and is therefore a fluid notion. For example, the poor are the *ochlos* in relation to the rich or the ruler. The tax collector is *minjung* only in relation to the ... nationalist establishment.

3. The *ochlos* are feared by the unjust and powerful, but they are not organized into a power group. . . . They are *minjung* not because they have a common destiny, but simply because they are alienated, dispossessed and powerless. They are never represented as a class which has a power base.

4. Jesus sides with the *ochlos* and accepts them as they are without making any conditions.[9]

4. The churches in China provide us with further examples of a new reading of the Bible. Much is being written today about the new life of the Christian community in China since the religious repression was lifted some seven or eight years ago. Again and again, the central feature of the Chinese church is being described in terms of a resurrection experience, of having died and come to life again with Christ.

In a report about a visit to China H.R. Weber writes: 'Visiting Christians in China I felt in many ways as if transplanted into the time of the Acts of the Apostles. Many of the older members of the congregations have their roots in the long tradition of pre-liberation church history in China which was strongly marked by Western missionary influence. Yet they have gone through a death and resurrection experience (like the Jews who became Judeo-Christians in apostolic times). Together with them are the growing number of first-generation Christians (like the Gentile believers in the Acts).

Church life is thus characterized by zeal for God and the fervour of a new beginning, but also by all the confusions, dangers, potential heresies and the many open questions we know from the Acts and the New Testament letters'.[10]

There is no doubt that the Bible is the most important link among the 3.5-4 million protestant Christians in China, most of whom are first-generation Christians who have grown into a post-denominational and a post-liberation Christianity. This clearly distinguishes China from the three other contexts referred to. While more and more church-buildings are being re-opened for worship, the small house church groups which developed during the time of the cultural revolution remain the centres for intensive Bible study.[11] During the years when all organized religious practice was forbidden and most Bibles had been destroyed or confiscated, Christians had learned central passages from the Bible by heart or had copied them into their note-books. This intimate living with the Bible under external pressure and persecution contributed to a reading of Scripture from the perspective of the people who had few if any experienced interpreters to help them.

A number of features characterize this new Chinese reading of the Bible: (1) Much emphasis is placed on the incarnation and on the passages affirming Christ as the 'head of the universe'. 'In the New Testament they have come to appreciate St. John's Gospel, Ephesians, Colossians and Hebrews: The cosmic Lordship of Jesus Christ is very meaningful to their new understanding of Jesus Christ. To Him alone, they confessed, is the Chinese Church ultimately committed'.[12] (2) There is a strong emphasis on the call to conversion, on reconciliation with God, on personal salvation and new life in Christ—as for all first-generation Christian communities. (3) Finally, Chinese Bible-reading is closely related to the experience and challenge of everyday Christian living in faith, hope and love.

The obvious difference from the earlier examples with their strong emphasis on the social and political dimension of the biblical message is addressed by H.R. Weber in his report:

> None of the sermons I heard directly touched social-political questions, but there was also no exclusively other-worldly or escapist message. God's action in history is affirmed, and the prophetic role is more seen in discerning where and how God acts than in confronting or denouncing social evil. The Church in China clearly lives in a post-liberation situation. Much of the good

news proclaimed by Jesus in the synagogue of Nazareth (Luke 4, 16ff.) has been realized. This means also that Chinese Christians have probably a deeper understanding of the fact that social-political liberation and economic development are not yet the whole of the Gospel. Life is more than what we live now. Human history is surrounded and penetrated by transcendence.[13]

III

Four very different examples: one from a meditative context, one catechetical, one a very specialized piece of exegetical research and finally impressions from church life in China. In what sense do they represent a *new* reading of the Bible?

The common point in all four examples, which could be multiplied, is the fundamental change of perspective as compared to the tradition of most Christian communities. Here the Bible is being read through the eyes of people who have become conscious of their condition as victims of history, as those who have no voice and whose primary experience is suffering or who, as in the Chinese case, have gone through an experience of dying and coming to life again. They discover in the Bible a human story that seems to correspond directly to their experience. They hear in the Bible a language that arises from the life of people who have encountered God as liberator in times of oppression, as comforter and healer in times of suffering, as the defender of the rights of the poor and powerless and as the ultimate source of all life. They read the Bible as the powerful word of God who through this web of human stories addresses them in their historical condition. They do not seem to be troubled by the fundamental historical gap of 2000 to 3000 years, by the difference of culture and thought forms. They understand the oral and narrative character of biblical language and, while respecting the integrity of the biblical stories as part of past history, they intuitively establish the symbolic or analogical merging of the horizons of past and present. Their primary interest is not to understand and interpret the Bible as a literary 'text', as the basis of Christian faith and the norm of all teaching of the church, but rather to understand their own life in the light of the Bible.

Carlos Mesters, the author of our first example and himself a distinguished biblical scholar, has not only been an important animator of this new reading of the Bible among Christian base

communities in Brazil, but he has constantly carried further the
theological reflection about this change of perspective. His observations
may help in assessing the ecumenical significance of the new
encounter with the Bible.

Reading the Bible, I said in the beginning, is in a sense an encounter
of life with life. 'All of human existence—says P. Ricoeur—is like a
text which is to be read'.[14] Reading the Bible just as reading any
other story of significant human experiences takes place in the midst
of our efforts to read the text of our own existence, starts from
questions—whether acknowledged or not—which call for clarification.
We try to read and to understand the text of our human life as we
enter into dialogue with the Bible. All biblical interpretation,
therefore, begins with the recognition of familiar features in the
biblical story.

'Never go alone into the world of the Bible. Take with you the
suffering of the people to whom you belong' (Mesters). Our existence
includes those, to whom we belong. Thus, it becomes an important
question whom we take along as our partners as we enter into
dialogue with the Bible. Our understanding of the Bible has
benefited a lot by the fact that biblical exegesis in our century has
taken seriously the questions of secular contemporaries or the doubts
of the unbeliever in ourselves. For Christians in Latin America,
Korea and in most countries of the so-called Third World the
primary partner—in the words of Mesters—is not the unbeliever but
the 'non-person'.

For the secular, rationalist mind the narrative and symbolic
language of the Bible has become strange and sealed. Much critical
effort has gone into the project of a 'non-religious interpretation of
the Bible' guided by the criterion of intellectual honesty. The Bible
has been liberated from dogmatic captivity and received new
meaning for many Christians.

Today, however, we are challenged by the fact that people in Latin
America and elsewhere who are plagued by the hard reality of their
life, rather than by intellectual doubts, can establish an immediate
relationship to the language of the Bible and unlock its symbolic
message of liberation. This intuitive reading of the Bible with the
same eyes that try to read the text of present human reality should
not be disregarded as being naive, uncritical or even ideologically
misguided. In fact, it can, and does, lead to renewed interest in
critical exegesis as the example of Ahn's study on the meaning of

'ochlos' shows. However, exegesis here is not the first but a second step, the result of the primary effort to probe more deeply into the meaning which the people have discovered for their life and their struggle in the biblical story. 'Scholarly exegesis is now being questioned by a Christian community which has taken the Bible back into its own hand and which does not want to start from the questions which the exegete considers important, but by those which are being posed by the reality of the life of the people.'[15] Scholarly exegesis thus takes on the function of 'spectacles' which sharpen the eyes of the people in their reading.

I believe that the ecumenical significance of this new reading of the Bible lies in the fact that it restores to the Bible its basic character as an account or witness of human life lived in the presence of the living God, which in our reading and entering into its story can become Word of God for us. Each culture, each people, each community will do its own reading of the Bible in the context of trying to answer the basic question of life. The differences between our readings, past and present, will not separate us but rather challenge and enrich us mutually as long as we expose our lives to one another even as we expose ourselves to the story of the Bible. The ecumenical problem starts where life and suffering are being replaced by theories about life and suffering, where theology, whether in the form of exegesis or of systematic reflection and teaching, becomes the starting point rather than the second step, the norm for understanding rather than the spectacle or the looking glass.

I put a question mark after the title of this paper: A new reading of the Bible? What may appear new to one is old to another. The challenge coming from Latin America and Asia has been received and appropriated in Europe and this has led especially Dutch exegetes to rediscover the tradition of Jewish Bible reading. There may in fact be very old elements in what I have described. But this is precisely the character of genuine ecumenical dialogue: you discover your own true identity of faith through encounter with the other.

NOTES

1. Carlos Mesters, *Missião do Povo que Sofre*, Petropolis (1981); quotations follow the German translation C.M. *Die Botschaft des leidenden Volkes*, Neukirchen-Vluyn (1982), (trans. H. Brandt).

2. *Op. cit.*, pp. 23f.

3. *Vamos Caminando*, ed. Bambamarcea Gruppe, Freiburg, Münster (1983).

4. *Op. cit.*, p. 159.

5. *Op. cit.*, p. 406.

6. Kim Yong Bock, ed., *Minjung Theology. People as Subjects of History*, Singapore (1981), p. 18.

7. *Op. cit.*, p. 25.

8. *Op. cit.*, pp. 136ff.

9. *Op. cit.*, pp. 149f.

10. H.R. Weber, 'Impressions on the Bible and Church life in the new China, Febr. 18-29, 1984', mimeographed text, Geneva (1984), p. 6 (in excerpts published in 'Bridge: Church Life in China today, Hongkong, No. 6, July 1984').

11. Cf. R. Fung, *Households of God on China's Soil*, Geneva (1982).

12. S. Amirtham, 'A Resurrection Experience: Life of the Church in China', in *Ministerial Formation* 29/30, Geneva (March + June 1985); quote in No. 30 p. 32.

13. *Op. cit.*, p. 11.

14. Quoted from G. Casalis, *Les idées justes ne tombent pas du ciel. Eléments de 'théologie inductive'*, Paris (1977). Quote from German translation: *Die richtigen Ideen fallen nicht vom Himmel*, Stuttgart (1980), p. 78.

15. C. Mesters, 'Das Verständnis der Schrift in einigen brasilianischen Basisgemeinden', *Concilium* 16 (1980), p. 565.

10

THE BIBLE AND ITS EXEGESIS IN THE CONTROVERSIES ABOUT REFORM AND REFORMATION[1]

H. Smolinsky

If you talk about the sixteenth-century Reformation emphasizing that the controversy over the Bible, over its interpretation and over its theological importance was a central subject of the denominational arguments, you can be sure you tell your listeners nothing new. In every good handbook on church history you can read that the German Reformer Martin Luther—according to his own state-ment—found the answer to the tormenting question 'How can I find a merciful God?' by a new interpretation of Rom. 1.17, where it says: 'The righteous man lives through his faith' (Hab. 2.4).[2] The Reformer's singular reverence for the Holy Writ as the source of all theology was reduced to the conclusive formula of 'Sola-Scriptura' and confronted with the Catholic Church's principle of tradition. Martin Luther's translation of the Bible, which was finished in 1534 with the Complete Bible and whose effect can hardly be overestimated, had since 1522 served as means of communication between the theology of Wittenberg University and the masses.[3]

The consequences of the Reformer's focus on the Holy Writ, concerning both the methods and the contents, have been frequently and intensively examined, for example, in Leif Grane's impressive book *Modus loquendi theologicus: Luther's Fight for the Renewal of Theology (1515-1518)*, published in 1975.[4] In contrast to this, Catholic Church historiography has only in places analysed the critical and creative function of the Bible in the sixteenth century. In so doing, emphasis has been place on leading humanists, and no exhaustive study of the exegesis of the time has been made.[5] An apologetically conditioned mistrust of a one-sided emphasis on the Bible may have had an obstructive effect in this.

My contribution to this symposium consists in the attempt to take

up aspects of the history of Reform and Reformation of the Early
Modern Times under the title of 'The Bible and its Exegesis in the
Controversies about Reform and Reformation', an approach which,
in my opinion, should make clear some creative elements of the
Bible.

As it is impossible to treat such a subject exhaustively, two points
of emphasis are chosen: in the first place, remarks about humanism,
its relationship to the Bible and to Catholic Reform; in the second
place, the controversy over the Bible and its interpretation during the
period of the Reformation. The separation of humanism from
Reform and Reformation, which has here been practised for
methodological reasons, is not a real division. On the contrary, to my
mind, the single elements merge into each other far more than has
been stated in historiography.

I. *The Starting-point: Humanists and Holy Writ*

The humanism of the fifteenth/sixteenth century was a great
educational movement. Paul Oskar Kristeller has described it as
follows: 'The humanist profession as a whole was a scholarly and
literary profession'.[6] Following this definition, philology and the
cultivation of the 'bonae litterae' were centres of humanist interests.
People devoted themselves not only to pagan antiquity, but also to
the Bible and to the old Christian literature. Especially the German
humanists, such as Peter Luder, Rudolf Agricola and Jakob Locher,
pleaded for a new theology which orientated itself to the Bible and
the Early Fathers, but no longer to the scholasticism of the Middle
Ages. This form of humanism found its unquestionable climax in
Erasmus of Rotterdam (1469-1536) whose genuine religious interests
have been identified more and more distinctly during the last
decades.[7] Together with the English Thomas More, the French
Lefèvre d'Étaples (Faber Stapulensis) and the German Johannes
Reuchlin, Erasmus is the main representative of a movement which
has been called 'biblical humanism' since the publication of the work
of the Dutch scholar Lindeboom in 1913.[8] Characteristic of this
'biblical humanism' is the interest in the genuine, original text of the
Christian sources of faith, that is, the Bible; in the Early Fathers; its
accentuation of the classical languages Latin, Greek and Hebrew;
knowledge about the close relation between language and truth; and
care for an interpretation appropriate to the Bible. On this

foundation, the humanist Hermann van dem Busche developed in his book *Vallum humanitatis* (The Rampart of Humanity), published in 1518, what was almost a programme for a new theology.[9] Its intention was to refer to the original language for biblical exegesis and to make use not only of textual criticism, but also of rhetoric, poetry, history, and knowledge of the real facts.[10] It was typical of humanism that for van dem Busche classical education and theology belonged indissolubly together and should both be taught at the university.[11]

This new system of methods to understand the Bible was developed most impressively by Erasmus of Rotterdam in his two works: 'Ratio seu Methodus compendio perveniendi ad veram Theologiam' and 'Methodus',[12] the consequences of which we shall deal with later on.

The demands for a new theological method would have made no sense, if the humanists had not themselves been concerned with the essential foundation of all theology, the text of the Bible. Therefore, the system of methods for understanding the Bible and working on the text belong indissolubly together, as the example of Erasmus shows. Already in 1505, he had edited the Annotationes to the New Testament by the Italian humanist, Laurentius Valla, in which the Vulgate was criticized.[13] In 1516, Erasmus published the critical edition of the New Testament to which he added the 'Paraclesis' and the 'Methodus' as prefaces and guiding introductions; at the same time he himself produced a new Latin translation.[14] The second edition of the Greek New Testament of 1519 to which he added the 'Ratio' was later on used by Luther as a basis for his September Testament, the German translation of the New Testament which he made on the Wartburg in 1522.[15]

It is beyond question that the work on the text of the Bible and on its interpretation was not a neutral, purely philological exercise, but resulted in a development of extremely grave consequences. Creative and critical forces were set free which could change theology and religious practice.

This creativity of the Holy Writ was nothing new. Already the Poverty Movement of the twelfth and thirteenth centuries had found in the Bible its ideal of the unconditional Imitation of Jesus, an ideal which was inseparably connected with the sermon and with radical poverty, and which the members of the movement tried to realize concretely in life.[16] The Spiritual Movement of the Franciscan Friars

orientated itself later on to the historical speculations of Abbot
Joachim of Fiore who, among others had been inspired by the
Apocalypse of the New Testament.[17] With John Wyklif and Jan Hus a
religious movement started which also appealed to the Bible, was
basically critical of the Church, and aimed at a change of heart.[18]

Biblical humanism differed from such an immediate religious-
practical transposition of the Holy Writ in two important respects: in
the first place, it worked on the actual biblical text and did not take it
for granted; and, in the second place, it found its way to the contents
of the Writ through its own approach, the rhetorical-scholarly
method previously mentioned. The creative elements, thus released,
had necessarily to develop in directions other than earlier Bible
movements had taken. In the sense of the general direction of
humanism this happened, first of all, on the level of education and
rhetoric, concretely of theology, sermon, catechesis etc. and, secondly,
on the level of religious practice.

These problems had not yet been clearly recognized by the
contemporaries of Erasmus, but they could already sense the heart of
the matter. Therefore, it is not astonishing that, from the start, his
edition of the Bible and his humanistic demand for three languages
in theology were controversial. The Italian prince, Alberto Pio Carpi,
rejected the Christian biblical humanism entirely,[19] and a theologian
of Louvain, Jakob Latomus, turned against Erasmus' system of
methods to understand the Bible in a comprehensive work under the
title of 'De trium Linguarum et studii theologici ratione dialogus' in
1519.[20] On one hand, the Archbishop of Mainz, Albrecht von
Brandenburg, admired the work of this great humanist. In a letter
dated from September 13th, 1517, he wrote: 'What could have been
desired more in our times but the improvement of the editions of the
NT'.[21] The Ingolstadt theologian Johannes Eck, on the other hand,
already criticized the attempts at interpretation by the great
humanist who in Eck's opinion bound the Holy Writ too strongly to
its time and environment.[22]

What announced itself during these first years of controversies
soon developed into two fundamental standpoints which, however,
were interlocked for a long time. One of them was a Catholic Reform
movement which in spite of all criticism of theology and piety
remained within the Catholic Church. The other was a movement
which, as a final consequence, destroyed the borderlines of the Old
Church and involuntarily created a new church; reform became

Reformation. This result becomes even more complicated if you consider the circumstance that also within the Reformation, in spite of the common recourse to Holy Writ, fundamental divisions took place. Therefore, the principle of Sola-Scriptura and the text alone could not be the determinative factors. For that reason, hermeneutics and the theological pre-understanding were soon to play a most decisive part in the differences about the Bible.

II. *Three Models*

As it is impossible to enumerate in a short time the whole complexity of the exegesis, its improvements, its controversies and its consequences, three models—as a scheme—will be presented into which the developments of that time can be divided. There are the following points: 1. a philology without consequences for theology; 2. the biblical-New Testament Reform programme of biblical humanism; 3. the controversy over the Bible and its interpretation during the Reformation.

1. *A Philology without Consequences for Theology*
As an example of the model which is here to be characterized we can take the above-mentioned Johannes Eck (1486-1543).[23] His letter to Erasmus had already revealed how small his agreement was with the biblical humanism. Although this negative attitude of Eck was to grow even stronger over the years,[24] it should not lead to the conclusion that he did not recognize the worth of the Holy Writ and of the classical languages. Eck, who was three years younger than Luther and belonged to his bitterest enemies, had lectured on theology in Ingolstadt since 1510 and was quite interested in reforms. Several of his publications which deal explicitly with the Bible group themselves around the years 1537 and 1538. A linguistically bad Bible translation of his own, an interpretation of the twentieth psalm in the Vulgate and a comprehensive exegesis of the prophet Haggai appeared in print.[25] Beyond that, he had delivered numerous exegetical lectures since 1520. They have only been preserved in manuscript and not been interpreted till today.[26] In the following, his 'Explanatio Psalmi Vigesimi' may be introduced as an example.[27]

First of all, it can be observed that the humanist textual criticism as well as the new Latin and German translations, which were numerous at that time, no longer allowed Eck in 1538 to assume that the Vulgate was correct and valid. He had to prove its textual foundation philologically and defend it. As a control instance he accordingly used the *Psalterium iuxta Hebraeos* of Hieronymus as well as the new Latin translations of Felinus Aretius (pseudonym of Martin Bucer), Felix Pratensis, Konrad Pellikan and Sebastian Münster.[28] To come to a judgment of his own, Eck consulted the Hebrew psalter and the Targum. It is amazing to see how extensive his knowledge of the Jewish exegesis is, a knowledge he had probably acquired through Johannes Reuchlin.[29] On the basis of the rabbinic Bible, which was edited in Venice by Daniel Bomberg, he quoted the following Jewish commentaries: Ibn Esra, David Kimchi (David ben Josef, 1160–1235, Narbonne) and Rashi (Salomon Jizchaki).[30] In the system of his interpretation, the Rabbis are consulted in a twofold manner: first of all, philologically concerning their variant readings and their explanations of the Hebrew language. As the Vulgate is decisive for Eck, he decides himself basically for such interpreters who stand nearest to the *lectio ecclesiastica*. Secondly, he also uses the theological interpretation of the Rabbis as far as they represent the Messianic interpretation of the psalm. That is the case with the Targum and with David Kimchi. But on the whole, Eck does not only understand the psalm as Messianic prophecy, but as the direct prediction of Christian christology. This decision, which follows the traditional Christian interpretation, finally prevents his entering into a serious controversy on the rabbinic theology. Instead, he is guided by the interpretations of the Early Fathers, of the Middle Ages and contemporary scholasticism, especially by the Thomist Cajetan.

Just as little as it came to a serious controversy with the Rabbis, he does not succeed in making his extensive philological work fertile for the essential theology of the psalm. In this, he equals his teacher Reuchlin whose purely philological exegesis 'de verbo ad verbum', concerning the seven psalms of penance, Eck knew well.[31] Although the decisive step of a transposition of philology to theology was not achieved, this first model can be defined as significant, in that as far as future biblical exegesis was concerned it did not close the gate on the reason for the present biblical text; rather, it opened it.

2. *The Biblical-New Testament Reform Programme of Biblical Humanism*

Essentially more extensive than Eck's exegesis was a reform programme which was represented by the biblical humanists. Here we find, to a high degree, creative elements of the Bible and its interpretation. For that purpose, Erasmus serves as an example, not that there have been no other original representatives of biblical humanism.

Already the Greek edition of the New Testament and the new Latin translation of Erasmus were sufficient to relativize the theological consequences which since then had been drawn from the Vulgate text, and to call in question the scholastic-Latin exegesis. Added to that, came the recourse to the Early Fathers, especially to Origen and Hieronymus, as well as a distinct focussing on Christ, concerning the interpretation of the New Testament. The 'Ratio . . . ad veram theologiam' contains a whole theological reform programme and was placed in front of the edition of the New Testament as an introduction.[32] Here Erasmus developed his hermeneutics and his understanding of the Bible.

The focussing on Christ is developed in such a way that Jesus is seen as teacher and educationalist. The true theology understands the life of Jesus as 'doctrina pietatis'. In an ethically understood succession Christian life realizes itself. For the interpretation of the Writ, the particular contemporary circumstances have to be observed, the forms of language, the geography, the historical-political situation, etc. Erasmus does not regard the Writ as clear in itself, but sees many dark passages in it.[33] He consciously relies on the Fathers' exegesis and on the system of spiritual sense of Scripture as represented by Origen.[34]

Therefore it is no wonder that he carried the Platonic philosophy and its sharp separation between the visible and invisible into his exegesis. This happened strikingly in 'Enchiridion Militis Christiani' (Handbook of the Militant Christian), published for the first time in 1503.[35] Concerning the Pauline distinction between 'flesh and spirit', it is said: 'What the philosophers call reason, that is called by Paul sometimes spirit, sometimes inner man, sometimes law of the conscience . . . You read in Paul of the outer man who is depraved and of the inner man who is renewed every day. Plato has postulated two souls in man. Paul creates two men in the same man'.[36] Priority is given to the interior and the invisible, the spirit is interpreted platonically and so misunderstood. Concerning this exegesis, this leads in consequence to a depreciation of the outward ceremonies and so, as well, of the Old Testament and all religious practice. The inner law of love is confronted with the outer law. A spiritualized ethical piety characterizes the reform programme offered by Erasmus for Christian practice.[37]

An extraordinarily passionate controversy developed when Erasmus applied his theory of accommodation, i.e. the teaching of the assimilation of the Revelation to the particular time and to the inner law of love, to the dissolution of marriage. Already Laurentius Valla and Lefèvre d'Étaples had taken divorce into consideration on account of the biblical results, and they had criticized the text of the Vulgate.[38] Erasmus went more deeply into this position in his interpretation of Mt. 5.31 Mk 10.4 and especially 1 Corinthians 7.[39] In his opinion, Jesus had admitted the dissolution of marriage in case of 'hardness of heart'. Quite in the sense of his anti-legal attitude, the law of the indissolubility of marriage, which is in force as such, has to be repealed when salvation is at stake.

Later on, Erasmus wrote that he had wanted only to draw attention to such a possibility.[40] But because here the canon law and the whole practice of the Catholic Church were called into question, it was no surprise that this 'slight remembrance' evoked an exceptionally loud controversy, in which Jakob of Hochstraten, Stunica, Edward Lee and Johannes Dietenberger took part.[41] Concerning this point, his exegesis could not assert itself. Of importance, perhaps, was the fact that the Reformers no longer accepted marriage as a sacrament, and therefore its significance had to be increased on the Catholic side.

What we have recognized by this example, was already understood by contemporaries: In the work of Erasmus on the Bible and in biblical humanism could lie a dangerous explosive, especially if you consider that his works were soon translated into German and printed in large quantities.[42] Erasmus himself had never thought of overstepping the border-lines of the church. But as early as 1521, a picture was published with the title 'The Divine Mill'. Here he was presented as a miller producing the flour out of which Martin Luther could bake his bread.[43] The inner connection between biblical humanism and the Reformation, which has not been fully analysed until the present day, was suggested in that image, while the qualitative difference between Luther and Erasmus was also visualized.

3. *The Controversy on the Bible and its Interpretation during the Reformation*

With the Reformation and its principle of Sola-Scriptura the differences over the Bible and its interpretation reached a new level. While the exegesis of many biblical humanists was still orientated to the tradition of the Old Church, a liberation from it—connected with many other factors—led to a theology which finally was to destroy the frame of the Old Church.[44] At this point of decision, the humanists separated themselves into different groups, with, however, a common conciliatory attitude as their characteristic feature. Among this group were, for example, Melanchthon, Martin Bucer and Erasmus himself.[45]

It is impossible to enumerate all the negative and positive elements of the controversies during the Reformation. A few examples must suffice. They are chosen in such a way that the positive and negative sides of the dispute can be recognized.

The first example is taken from a literary conflict between Martin Luther and Hieronymus Emser from 1521 to 1522.[46] Emser was court chaplain in Dresden, influenced by humanism and Erasmus, an expert on the Early Fathers, and therefore he felt himself— however mistakenly—able to conduct a theological dispute with Luther. One of the points of the controversy was the interpretation of 2 Cor. 3.6. The text says: Τὸ γὰρ γράμμα ἀποκτείνει, τὸ δὲ πνεῦμα ζωοποιεῖ ('For the letter kills, but the spirit makes alive'). Erasmus had related this passage to the polyvalent sense of Scripture and named the letter as the literal sense and the spirit as the spiritual sense. At the same time, he related the Old Testament to the letter and so depreciated its significance.[47] This complex interpretation was soon employed very simplistically against Luther and the Reformers during the controversies. Emser and others reproached them by maintaining that they knew only the dead letter, ie. the literal interpretation.[48] They ignored the spirit, which came to full effect in the interpretation of the church and its tradition. Emser's dispute with Luther had a creative effect in that the Wittenberg reformer was hereby forced to define his own teaching on the spirit and the letter.[49] Luther emphasizes that there is only one meaning to the Holy Writ. The literal and the spiritual sense, which refers to Christ, may not be separated. Therefore the passage 2 Cor. 3.6 should not be related to the interpretation of Holy Writ, but to the sermon on the law and to the sermon on mercy. 'The letter is God's law in the Old Testament, which does not make people better, but even worse.' According to Luther, this law gives no mercy. 'But the spirit gives mercy to the heart and renews man.'[50] In this way,

Luther succeeds in giving the literal text of the Bible a new worth and succeeds in overcoming the teaching of the fourfold sense of Scripture. At the same time, he could bring out the central teaching of the law and gospel through this passage.

But the subject of hermeneutics was in no way settled. Even in 1529, the Swiss theologian Johannes Buchstab wrote a book of his own with the title *That the biblical works have to have a spiritual interpretation*.[51] There he defended the spiritual sense which goes beyond the literal text. It is decisive for us to see that hermeneutics was recognized as a problem, which could be of great moment for the history of exegesis on a long-term basis. Luther and Erasmus are thought to have taken up the most profound standpoints. They had in common the connection between the spiritual sense and Christology but, in contrast to Luther, Erasmus held firmly to the multiple senses of Scripture during his lifetime and refused to accept the teaching of the 'Claritas Scripturae'.

The second example is taken from an exchange of letters by two humanists which was published under the title: *De Sacrae Scripturae dissonis translationibus* in 1542.[52] Here the Augsburg Canon Konrad Adelmann von Adelmannsfelden asked the Augustinian Canon Kilian Leib in Rebdorf near Eichstätt why the different translations of the Bible differed so much from each other, concerning the text. Leib, a good hebraist, answered with arguments from the Old Testament. He stated two reasons: first, each translation is formed by a basic theological decision which has been made in advance. Secondly, the Hebrew language presents philological difficulties. As evidence for the first thesis, he uses Luther's teaching of justification, 'sola fide', which is the determinative perspective for the translation by Luther. The Hebrew language, however, is difficult in a twofold manner: because of its punctuation, which can be different even with the same number of consonants, and because of the manifold meanings of one and the same word. As a paradigm, he mentions 'Ruach', which could be translated either by 'wind' or 'spirit'.

It is no mere accident that Adelmann and Leib were humanists. In their letters, they pointed out a problem to which humanism had already directed its attention for a long time. It was the relationship between language, translation and interpretation. They were conscious of the circumstance that each translation was, as well, an interpretation which had to be made clear to the reader in a convincing linguistic form.

The controversies over the Bible deepened this knowledge during the Reformation. The criticism of Luther's September Testament of 1522 (which lasted for years) is especially applicable to this thesis. The crucial point of the dispute shifted very quickly from the actual state of the text to the glossing of the text and to the prefaces which Luther placed in front of the individual biblical books. Leib's opinion can already be observed during the twenties: people argued more about the basic theological decisions and the hermeneutic rules than about the actual text. The first comprehensive criticism of Luther's translation, written by Emser, proves this.[53] Later on, other Catholic theologians such as Johannes Dietenberger, Georg Witzel and Johannes Eck argued similarly.[54] Therefore, the following subjects run through the particular controversies like a red thread: *Claritas Scripturae*, Writ and Church, Canon of the Writ, Law and Gospel, Writ and Tradition, Spirit and Letter. In his own way, Erasmus of Rotterdam indicated this problem when he wrote against Luther in 'Hyperaspistes' in 1526: 'By the way you always fail in your attempt to impose on us your interpretation as God's word'.[55]

With these necessarily very short remarks the interconnectedness of the controversy on the Bible and its interpretation in the sixteenth century becomes once again evident: It is the complex interweaving of language, methods of interpretation and theological content as well as their consequences for the image of the Church and the Christian Life.

Here the controversies showed themselves to be creative by developing further the work on the Bible and by deepening reflection. They proved themselves to be obstructive when their denominational fixation blocked the view and set limits which could not be overstepped without penalties.

NOTES

1. Selected bibliography: George H. Tavard, *Écriture ou Église? La crise de la réforme*, Paris (1963); Richard Stauffer, *Interprètes de la Bible. Études sur les réformateurs du XVIᵉ siècle*, Paris (1980); Hans-Joachim Kraus, *Geschichte der historisch-kritischen Erforschung des Alten Testaments*, Neukirchen-Vluyn (3rd edn, 1982); Henning Graf Reventlow, *Bibelautorität und Geist der Moderne*, Göttingen (1980), pp. 16-160; Jerry H. Bentley,

Humanists and Holy Writ. New Testament Scholarship in the Renaissance, Princeton, New Jersey (1983); Heinrich Karpp, Bibel IV: *Theologische Realenzyklopädie*, VI, pp. 66ff. (with copious bibliographical notes). For a brief and illuminating survey of recent research concerning the Middle Ages, see Pierre Riché—Guy Lobrichon (ed.), *Le moyen âge et la Bible*, Paris (1984). Cf. also B. Smalley, *The Study of the Bible in the Middle Ages*, Oxford (3rd edn, 1984).

2. *Weimarer Ausgabe* (WA) 54, pp. 185-186. See, for example, the excellent *Handbuch der Kirchengeschichte*, ed. Hubert Jedin, Vol. IV, Freiburg/Basel/Wien (1967), pp. 36ff.

3. Cf. Herbert Wolf, *Martin Luther. Eine Einführung in germanistische Luther-Studien*, Stuttgart (1980); Siegfried Raeder, 'Luther als Ausleger und Übersetzer der Heiligen Schrift', *Leben und Werk Martin Luthers von 1526 bis 1546*, ed. Helmar Junghans, Göttingen (1983), pp. 253-78. See also *Biblia deutsch. Luthers Bibelübersetzung und ihre Tradition*, ed. Heimo Reinitzer, Herzog August Bibliothek Wolfenbüttel (1983).

4. Leif Grane, *Modus Loquendi Theologicus. Luthers Kampf um die Erneuerung der Theologie (1515-1518)*, Leiden (1975).

5. On the whole subject see n. 1. Special attention is paid to Erasmus of Rotterdam and Lefèvre d'Étaples. See below nn. 12, 14. Cf. also Guy Bedouelle, *Lefèvre d'Étaples et l'intelligence des Écritures*, Genève (1976); Jean-Pierre Massaut, 'Lefèvre d'Étaples et l'exégèse au XVIᶜ siècle', *Revue d'Histoire Ecclésiastique* 78 (1983), pp. 73-78.

6. Paul Oskar Kristeller, 'The Role of Religion in Renaissance Humanism and Platonism', *The Pursuit of Holiness in Late Medieval and Renaissance Religion*, ed. Trinkaus-Oberman, Leyden (1974), p. 369.

7. See the following notes.

8. J. Lindeboom, *Het Bijbelsch Humanisme in Nederland*, Leiden (1913). Cf. Cornelis Augustijn, 'Die Stellung der Humanisten zur Glaubensspaltung', in: *Confessio Augustana und Confutatio*, ed. Erwin Iserloh, Münster (1980), pp. 36-61.

9. Hermanni Buschii . . . *Vallum humanitatis*, Cologne (1518). Cf. Hermann Joseph Liessem, *Hermann van dem Busche. Sein Leben und seine Schriften*, Köln (1884/1908), repr. Nieuwkoop (1965).

10. *Vallum humanitatis* D IVbff.

11. *Vallum humanitatis* A Vbff.

12. Erasmus of Rotterdam, *In Novum Testamentum Praefationes*, ed. Gerhard B. Winkler, Darmstadt (1967). Cf. Gerhard B. Winkler, *Erasmus von Rotterdam und die Einleitungsschriften zum Neuen Testament. Formale Strukturen und theologischer Sinn*, Münster (1974); M. Hoffmann, *Erkenntnis und Verwirklichung der wahren Theologie nach Erasmus von Rotterdam*, Tübingen (1972).

13. *Laurentii Vallensis . . . in Latinam Novi testamenti interpretationem ex collatione Grecorum exemplarium Adnotationes apprime utiles* (edited, with a

prefatory letter, by D. Erasmus), Paris (1505). Cf. H. Holeczek, *Humanistische Bibelphilologie als Reformproblem bei Erasmus von Rotterdam, Thomas More und William Tyndale*, Leiden (1975), pp. 79ff.; cf. W. Schwarz, *Principles and Problems of Biblical Translation: Some Reformation Controversies and their Background*, Cambridge (1955).

14. Cf. n. 12; see also Robert Stupperich, *Erasmus von Rotterdam und seine Welt*, Berlin/New York (1977), pp. 120ff.

15. Cf. Raeder, p. 271 (see n. 3).

16. For a survey, see Malcolm D. Lambert, *Medieval Heresy. Popular Movements from Bogomil to Hus*, London (1977).

17. Cf. Henri de Lubac, *La posterità spirituale di Gioachino da Fiore*, I, Milano (1981), pp. 85ff.

18. Cf. Reventlow (see n. 1), pp. 55ff.

19. Cf. G. Fussenegger, 'Alberto Pio von Carpi', *Lexikon für Theologie und Kirche*, 2nd edn, II, col. 955; M.P. Gilmore, 'Erasmus and Alberto Pio Prince of Carpi', *Action and Conviction in Early Modern Europe. Essays in Memory of E.H. Harbison*, ed. Th.K. Rabb and J.E. Seigel, Princeton, New Jersey (1969), pp. 266-318.

20. 'De trium linguarum et studii theologici ratione dialogus', per Jacobum Latomum ed., in *Primitiae Pontificiae Theologorum Neerlandicorum Disputationes contra Lutherum*, ed. F. Pijper, Hagae-Comitis (1905) = Bibliotheca Reformatoria Neerlandica, 3. Cf. J. Étienne, 'Latomus', *Lexikon für Theologie und Kirche*, 2nd edn, VI, col. 822.

21. Letter from Albrecht of Brandenburg to Erasmus, September 13, 1517: 'Quid enim desiderari magis etate nostra potuit quam ut emendatiora essent Veteris (corr.: Novi) Instrumenti exemplaria? . . At per te in lucem est reductus et quasi a morte in vitam revocatus (scl. Hieronymus)' = Allen (ed.), *Opus epistolarum D. Erasmi*, 12 Vols., Oxford (1906-58), n. 661.

22. Letter from Johannes Eck to Erasmus, February 2, 1518: 'Primo autem omnium, ut hinc exordiar . . . Istis enim verbis innuere videris Euangelistas more humano scripsisse . . . Ad aliud ascendamus. Acta Apostolorum elucidaturus cap. X adnotasti haec verba: "Tamen etiam cum Graece scribunt Apostoli, multum referunt ex proprietate linguae suae" . . . Hoc minus sobrie a te homine Christiano fore scriptum plerique opinantur . . . Postremo pluribus praeteritis . . . hoc ex meo addam, qui Augustini doctrinam eminentissimam in primis post sacrum canonem ac Ecclesiae sanctae decreta suspicio et veneror. Idcirco displicet mihi iudicium tuum, quod de Augustino super Joanne affers; "Impudentissimum" asseris "alterum alteri comparari"' = Allen n. 769. The answer of Erasmus to Eck dated May 15, 1518 = Allen n. 844.

23. Cf. Erwin Iserloh, *Johannes Eck (1486-1543). Scholastiker, Humanist, Kontroverstheologe*, Münster (1981); *idem*, 'Eck', *Theologische Realenzyklopädie* IX, pp. 249-58 (with copious bibliographical notes).

24. Cf. the letter from Eck to Contarini, March 13, 1540: 'At ut perveniam ubi volebam, Erasmus et Luderani ad solas bonas literas... scholasticos adhortantes. Philosophiam et theologiam una pessundederunt...': Beiträge zum Briefwechsel der katholischen Gelehrten Deutschlands im Reformationszeitalter. Ed. Walter Friedensburg: *Zeitschrift für Kirchengeschichte* 19 (1899), p. 256.

25. *Bibel. Alt und new Testament, nach dem Text in der hailigen kirchen gebraucht, durch doctor Johann Ecken, mit fleiß... verdolmetscht*, Ingolstadt (1537); *Explanatio psalmi vigesimi a Johan. Eckio...*, Augsburg (1538); *Super Aggaeo propheta Jo. Eckii commentarius, Salingiaci* (Solingen) 1538. The 'Explanatio' is edited, with an introduction, by Bernhard Walde: *Corpus Catholicorum* Vol. 13, Münster (1928).

26. See, for example, Universitätsbibliothek Munich: 2° Cod. 37, 8° Cod. 8, 8° Cod. 9 with lectures of Eck on the Psalms, Malachi, Genesis, Exodus, Leviticus etc.

27. For useful discussion, see the introduction of Walde (see n. 25).

28. Cf. *Explanatio*, pp. xxxiif. (ed. Walde).

29. Cf. *Explanatio*, pp. xxxff. (ed. Walde).

30. Cf. *Explanatio*, p. xxxvii (ed. Walde); Alice Magee Brunot, 'Kimchi (Kimhi) David', *New Catholic Encyclopedia* VIII, pp. 181f.; *idem*, 'Rashi (Rabbi Shelomoh ben Yishaq)', *New Catholic Encyclopedia* XII, pp. 85f. In 1521, Eck had participated in the lectures of Reuchlin at the university of Ingolstadt. Cf. also Clm 11602, Bayerische Staatsbibliothek Munich: Joh. Eckii regestum super lexico hebraico Capnionis (= Reuchlin)... collectum..., Fol 3ff. See Kraus (see n. 1), pp. 12ff.

31. Cf. Kraus *ibid.*, p. 26: 'Den "Rudimenta linguae Hebraicae" aber läßt Reuchlin eine aufschlußreiche Erklärung der sieben Bußpsalmen folgen... Es handelt sich um eine philologische Methode der Exegese ("de verbo ad verbum")'.

32. Cf. n. 12; see also M. Hoffmann, *Erkenntnis und Verwirklichung der wahren Theologie nach Erasmus von Rotterdam*, Tübingen (1972).

33. Cf. Reventlow (see n. 1), pp. 68-89.

34. Cf. Reventlow (see n. 1), p. 75.

35. Cf. the introduction: *Erasmus von Rotterdam, Ausgewählte Schriften*, ed. W. Welzig, Vol. I, Darmstadt (1968), p. xi.

36. *Erasmus, Enchiridion* (ed. Welzig), Darmstadt (1968), pp. 127-29. Cf. J. Étienne, *Spiritualisme érasmien et théologiens louvanistes*, Louvain (1956), p. 14.

37. Cf. Augustijn (see n. 8), p. 40; Reventlow (see n. 1), pp. 72-79; C. Augustijn, *Erasmus. Vernieuwer van kerk en theologie*, Baarn (1967); H. Holeczek, *Humanistische Bibelphilologie als Reformproblem bei Erasmus von Rotterdam, Thomas More und William Tyndale*, Leiden (1975).

38. Cf. É.V. Telle, *Érasme de Rotterdam et le septième sacrement*, Genève (1954).

39. Erasmus of Rotterdam, *Novum Testamentum: Opera Omnia* VI, Leiden (1705), repr. London (1962): ad Matth 5,31, cols. 29-30; ad Mk 10,4, col. 190; Glossa ad 1 Cor 7,39: 'liberata est a lege, cui autem vult, nubat'. Erasmus translated: 'libera est ad cui velit nubendum'. The whole gloss cols. 692-703. See Erasmus' letter to Jakob Hochstraten dated August 11, 1519, Allen IV, n. 1006.

40. Letter from Erasmus to Hochstraten, August 11, 1519, Allen IV n. 1006, p. 49: 'Cum viderem Christi spiritum mire pro temporum ratione dispensare suos afflatus, et animadverterem quanta sit autoritas Ecclesiae, submonebam, si qua fieri posset, ut tot hominum pereuntium saluti consuleretur'.

41. See *Johannes Dietenberger OP, Phimostomus scripturariorum*, Köln (1532), edited, with an introduction, by Erwin Iserloh and Peter Fabisch, Münster (1985), pp. lxxxiff.

42. Cf. Heinz Holeczek, *Erasmus Deutsch*, Vol. I: *Die volkssprachliche Rezeption des Erasmus von Rotterdam in der reformatorischen Öffentlichkeit 1519-1536*, Stuttgart (1983), p. 21: 'Der erste und wichtigste Themenkomplex umfaßt die biblizistischen Arbeiten des Erasmus, das sind seine biblischen Ausgaben und seine Schriften zur Erschließung der Hl. Schrift sowie ihre Ausdeutung für die Reformdiskussion. Im Mittelpunkt stehen hierbei sein Novum Testamentum einschließlich seiner Annotationes, sowie seine Paraphrases zum NT. Diese Gruppe ist die umfangreichste, sie umfaßt über hundertzehn Einzeldrucke'; p. 22: 'Aus dieser generellen Übersicht der überlieferten deutschen Ausgabe des Erasmus läßt sich auf eine starke Präsenz desselben in der volkssprachlichen Öffentlichkeit der Reformationszeit in den drei Themenbereichen des Biblizismus, der Reform von Pietas und Moral schließen'.

43. Cf. Peter Hegg, 'Die Drucker der "Göttlichen Mühle" von 1521', *Schweizer Gutenbergmuseum* 4 (1954), pp. 135ff, cited by Holeczek (see n. 42), p. 13.

44. Cf. Bernhard Lohse, *Martin Luther. Eine Einführung in sein Leben und sein Werk*, München (1981), pp. 160ff.; Kraus (see n. 1), pp. 6ff. Raeder (see n. 3); Stauffer (see n. 1).

45. Cf. Augustijn (see n. 8); Robert Stupperich, *Der Humanismus und die Wiedervereinigung der Konfessionen*, Leipzig (1936).

46. Cf. Heribert Smolinsky, *Augustin von Alveldt und Hieronymus Emser. Eine Untersuchung zur Kontroverstheologie der frühen Reformationszeit im Herzogtum Sachsen*, Münster (1984), pp. 256ff.

47. Erasmus, *Novum Testamentum* (see n. 39), col. 759: '. . . et intelligas novum Testamentum spiritum, vetus litteram. At Apostoli delecti sunt ut spiritum administrarent, non ceremonias Legis tantum ac praecepta Legis, quae suo more litteram vocat'; *idem, Enchiridion Militis Christiani* (ed. Welzig, see n. 35), p. 80: 'Erue sensum spiritalem, iam nihil suavius, nihil succulentius'; p. 84: 'Sed uti divina scriptura non multum habet fructus, si in

littera persistas . . . '; p. 90: '. . . neque ad spiritalem scripturarum cognitionem elaborant . . . non Paulum magistro astruentem: Littera occidit, spiritus est, qui vivificat'. Cf. Reventlow (see n. 1), pp. 74f.

48. Cf. Smolinsky *op. cit.*, pp. 260ff.; *Johannes Eck, Enchiridion locorum communium adversus Lutherum et alios hostes ecclesiae*, ed. Pierre Fraenkel, Münster (1979), ch. 1, p. 31; Johannes Dietenberger (see n. 41), p. xliii, ch. 4, pp. 54ff.

49. Cf. Smolinsky *op. cit.*, pp. 263ff.; Luther, *Auf das überchristlich Buch*, WA 7, pp. 647ff.

50. Smolinsky *op. cit.*, p. 263.

51. Johannes Buchstab, *Daß die Biblischen geschrifften mussen eyn geystliche ußlegung han* . . . s.a.e.l. (1529); Cf. E.W. Zeeden, 'Buchstab': *Lexikon für Theologie und Kirche*, 2nd edn, II, col. 749.

52. De Sacrae Scripturae Dissonis Translationibus Autore *Kiliano Leib* . . . D. Chunradi Adelmanni Epistola, s.l. (1542); cf. Josef Deutsch, Kilian Leib, Prior von Rebdorf. *Ein Lebensbild aus dem Zeitalter der deutschen Reformation*, Münster (1910), pp. 134-36; Monika Fink-Lang, *Untersuchungen zum Eichstätter Geistesleben im Zeitalter des Humanismus*, Regensburg (1985), pp. 208-13, 243-46.

53. Hieronymus Emser, *Auß was grund unnd ursach Luthers dolmatschung uber das nawe testament* . . . *vorbotten worden sey*, Leipzig s. a. Cf. Kenneth A. Strand, *Reformation Bibles in the Crossfire. The Story of Jerome Emser, His Anti-Lutheran Critique and His Catholic Bible Version*, Ann Arbor (1961); Karl-Heinz Musseleck, *Untersuchungen zur Sprache katholischer Bibelübersetzungen der Reformationszeit*, Heidelberg (1981).

54. Cf. Dietenberger (see n. 41); Georg Witzel, *Annotationes in Sacras Literas*, Mayence (1537); Eck, *Enchiridion* (see n. 48).

55. Erasmus, *Hyperaspistes diatribae* . . . ed. W. Lesowsky, Darmstadt (1969), p. 390: 'Caeterum in hoc peccas, quod nobis perpetuo tuam interpretationem obtrudis pro verbo Dei'.

11

COURANTS ET CONTRE-COURANTS DANS L'EXEGESE BIBLIQUE JUIVE EN FRANCE AU MOYEN-AGE

Elazar Touitou

La contribution du judaïsme espagnol au patrimoine religieux et intellectuel du peuple juif pendant les 10-13ème siècles fut, comme on le sait, très riche et très variée. Les Juifs d'Espagne créèrent des œuvres de valeurs dans tous les domaines culturels que le monde médiéval connaissait: exégèse biblique, études talmudiques, philosophie, lettres—sur des sujets sacrés et profanes—philologie, codification juridique, littérature scientifique (astronomie, médecine) etc... Par contre, l'activité intellectuelle du judaïsme franco-allemand au moyen-âge était relativement restreinte et se confinait aux domaines spécifiquement juifs, c'est-à-dire aux études bibliques et talmudiques.

Cette différence serait due, selon les historiens, à la conception différente qu'avaient les Juifs de chacun de ces deux grands centres quant à la relation qu'il faut entretenir avec le monde étranger environnant. Le judaïsme espagnol était ouvert au monde arabe et à sa culture; les Juifs sépharads ne se sont donc pas empêchés de se former aux disciplines intellectuelles de la civilisation arabe, laquelle était, on s'en souvient bien, très riche en ce moyen-âge. Ce n'est donc pas par hasard que les grandes œuvres des docteurs juifs espagnols étaient écrites, pour la plupart des cas, en arabe. Le judaïsme franco-allemand, au contraire, se replia sur lui-même, s'enferma dans les limites bien définies de la culture juive classique—la Bible et surtout le Talmud—et s'immunisa pour ainsi dire contre toute influence culturelle étrangère. C'est ce qui explique l'utilisation quasi exclusive de l'hébreu par les docteurs juifs franco-allemands.

La réalité était, croyons-nous, beaucoup plus complexe. La civilisation arabe avait, dans la plupart de ses domaines, un caractère profane, ou tout au moins neutre du point de vue religieux. La langue

qui véhiculait cette civilisation, je veux dire l'arabe, était la langue
pratiquée par tout le monde. Enfin les intellectuels arabes étaient
souvent des laics et leur enseignement ne s'identifiait pas forcément
avec celui de l'establishment musulman religieux. Il n'y avait donc
pas de cloison étanche entre le monde arabe—et je spécifie: arabe et
non musulman—et le monde juif. La situation, dans l'Europe
occidentale chrétienne, était tout à fait différente. Les divers
domaines de la culture occidentale—et ils n'étaient pas très
nombreux au début de notre période—étaient fortement imprégnés
de christianisme; la langue des écoles, des sciences était exclusivement
le latin, c'est-à-dire la langue officielle de l'Eglise. Quant aux
intellectuels, ils étaient tous des clercs, gens d'église. Les Juifs ne
pouvaient donc pas avoir accès à cette ambiance culturelle, même
s'ils le voulaient.

Telle était, à peu près, la situation jusque vers le milieu du 11ème
siècle. Elle changea sensiblement et rapidement à partir de la seconde
moitié du siècle. Notons d'abord ce qui se passe dans la Chrétienté.
Citons un témoignage précieux, celui de Guibert de Nogent qui, né
en 1053, écrivait vers 1115 ses Confessions et opposait en ces termes
les deux extrémités de sa vie:

> Dans le temps qui précéda immédiatement mon enfance et durant
> celle-ci même, la pénurie de maitres d'école était telle qu'il était à
> peu près impossible d'en trouver dans les bourgs: à peine s'il s'en
> rencontrait dans les villes. En découvrait-on par hasard? Leur
> science était si mince qu'elle ne saurait se comparer même à celle
> des petits clercs vagabonds d'aujourd'hui.[1]

Les écoles se multiplient, les étudiants, de plus en plus nombreux,
assoiffés de savoir, parcourent, le pays à la recherche des maîtres les
plus illustres, de plus en plus nombreux eux aussi. Les matières
enseignées se diversifient et l'enseignement devient plus approfondi.
Surtout une nouvelle approche émerge, celle de faire passer toute
chose au crible de la raison humaine. Attention, cela ne veut pas du
tout dire un rejet de la tradition—le moyen-âge était très empreint de
religiosité et assumait très sincèrement ses attaches aux racines de la
tradition—cela veut dire un ardent désir de comprendre sa foi, son
monde, son histoire, donc connaître et comprendre, 'auctoritas et
ratio'. Trouver l'équilibre adéquat entre l'autorité de la tradition et
celle de la raison humaine serait même, selon certains, le trait
caratéristique de la renaissance du 12ème siècle.[2] Dans le domaine
des études bibliques cela se traduit par l'épanouissement, en ce siècle,

d'une exégèse littérale, historique, à côté de l'exégèse spirituelle pratiquée depuis toujours.[3] Dans la domaine de la controverse judéo-chrétienne cela s'exprime, chez les chrétiens, par une floraison de traités contre les Juifs, basés certes sur les arguments traditionnels, mais présentés plus rationnellement; les sujets sont triés et appropriés aux centres d'intérêt de l'époque. La matière ne change pas, mais la manière est nouvelle.[4] Spicq, spécialiste de l'exégèse chrétienne du moyen-âge, souligne que 'ce sont les besoins de la polémique contre les Juifs plus encore que les exigences de l'exégèse qui imposèrent aux auteurs du 12ème siècle une initiation plus ou moins sommaire aux langues orientales'.[5] Et il conclut quelques lignes plus loins: 'C'est donc d'abord et avant tout pour des fins apologétiques que les exégètes du Moyen-Age apprirent l'hébreu et analysèrent le sens littéral'.

Clercs et laïcs participaient à ces controverses. Les plus instruits y exposaient les thèses savantes apprises dans les fameuses écoles du temps; les moins instruits y répétaient les enseignements que dispensaient les représentants de l'Eglise. C'est qu'au moyen-âge 'on s'instruit d'avantage par l'ouïe que par la lecture'.[6] Les moyens de cet enseignement oral étaient nombreux et divers. D'abord la prédication.

> On prêchait un peu partout, pas seulement dans les églises, mais aussi dans les marchés, sur les champs de foire, au carrefour des routes,—et de façon très vivante, pleine de flamme et de fougue. Le prédicateur s'adressait à l'auditoire, répondait à ses questions, admettait même ses contradictions, ses rumeurs, ses apostrophes. Un sermon agissait sur la foule, pouvait déchaîner sur l'heure une croisade, propager une hérésie, entraîner des révoltes. Le rôle didactique des clercs était alors immense: c'étaient eux qui enseignaient aux fidèles leur histoire et leurs légendes, leur science et leur foi.[7]

Au cours de ces prédications on déclamait aussi, après les avoir traduit en langue vernaculaire, des écrits théologiques populaires, rédigés à l'origine en latin.

Il y avait aussi les spectacles; ceux-ci sont, bien entendu, à base religieuse.

> Toute fête commence par les cérémonies du culte . . . Celles-ci se prolongent de spectacles qui, donnés primitivement dans l'église même, n'ont pas tardé à se voir rejetés sur le parvis; . . . Ces spectacles sont essentiellement populaires; ils ont le peuple pour acteurs et pour auditoire—auditoire actif, vibrant au moindre

détail de ces scènes qui réveillent en lui sentiments et émotions d'une qualité tout autre que celle du théâtre actuel, puisque ce ne sont pas seulement l'intellect ou la sentimentalité qui entrent en jeu, mais aussi des croyances profondes.[8]

Comment réagit la communauté juive de France aux assauts de ce renouveau? La plupart des historiens prétendent que la communauté juive franco-allemande demeura imperméable aux idées nouvelles qui remuèrent le monde chrétien environnant. La société juive du 12ème siècle ne serait que la continuation calme, tranquille, des générations précédentes. La vie juive se serait poursuivie sans failles, sans problèmes, à côté pour ainsi dire des grands courants spirituels qui firent vibrer leurs voisins chrétiens. Pour revenir au domaine de l'exégèse biblique qui nous concerne, l'école exégétique littérale de Rachi serait, selon ces historiens, une production proprement et intrinsèquement juive, tant pour ses sources que pour ses tendances, sans aucune relation, ou presque, avec le monde chrétien environnant.

Nous trouvons cette conception inacceptable.[9] D'abord il y a un fait irrécusable: c'est précisément au début de notre époque que se crée chez les Juifs de France une école exégétique visant à faire valoir l'aspect littéral des textes sacrés, sans pour autant en dévaluer le sens midrachique. Puis, parallèlement à ce qui se passe chez les Chrétiens, cette école se développe pendant deux ou trois générations, atteint son apogée et, vers le dernier quart du siècle, décline, comme chez les Chrétiens. Est-ce par simple hasard que le même phénomène culturel se produit simultanément dans les deux communautés voisines? Samuel ben Meïr (=Rachbam) parle au nom de son grand-père Rachi des 'explications littérales qui se renouvellent chaque jour'.[10] Nous présumons qu'il y a là un écho des tendances nouvelles. Joseph Qara et Rachbam parlent plusieurs fois d'un nouveau genre d'étudiant juif qui ne peut plus se suffire des commentaires midrachiques traditionnels; ce sont des 'maskilim'—intellectuels juifs faisant pendant pour ainsi dire aux intellectuels chrétiens si bien décrits par Le Goff.[11] C'est pour ces 'maskilim' que nos rabbins ont rédigé leurs commentaires littéraux.

Mais il y a aussi autre chose. La vitalité religieuse des Chrétiens impressionnait les Juifs. Nous en avons un témoignage poignant émis par un exégète liturgique, très probablement R. Joseph Qara, jeune contemporain de Rachi. Joseph Qara met, dans la bouche de la Synagogue, la confession suivant: 'Quoique mon esprit enregistre leurs paroles, et dans mon cœur une flamme ardente m'attire vers eux subrepticement, malgré cela mon attachement à Toi est pour moi le Bien'.[12] Il était certainement urgent de préserver les jeunes Juifs contre l'influence chrétienne. Rachi le dira expressément: 'Prouve la véracité de mes paroles, ne soit pas séduite par les nations (étrangères) et que les bons et intelligents parmi toi soient tenaces dans leur foi et sachent répondre à leurs séducteurs, de manière que les jeunes apprennent d'eux'.[13] Il faut croire que ces 'jeunes' n'étaient pas préparés à ce genre de discussion.

Quel était, en France vers la fin du 11éme siècle, le bagage culturel d'un Juif moyen? D'abord une intimité à double aspect avec la bible hébraïque—d'un côté une connaissance du mot-à-mot du texte, enseigné en vieux français à l'aide de ces lexiques dont une version tardive nous a été admirablement présentée par M. Banitt;[14] d'un autre côté des explications midrachiques, éparses dans le Talmud ou amassés dans ces Sommes riches et touffues que sont Midrach Rabba, Midrach Tanhuma et autres midrachim. Ensuite une solide connaissance du Talmud. Cette instruction, toute axée vers le dedans juif, s'avèrera inadéquate aux idées nouvelles qui exigeaient des explications rationnelles. Surtout elle ne prépare guère à l'éventuelle joute verbale avec les Chrétiens. Il fallait former les étudiants selon les méthodes nouvelles; entre autre, il fallait les initier à une nouvelle approche de l'Ecriture, approche moderne, rationnelle, voire même audacieuse.

Résumons et concluons jusque là. Le 12ème siècle a connu un important développement de l'exégèse biblique littérale en Europe occidentale, tant chez les Chrétiens que chez les Juifs. Les deux facteurs essentiels de ce développement, à savoir l'influence de la renaissance intellectuelle et les besoins de la controverse religieuse, valent autant pour les Chrétiens que pour les Juifs.

Nous parlons sans cesse de controverse judéo-chrétienne; il faut savoir qu'il y avait aussi des échanges d'idées entre Chrétiens et Juifs, et il nous paraît nécessaire de faire une distinction entre des deux genres de contact. Les deux s'engagent, bien entendu, sur des sujets bibliques, mais leurs caractères sont tout à fait différents. Dans la controverse les partenaires sont adversaires; le point de départ est le même pour tous les deux, c'est le texte biblique, ce qui les sépare, c'est l'interprétation de ce texte. Lorsque le commentateur prépare son travail d'exégèse, c'est certes le texte qu'il entend expliquer, mais à l'arrière-plan, consciemment ou non, se trouvent les thèses de l'adversaire; c'est donc non seulement pour exposer ses propres idées qu'il écrira son commentaire, mais aussi pour combattre les idées de l'adversaire, que cela soit dit explicitement ou non.

Dans les échanges d'idées, par contre, point d'adversaires mais des interlocuteurs. Il y a là information mutuelle et parfois même fructification mutuelle. Les exégètes du temps, Chrétiens et Juifs, mais beaucoup plus les Chrétiens que les Juifs, relatent ces échanges d'idées. La regrettée Miss Beryl Smalley puis d'autres après elle l'ont copieusement prouvé pour le côté chrétien. Pour le côté juif, rappelons que Rachi, déjà, à propos d'Ezéchiel 2,1 écrivait: 'il nomme Ezéchiel fils de l'homme, c'est que le prophète voit le Char (divin) et s'en sert au même titre que les anges, il était donc nécessaire de souligner qu'il n'y avait là-bas aucun être humain, Ezéchiel exclus'. Et le copiste qui assistait lui-même au cours de Rachi ajoute là une phrase très intéressante: 'et tout ceci, c'est un Chrétien[15] qui l'a expliqué à notre maître, et celui-ci en fut bien satisfait'. Cet épisode mérite d'être analysé. Où a eu lieu la conversation entre Rachi et le Chrétien? Au hasard d'une rencontre dans les rues de Troyes ou à l'école même de Rachi? Etait-ce là un épisode unique, inhabituel, ou plutôt y en avaient-il d'autres, que les copistes n'ont pas pris garde de relater? Ne sommes-nous pas en présence, déjà du temps de Rachi, de ce que nous raconte R. Yehiel de Paris quelques générations plus tard, à savoir que des clercs participaient régulièrement aux cours des maîtres juifs?[16] En tout cas il était homme bien instruit, ce Chrétien qui enrichissait Rachi d'une explication puisée probablement dans Jérôme.

Rachbam écrit, à propos de Lévitique 19,19: 'J'ai dit aux Chrétiens . . . et ils ont reconnu que j'avais raison'. Ici aussi il aurait été très important de connaître les modalités de cette rencontre. Un autre commentaire de Rachbam démontre encore plus que le précédent l'intensité et le sérieux de ces échanges d'idées. Rachbam explique le fameux verset de Genèse 49,10 et termine par la phrase suivante:

אין לעז במקרא ולא 'שלו' כת כאן כדברי העברים ולא 'שליח' כדברי הנוצרים

Les Chrétiens sont nommés ici non pas 'minim' comme de coutume, mais 'nozrim'; quant aux Juifs ce ne sont pas 'nos maîtres' ou 'les sages d'Israël' habituels, mais un nom absolument inattendu, 'les Hébreux'. Il y a là, je crois, un lapsus linguae qui dévoile que Rachbam pensait latin quand il écrivit cette phrase, c'est en effet le mot 'hébreu' qui revient le plus souvent sous la plume des Chrétiens du 12ème siècle pour désigner les Juifs.

A partir de la seconde moitié du 12ème siècle le ton des discussions change; il devient âpre et souvent insultant. La sérénité, preuve de relations correctes, fait place à l'ambiance injurieuse, voire haineuse. Les Juifs sont des hérétiques qu'il faut traquer, le Talmud, le livre juif par excellence, est plein d'insanités et il faut l'expurger, sinon le brûler. La controverse s'engage de plus en plus sur le Talmud et de moins en moins sur la Bible où les Juifs, plus forts que les Chrétiens dans l'exégèse littérale, avaient le dessus. Vers la fin du 12ème siècle et au début du 13ème, on abandonne l'exégèse littérale dans les deux camps, vus les nouveaux besoins de la controverse et la 'fermeture' du siècle aux idées nouvelles. L'exégèse midrachique chez les Juifs et spirituelle chez les Chrétiens redevient prédominante.

Les lignes principales de la thèse que nous présentons sont donc les suivantes: vers la fin du onzième siècle Rachi donna le branle à un fort mouvement exégétique à double courant—un courant littéral (פשוטו של כתוב), nouveau à l'époque, et un courant semi-midrachique (האגדה המיישבת דברי המקרא על אופניו). Le Peshat fut cultivé pendant deux ou trois générations par des écolâtres illustres—R. Joseph Qara, Samuel ben Meïr (Rachbam), R. Joseph Bekhor Chor d'Orléans (Rivash), R. Eliézer de Beaugency. Le Derash fut pratiqué, d'abord par Rachi lui-même, puis par d'autres maîtres qui, s'estimant simplement être glaneurs dans le champ midrachique traditionnel, sont restés en général dans l'anonymat.[17] Le Peshat était volontairement ouvert aux idées modernes de la renaissance du 12ème siècle et se présentait explicitement comme instrument utile pour la controverse judéo-chrétienne. Le Derash, lui, demeurait dans le sillon de la tradition et ne voulait qu'édifier les Juifs eux-mêmes. Le Peshat satisfaisait les besoins extérieurs de la communauté juive, le Derash continuait à remplir la vie intérieure juive. Il y avait, évidemment, au sein de chacun de ces deux grands courants, des nuances exégétiques qui départageaient nos docteurs, selon les nécessités du temps et selon la personnalité de l'exégète; mais l'aspect général du mouvement est, je crois, comme nous le décrivons.

Nous voudrions étayer succinctement notre thèse par deux exemples, le premier touche un point de psychologie sociale, le second concerne un problème de foi religieuse. Nous suivrons, pour chaque exemple, le mouvement exégétique qui s'amorce avec Rachi puis se développe ou au contraire change de direction avec Rachbam

(1ère moitié du 12ème siècle), Rivash (2ème moitié même siècle) et Hiskia ben Manoah, surnommé Hiskouni (13ème siècle).

1. *E S A U*. Dans la tradition midrachique Esaü représente Rome et, par extension, les peuples hostiles à Israël, Chrétiens inclus. Rachi adopte cette conception préfigurative comme base de son commentaire. C'est ainsi qu' Esaü fut prédisposé, dès sa conception, à adorer les idoles.[18] Sa rousseur (v. 25) est 'le signe qu'il versera le sang'. La chasse est, pour Esaü, une école de tromperie (v. 27). Il est fatigué (v. 29) à force de tuer. Son impiété risque tellement d'affliger son grand-père que Dieu raccourcira la vie d'Abraham de cinq ans pour lui ménager le triste spectacle d'un petit-fils délinquant. Le droit d'aînesse, c'est en réalité le service de Dieu à l'autel, et Esaü 'l'impie', comme le nomme son frère Jacob, n'a que faire de ce droit. Après vingt-deux ans de séparation, Esaü continue de haïr son frère (Gen. 32,7) et se prépare à lui faire la guerre. Rachi note bien, çà et là, que tel ou tel commentaire est d'origine midrachique, mais pour la majorité des cas il ne le dit pas; il présente donc son explication comme étant littérale. Cela montre à quel point l'image midrachique d'Esaü était encore vivace du temps de Rachi, et c'est cette image que Rachi a trouvé nécessaire de transmettre à ses élèves et lecteurs.

La tradition chrétienne prit, bien entendu, le contrepied de cette position. Esaü est bien une 'figure', un 'type', mais c'est la figure du peuple juif. Les commentaires de la Genèse d'Etienne Langton, sorte de 'somme' de l'exégèse chrétienne du 12ème siècle, reprennent tous les détails de l'allégorisation: Esaü est

> roux et couvert de sang, comme le sera le peuple juif après la Passion; son poil abondant ainsi que sa qualité de chasseur désignent les appétits matériels des Juifs; la vente du droit d'aînesse préfigure la renonciation du peuple juif à une loi spirituelle au profit de l'observance charnelle etc . . .[19]

Au niveau de la controverse populaire vivante, Jacob non plus n'est pas épargné. Nous lisons dans le Livre de Joseph le Zélateur, compilation de controverses probablement vécues, rédigée vers la fin de notre période, l'anecdote suivante:

> Un Jacopin (Dominicain ou Frère Prêcheur) rencontra Rabbi Joseph sur la route de Paris et lui dit: votre patriarche Jacob était un voleur et il n'y a pas d'usurier comme lui—au prix d'un seul plat qui valait la moitié d'un sequin, il acheta le droit d'aînesse qui vaut mille sequins.[20]

Face à l'allégorisation et aux invectives des polémistes, les intellectuels juifs répondront par l'exégèse littérale. Rachbam, quelques décennies après Rachi, changera totalement la direction de l'exégèse de notre récit: les difficultés de grossesse de Rebecca n'ont rien de mystique, ils proviennent simplement du fait qu'elle a des jumeaux (sur Gen. 25,22-23); 'admoni' veut dire 'roux' et pas plus, de même *'yode'a saïd'*—chasseur de métier. La fatigue d'Esaü est la conséquence normale de son dur travail, et s'il fait peu de cas du droit d'aînesse, c'est qu'il réalise les dangers mortels que courre tout chasseur dans ces forêts infestés de lions, d'ours et d'autres bêtes féroces. Les défauts d'Esaü sont bénins—notre chasseur est glouton et quelque peu sot. Le prix qu'il reçoit pour la vente de son droit d'aînesse n'est pas, comme tout le monde se l'imagine, un plat de lentilles, mais une certaine somme d'argent dont le récit ne souligne pas le montant. Rachbam continue, tout au long de son commentaire, de s'évertuer à donner une description impartiale d'Esaü. Quelques chapitres plus loin, toutefois, pointe assez clairement une note apologétique. Jacob se prépare à rencontrer son frère. Les messagers de Jacob lui rapportent qu'Esaü vient à sa rencontre avec, sous ses ordres, 400 hommes. 'Jacob eut grand peur et se sentit angoissé' souligne le texte (32,8). Rachbam, lui, interprète autrement les intentions d'Esaü: c'est par amour pour son frère, pour lui exprimer sa joie et pour l'honorer qu'il vient à lui flanqué de toute cette troupe. C'est, croyons-nous, un commentaire tendancieux. Quel est le but de Rachbam? Serait-il tellement téméraire de supposer que, au delà de l'intention exégétique, il y ait, de la part de Rachbam, une réaction contre toute allégorisation figurative? Esaü ne représente pas les Chrétiens, mais ceux-ci n'ont pas intérêt non plus à en faire une figure d'Israël—ce peuple serait alors bien sympathique ...

Joseph le Zélateur a bien saisi l'aspect apologétique du commentaire de Rachbam puisqu'il s'en sert dans sa controverse avec le frère dominicain. Par contre Rivash n'adoptera ce commentaire que partiellement: lui aussi voit en Esaü un chasseur habile, au fond bien sympathique, qui renonce, dans un moment de faiblesse, à son droit d'aînesse, étant sûr de le récupérer en fin de compte, grâce à l'amour de son père. En effet Isaac essaiera de le lui rendre:

> Isaac dit à son fils: prépare-moi un repas; tu as renoncé à ton droit d'aînesse pour un repas, moi je te le rendrai, ce droit, au prix d'un repas (que tu m'offriras) et là je te ferai dominer, et c'est d'ailleurs la coutume des grands de faire un repas quand ils reçoivent (le titre) de noblesse.[21]

L'approche littérale demeure chez Rivash la même que chez Rachbam et même s'affirme. Ce que Rivash repousse, c'est l'explication relative au droit d'aînesse. Quant aux intentions d'Esaü et de sa troupe, Rivash en propose une interprétation originale: 'les messagers dirent à Jacob: nous ne savons pas qu'est-ce qu'il pense faire, mal ou bien'.

Au 13ème siècle les conditions changent, et, avec elles, l'approche exégétique. Hiskouni revient à l'allégorisation traditionnelle et même l'élargit. Esaü est, de nouveau, l'impie par excellence. L'explication de Rachbam concernant le prix payé pour le droit d'aînesse est retenue par Hiskouni, et ceci était prévisible, vus les besoins de la controverse judéo-chrétienne. Ce qui était moins prévisible et qui étonne, c'est l'adoption par Hiskouni de l'explication de Rachbam relative aux bonnes intentions d'Esaü lors de sa rencontre avec son frère Jacob. C'est le patriarche Jacob qui douta à tort de la sincérité de son frère. Il y a quand même une certaine dynamique de l'exégèse...

2. Abordons maintenant notre deuxième exemple—*l'angélologie*. C'est un sujet extrêmement vaste et nous ne le cernerons que dans quelques uns de ses aspects—ceux exprimés par l'exégèse biblique, et plus exactement, par l'exégèse du Pentateuque, puisque les commentaires de Rachbam et de Rivash sur les autres livres bibliques ne nous sont malheureusement pas parvenus.

Les traditions rabbiniques sur l'angélologie sont recensés dans le Talmud et les Sommes midrachiques. (J'omets volontairement la littérature mystique juive.) Ces traditions sont nombreuses et variées.[22] Certaines s'efforcent de s'appuyer sur les textes sacrés mais la plupart sont le fruit des méditations et des spéculations des rabbins. Lorsque Rachi et son école entreprirent de doter la communauté juive d'un commentaire suivi et clair, ils se devaient immédiatement de faire un choix parmi les traditions. Ce choix— c'est la somme des croyances en angélologie que voulaient transmettre aux intellectuels juifs Rachi et ses continuateurs. Le choix s'efforcera, bien entendu, de répondre aux exigences du texte. Pourtant nous verrons tout à l'heure que nos docteurs touchent certains points angélologiques auxquels le texte ne fait aucune allusion, par exemple la date de la création des anges. C'est qu'il y avait aussi la nécessité de meubler le lecteur juif d'une conception plus ou moins cohérente et surtout viable en cette période houleuse qu'est le 12ème siècle.

Dans le monde chrétien, l'éveil intellectuel touche aussi notre problème.

> Le haut Moyen Age s'intéresse très peu à l'angélologie. Ce n'est qu'avec l'éveil théologique du 12ème siècle que nous assistons à une recrudescence de l'intérêt pour l'angélologie. Honorius, Rupert, Anselme exposent les opinions courantes à ce sujet et précisent leurs idées sur plusieurs points particuliers... A partir du milieu du 12ème siècle les sommes théologiques publient toutes un traité assez développé sur les anges.[23]

Surtout ne croyons pas que ces développements théologiques restaient l'apanage des théologiens et des écolâtres; ils étaient vulgarisés, grâce à ces adaptations en français vernaculaire dont nous parlions tout-à-l'heure. Nous possédons sur ce sujet un document très intéressant, c'est une traduction en vieux français du fameux Elucidarius d'Honorius Augustodunensis; l'œuvre fut rédigée vers l'année 1100 et traduite probablement quelques années plus tard. Une adaptation, tardive il est vrai, de cette œuvre nous est parvenue en plusieurs manuscrits. Elle s'intitule 'La Lumiere as lais'. Citons-en quelques extraits; cela nous aidera, je crois, à mieux comprendre nos exégètes:

> Q. Quand les anges furent-ils créés? R. Avant que le temps commença et que les éléments fussent ordonnés. Le ciel qui est celui des anges, est le premier qui fut peuplé.
>
> Q. En quel état Dieu fit-il les anges? R. Il les fit entre le souverain bien et le changeable, c'est-à-dire avec la liberté de se tourner vers Dieu ou de s'en éloigner... L'ange Lucifer fut le premier à s'enorgueillir de sa beauté et de sa vertu. De là sa chute et ce qui s'ensuivit.
>
> Les bons anges—Après la chute de Lucifer, les bons anges ont reçu le privilège de ne mal faire et de ne pas pêcher.
>
> Hiérarchie angélique—Il y a neuf 'ordres' d'anges, hiérarchisés: Séraphins, Chérubins, Trônes etc...[24]

Revenons à nos rabbins. La Bible, on le sait, ne souffle pas un mot sur la création des anges, ni, par conséquent, sur la date de celle-ci. Le lecteur s'aperçoit tout d'un coup que les anges existent et servent Dieu. C'est tout ce que nous pouvons déduire de la lecture des récits de la Genèse. Cela n'est pas suffisant. Rachi va donc compléter, partiellement au moins, les informations données. Commentant Genèse 1,5, Rachi choisit, parmi les diverses traditions rabbiniques, celle qui rapporte que les anges furent créés le deuxième jour.

D'après certains textes rabbiniques, les anges existaient bien avant la création du monde; d'après d'autres textes ils furent créés le premier jour et selon d'autres—le cinquième jour. Le choix de Rachi (le deuxième jour) est assez arbitraire, car rien dans le verset ne fait réellement allusion aux anges, même si nous admettons la pertinence de la question posée par Rachi, à savoir l'emploi de '*yom e'had*' (jour un) au lieu de '*yom richon*' (premier jour). Rachi souligne que la source de son commentaire est Genèse Rabba. En voici le texte:

> R. Yohanan dit: c'est au deuxième jour que les anges furent créés; R. Hanina dit: c'est au cinquième jour. R. Louliané, au nom de R. Yitshak dit: qu'on retienne l'avis de R. Yohanan ou qu'on adopte celui de R. Hanina tout le monde reconnaît que rien (aucun ange) n'a été créé le premier jour, et cela pour t'empêcher de dire: Mikhael tirait les cieux au sud, Gabriel au nord et Dieu mesurait au milieu... Personne ne s'est associé à Dieu pour créer le monde.

C'est la croyance que Rachi voulait inculquer à ses lecteurs—Dieu est le Créateur unique et exclusif.

Les anges sont, selon Rachi, dénués de toute individualité, de toute indépendance, même lorsqu'ils parlent à la première personne. L'ange qui a promis à Abraham: 'je reviendrai chez toi' (Gen. 18,10)—'ne lui annonce pas son propre retour, mais par l'injonction de Dieu il lui dit ces paroles. De même 'l'ange de Dieu lui dit (à Hagar): je multiplierai ta race', or il n'est pas dans son pouvoir de le faire et ce n'est qu'un message de Dieu (qu'il transmet)'.[25] Quant à ceux qui ont osé émettre la phrase: 'nous allons détruire cette localité' (Gen. 19,13), ils se verront obligés de reconnaître humblement 'je ne puis rien faire' (v. 22) et Rachi insiste: 'c'est la punition des anges. Ils avaient dit "nous allons détruire" comme si cela dépendait d'eux. C'est pourquoi avant de partir ils ont dû convenir qu'ils n'agissaient pas de leur propre pouvoir'. Pourtant, à y voir de plus près, ces explications ne semblent pas être déduites d'une lecture littérale du texte. Dans un même verset les anges disent 'nous allons détruire cette localité... et Dieu nous a envoyés pour la détruire', donc ils reconnaissent n'être que les envoyés de Dieu. Quant à la phrase 'je ne puis rien faire'—elle a été arrachée de son contexte par Rachi, car l'impuissance de l'ange n'est pas décrite comme inhérente à sa condition, mais elle est provisoirement causée par la présence de Loth.

Dénué d'individualité, l'ange s'identifie totalement avec le message qui l'habite. Une fois celui-ci transmis, l'ange disparaît.[26] Un ange ne peut donc véhiculer qu'un seul message. La dépersonnalisation des anges s'exprime à l'extrême, par leur anonymat. Rachi explique la phrase 'Pourquoi donc me demandes-tu mon nom?' (Gen. 32,30) de la manière suivante: 'nous n'avons pas de nom fixe, nos noms changent suivant les missions qui nous sont commandées'. Deux élèves-copistes de Rachi ont inscrit en marge l'enseignement qu'il faut déduire de ce commentaire: 'L'ange dit: il n'est d'aucune utilité que tu saches mon nom, car la force et la puissance n'appartiennent qu'à Dieu. Si tu m'invoques je ne te répondrai pas et de ta détresse je ne puis te sauver'.[27] Et voici l'autre note marginale: (l'ange ne communique pas son nom) 'pour que les gens ne puissent dire: "c'est l'ange qui a fait cela, alors qu'en fait il n'est que délégué"'.[28] Les deux exceptions à cette règle de l'anonymat—Raphael qui guérit Abraham (Gen. 18,2) et Gabriel qui apparaît à Joseph (Gen. 37,15)—sont dues, peut-être, au fait que dans les deux cas le nom s'identifie strictement au rôle: רפאל du verbe רפא, גבריאל du substantif גבר = איש dans la phrase où il est dit: וימצאהו איש. En tout cas les deux autres visiteurs d'Abraham restent pour Rachi dans l'anonymat complet, quoique les sources midrachiques de son commentaire précisent le nom des trois anges.

Rachbam changera, là aussi, les données du sujet. D'après lui, le véritable problème est plutôt l'aride paradoxe de la Transcendance et de l'Immanence divines. D'abord Rachbam dénie au récit de la Création (Genèse 1) tout aspect philosophique, théologique ou mystique. Le but de ce récit est didactique—il veut préparer les Israélites à comprendre ce que Dieu dira dans le quatrième commandement: 'tu te souviendras du jour du Chabbat et tu le sanctifieras... car en six jours Dieu a fait le ciel et la terre etc....' C'est donc le monde visible, tangible qui est décrit dans ce premier chapitre de la Genèse, et c'est pour cette raison qu'on n'y relate pas récit de la création des anges, ni d'ailleurs du Paradis et de l'Enfer.[29]

Rachbam développe la conception que, Dieu étant absolument transcendant, toute révélation divine relatée dans les textes n'est en réalité qu'une apparition d'anges. Rachbam expose sa conception dans son commentaire sur Genèse 18-19. La visite des trois anges chez Abraham racontée à partir du verset 2, c'est la traduction manifeste de la révélation de Dieu relatée au verset 1. La justification de ce commentaire, Rachbam la trouve dans Exode 23,20, 'car mon nom est en lui', qui veut dire: שלוחו כמותו (son délégué est comme lui)'. Pour Rachbam il y a deux significations à cette formule juridique: le délégué de Dieu est l'égal de Dieu par le nom, ange=Dieu; il est aussi son égal par le rôle qu'il remplit: il transmet Ses paroles et exécute Sa volonté. La justification exégétique de cette conception, Rachbam le découvre dans le récit de la révélation de Dieu à Moïse (Exode 3) où l'on parle indifféremment de Dieu ou de Son ange.

Rachbam est très conséquent avec lui-même dans sa conception. C'est l'ange qui demande à Abraham des comptes sur le rire de Sarah, c'est l'ange qui introduit Abraham dans le secret des intentions divines vis à vis de Sodome et Gomorrhe, c'est devant l'ange qu'Abraham est debout, c'est l'ange qui fait pleuvoir du feu et du souffre sur Sodome, et tout ceci, quoiqu'il soit expressément écrit: et Dieu dit, debout devant Dieu, et Dieu fit pleuvoir . . . Grâce à ce principe théologico-exégétique il sera facile à Rachbam de résoudre le problème posé par le verset 19,24 'et Dieu fit pleuvoir sur Sodome et sur Gomorrhe du souffre et du feu provenant de Dieu', verset fameux pour la controverse qu'il suscita depuis très longtemps,[30] fameux aussi pour la place que lui accorda l'exégèse chrétienne médiévale depuis Pierre Damiens. On se souvient que Rachi préféra la solution stylisante préconisée déjà par un des auditeurs de R. Meïr. Rachbam explique: 'et Dieu fit pleuvoir—c'est l'ange Gabriel, venant de Dieu—là c'est (la décision de) Dieu Lui-même'. Le sujet épineux de la 'descente' de Dieu sur terre (Gen. 18,21; Ex. 3,8) trouvera aussi sa solution—c'est l'ange qui descend. Dieu dirige son monde, certes, mais ce que nous voyons et entendons ici-bas, ce sont les anges et leurs faits et gestes.

Il y a trois exceptions à cette règle: elles concernent les trois fois où Dieu conclut une alliance avec des hommes: avec Abraham (Gen. 15), avec le peuple d'Israël (Ex. 19–24) et avec Moïse (Ex. 33). Là Dieu Lui-même se révéla.

Quels sont les mobiles des conceptions angélologiques de Rachi puis de Rachbam? Serait-il si osé de supposer qu'ils visaient, au-delà de l'explication obvie des textes, de former des intellectuels juifs 'modernes' et de les préparer à la controverse religieuse judéo-chrétienne? Nos deux exégètes ne le disent pas. Rivash, par contre, qui fleurissait, on s'en souvient, dans la deuxième moitié du douzième siècle, le dit explicitement, dans son commentaire sur Genèse 18–19.

D'après Rivash, la révélation de Dieu à Abraham n'est qu'annoncée au premier verset du chapitre 18; en fait, elle ne commence à se dérouler qu'à partir du verset 17. Entretemps, voici que trois hommes arrivent:

> Selon le Peshat, ce sont des hommes réels, car nous n'avons vu nulle part des anges manger. Certes—continue Rivash avec embarras—nous n'avons pas le droit de contredire nos Anciens qui étaient eux-mêmes égaux aux anges, pourtant *il est interdit d'enseigner* que ces hommes étaient des anges, car il y aurait là étaiement (de la thèse chrétienne qui prétend que) leur divinité a mangé.

Puis il se lance à une attaque en règle contre l'exégèse christologiste de ce récit.

Gardons-nous de croire que Rivash était rationaliste sur toute la ligne. L'homme qui lutta avec Jacob est bien un ange, et s'il ne veut pas dévoiler son nom à son adversaire humain, c'est, entre autres raisons, pour ne pas qu'on se serve du nom angélique comme talisman. Ce qui suscita l'exégèse de Rivash au récit de Genèse 18–19, c'est bel et bien le besoin de la controverse judéo-chrétienne.

On peut maintenant suivre clairement le développement de la conception angélologique dans l'exégèse juive en France au Moyen-Age: Rachi s'efforce de réduire au minimum les prérogatives des anges—ils n'ont aucune 'densité', aucune personnalité, aucune initiative, ils n'ont même pas de nom fixe; chaque ange est absorbé par le message qu'il colporte. Rachbam ne leur accorde pas plus de personnalité, mais il en fait les lieu-tenants de Dieu sur terre; ils portent Son Nom, exécutent Sa volonté, publient Ses ordres. Dieu, Lui, est absolument transcendant. Rivash est encore plus extrémiste et va même à l'encontre de ses prédécesseurs dans le commentaire des textes litigieux—là il n'y a pratiquement pas d'anges. Pour les autres textes, il suit les sentiers battus de la tradition juive. Avec Hiskouni, au treizième siècle, c'est le retour à l'ancienne exégèse. Hiskouni reviendra, pour l'essentiel, aux commentaires midrachiques de Rachi; dans certains détails il ira même plus loin et dira, par exemple, que les anges et les hommes ont la même physionomie (Gen. 1,27), que les anges mangent comme les humains (Gen. 18,8), qu'ils sont éternels etc....

Il est temps de terminer. Notre analyse est certainement insuffisante—c'est trop peu deux exemples pour étayer une thèse, surtout que l'étude de ces examples ne s'arroge aucune exhaustivité. Pourtant il est permis, je crois, de conclure que l'exégèse biblique littérale que pratiquèrent les Juifs en France au Moyen-Age est avant tout la réponse juive au renouveau du douzième siècle sous toutes ses formes. Les docteurs juifs français n'avaient pas coutume de rédiger des écrits théologiques ou philosophiques, ils ont donc exprimé dans leurs commentaires bibliques tout ce qu'ils avaient à dire, tant sur les textes commentés que sur les nouveaux problèmes qui agitaient leurs contemporains. Ainsi il s'avère que Rachi, Rachbam, Rivash n'étaient pas seulement des exégètes bibliques, ils étaient aussi les édificateurs de leur communauté.

NOTES

1. Cf. Marc Bloch, *La société féodale*, Paris (1968), p. 158.
2. Cf. J. de Ghellink, *L'essor de la littérature latine au 12ème siècle*, Bruxelles/Paris (1946).
3. Cf. C. Spicq, *Esquisse d'une histoire de l'exégèse latine au Moyen-Age*, Paris (1944). B. Smalley, *The Study of the Bible in the Middle-Ages*, Indiana (1970). H. de Lubac, *Exégèse médiévale*, Paris (1961).
4. Cf. A. Funkenstein, 'Changes in the Patterns of Christian Anti-Jewish Polemics in the 12th Century', *Zion, Quarterly for Research in Jewish History*, 33 (1968) (héb.).
5. C. Spicq, 'Pourquoi le Moyen-Age n'a-t-il pas d'avantage pratiqué l'exégèse littérale', en *Sciences Philosophiques et Théologiques*, I, 1941-1942, p. 176.
6. R. Pernoud, *Lumière du Moyen-Age*, Paris (1981), p. 131.
7. R. Pernoud, op. cit.
8. R. Pernoud, op. cit., p. 243.
9. Pour une plus ample exposition de nos vues sur ce point, voir nos travaux parus en hébreu: 'Peshat et apologétique dans les commentaires de Rashbam sur l'histoire de Moïse', *Tarbiz* 51 (1982), pp. 227-38; 'La méthode exégétique de Rashbam et l'actualité historique de son temps', *E.Z. Malamed Jubilee-Book*, Ramat-Gan (1982) pp. 48-74; 'La méthode exégétique de Rashbam dans l'exégèse de la partie halakhique de la Tora', *Millet 2*, University for Everyman, Tel-Aviv (1984). Voir aussi notre travail paru en français dans *Archives Juives*, Vingtième année (1984), pp. 3-12.

10. Commentaire de Rashbam sur Genèse 37,2, édition D. Rosin, Breslau (1882).

11. Cf. J. le Goff, *Les intellectuels au Moyen-Age*, Paris (1957).

12. Cf. Arugat Ha-bosem, *Commentaires sur des textes liturgiques hébraïques*, édition E.E. Urbach, T. 2, Jerusalem (1964), p. 220.

13. Cf. Rachi, *Commentaire de Cantique des Cantiques* 7,9-10.

14. M. Banitt, *Le Glossaire de Bâle*, Jérusalem (1972) (en français).

15. Dans les éditions imprimées la version est איש (un homme, quelqu'un). Cette version n'est pas originale, comme le témoignent l'édition de Venise (1524) et certains manuscrits. Ceux-ci notent מין, terme par lequel les Juifs médiévaux désignaient les Chrétiens. Cf. Rashi's Commentary on Ezechiel 40-48, edited by A.J. Levy, Philadelphia (1931), p. 7.

16. Cf. Vikuah Rabenu Yehiel mi-paris, Thorn (1873), p. 10 (hébreu). Voir aussi l'étude de I. Loeb, 'La controverse de 1240 sur le Talmud', *Revue des Etudes Juives*, T. I (1881), p. 258.

17. Les commentaires de ces docteurs anonymes ont été interpolés dans le commentaire original de Rashi, comme nous le montrons dans notre travail 'La version originale du commentaire de Rachi sur le Pentateuque', *Tarbiz* (sous presse).

18. Cf. Rachi sur Genèse 25,22, édition A. Berliner, Francfort sur-le-M (1905).

19. Cf. G. Dahan, 'Exégèse et Polémique', *Les Juifs au regard de l'histoire, Mélanges B. Blumenkranz*, Paris (1985), p. 142.

20. *Le Livre de Joseph le Zélateur*, édition J. Rosenthal, Jérusalem (1970), p. 40 (héb.).

21. Allusion probable aux coutumes féodales.

22. Pour plus amples détails, cf. E.E. Urbach, *The Sages, their Concepts and Beliefs*, Jerusalem (1975), pp. 135 et passim.

23. *Dictionnaire de théologie catholique*, col. 1222.

24. Cf. Ch. V. Langlois, *La vie en France au moyen-âge*, T. IV *La vie spirituelle*, Genève (1970), pp. 75-76.

25. Rachi sur Genèse 18,10, selon la traduction française du Rabbinat français.

26. Rachi sur Genèse 19,1.

27. Rapporté dans Hize Menache, Londres (1901), p. 31.

28. D'apres le manuscrit Sasoon, rapporté dans Tosaphot Ha-chalem, Jerusalem (1984), p. 228.

29. Rashbam sur Genèse 1,27.

30. Cf. Talmud Babylonien, Tract. *Sanhedrin* f. 38v.

12

LUTHER ON JEWS AND ISLAM

J. Wallmann

Until far into this century, church historians considered Martin Luther's Reformation as something which occurred entirely within Christianity. Thus they wrote about Luther in relation to Roman Catholic theology and the Catholic Church, to Renaissance and Humanism and to controversies within Protestantism. It was left to the missionary experts, not to church historians, to deal with Luther's relationship to Jews and Islam. It was a Jewish scholar, Reinhard Lewin, who in 1911 published the first monograph about Luther's position toward the Jews.[1] Lewin's work did not receive much attention. The most important scholar of the 'Luther Renaissance', Karl Holl, does not mention it anywhere. Neither does he himself deal with the topic of Luther and the Jews. Only after Hitler's rise to power in 1933 and only after the National Socialists quoted the harsh words of the older Luther against the Jews as a justification for their anti-Semitic policies, only then did scholars like Heinrich Bornkamm and Erich Vogelsang turn to the topic of Luther's attitude toward the Jews. After the Second World War, after the Holocaust, an intensive discussion arose. In the last few years, many articles and books about Luther's attitude toward the Jews have appeared. I only mention Heiko A. Oberman's *Roots of Anti-Semitism*, a good work with a misleading title[2] and Walther Bienert's *Martin Luther und die Juden* (1982), the best and most complete collection of all of Luther's writings on this topic.[3]

As Oberman points out, there is a certain danger in concentrating on Luther's opinion on the Jews, namely the danger of making the same mistake as the anti-Semitic forces, who sought out only those passages from Luther's writings which fitted their purpose. In doing so, one runs the danger of being unhistorical in two ways. First of all, in this way Luther is isolated and the question remains unasked what Luther's contemporaries thought about the Jews and whether their opinion differed essentially from that of Luther. In this context, Guido Kisch's book *Erasmus Stellung zu Juden und Judentum*[4] destroyed much of the illusion about this great humanist as an early advocate of tolerance. According to Kisch, Erasmus had 'a definitely hateful opinion' and 'a deeply rooted, unbounded hate for Jews' (p. 9 and further p. 20). Even if other scholars have since questioned some of Kisch's findings (for instance Cornelis Augustijn),[5] it still is no longer possible to talk about Erasmus as the propagator of a universal principle of tolerance. Erasmus' tolerance was an inner-Christian tolerance and excluded the Jews, and this is true just as much for the eighteenth-century Enlightenment on the European continent (for instance Voltaire).

Not only can one make the mistake of becoming unhistorical by isolating Luther, one can also make another mistake and isolate the topic. This happens when one considers Luther's anti-Judaism (which is a better term for Luther than anti-Semitism) without regard to Luther's other anti-positions, namely his position against the Pope as the Antichrist, which had the great influence on his overall thought, his position against the so-called 'Schwärmer und Rottengeister' (the sectarians and enthusiasts) and finally his position against the Turks and Islam. I will confine myself in this paper to comparing Luther's position toward the Jews with that toward Islam. Within the restraints of a short paper, I can discuss this topic only summarily. First of all (I) I would like to compare Luther's exhortations on Jews and Islam with those of the other reformers. Secondly (II) I will show that in the formative years of the Reformation, Luther appeared not only as an opponent of the medieval papal church but public opinion also saw him as a non-conformist in regard to Jews and Islam; that he was considered a 'friend of Jews and Turks' (in the Reformation, the Mohammedans are invariably referred to as Turks). Further I would like to trace the development which takes place over the years in Luther's position toward the Jews (III) and toward Islam (IV), and how, in the end, Luther occupies the same 'anti' position toward Jews and Islam as he does against the papacy. In doing so, it can be shown, that a change takes place in his attitude toward the Jews and Islam, to be sure at different times, quite early for Islam and somewhat later for the Jews. Based on this 'change at different times' I would like to draw some conclusions in regard to the effect of Luther's attitude toward Jews and Islam on the older Protestantism (V). I will show that Luther's 'anti' position against Islam, because it happened early on, penetrated Protestantism in general, whereas his rather late change of heart against the Jews had only a partial effect on older Protestantism.

I

Luther has dealt with Jews and Islam far more intensively than any of his contemporaries, definitely far more than any of the other reformers. Others like Zwingli and Calvin wrote against the Pope and against the radicals on the left wing of the Reformation. However, they said little about Jews and Islam, and definitely did not deal with this topic in special writings. Luther's opinion on Jews and Islam is far more visible. Even if one disregards the immense material in his lectures, his sermons, and his writings, one can find it in the so-called 'Juden- und Türkenschriften', which have been collected as a literary genre in the older Walch Luther edition of 1747 (vol. XX)[6] and then again in our century in the Munich Luther edition of 1936 (second edition, appendix vol. 3).

Why did neither Zwingli nor Calvin find it necessary to deal with Jews or Islam? As far as the Jews are concerned, either in Zurich or in Geneva, a position regarding the Jews was not an actual problem that one had to deal with. The Jews had been driven out of all Western European countries in the late Middle Ages, from England in 1290, from France in 1394, from Spain in 1492, from Portugal in 1496. They had also been driven out of most of the Swiss Cantons, from Zurich by an expulsion decree of 1436. In none of the places where Zwingli worked did he meet Jews who lived there; the same was true for Calvin in Geneva. The situation in the Holy Roman Empire of the German Nation was totally different. To be sure, at the end of the fifteenth century and in the first two decades of the sixteenth century, the Jews had been expelled from many cities and territories, but in the Empire they were further tolerated. As 'Kammerknechte' (chamber valets) they were immediately under the protectorate of the emperor. Throughout the Reformation era the German Jews formed a well organized religious minority, which possessed in the Alsatian Jew Josel von Rosheim, its own spokesman, who represented the interests of the Jews during the imperial diet. Luther met the Jews throughout his life. He was visited by Jews in Wittenberg and held disputations with them. He also met Jews during his travels. He calls Josel von Rosheim 'a good friend'.[7] If

Luther talks frequently about the Jews, then this is on account of the fact that in the German Empire the co-existence of Jews and Christians was a constant problem. The Strasbourg Reformer Martin Bucer and the Nürnberg Reformer Andreas Osiander were forced to form an opinion on the Jews. However, the Swiss reformers lived in areas, which had already practised what the later Luther preached to the princes: 'Drive out the Jews!' One should mention, however, that neither Zwingli nor Calvin is known to have objected to the forceful expulsion of the Jews from France and Switzerland.

The situation is different in regard to Islam. There were no Muslim minorities in the Christian States of Middle Europe in the 16th century. But there was a danger of the Turks. In the same year in which Luther refuses to recant at the Diet of Worms, the Turks conquer Belgrade (1521). In 1522 Rhodos is taken, and after a few years of respite the Turks appear for the first time before the walls of Vienna (1529). Now it has to be pointed out, that the Turks were fighting a war against the emperor and the Holy Roman Empire. They were not fighting against the king of France, who was even an ally of the Turks. Therefore, when Luther takes a position on Islam, he does not do so because of religious interests, but because he has to take a position on the war. Because Luther became an adviser to those protestant princes, he had to decide at the diet about the war against the Turks, about the aid the emperor was going to receive against the Turks. Calvin was in a totally different situation. For Calvin, it was far more advisable to refrain from any statement on Islam, the ally of France, because this could only strengthen the suspicion that Protestantism might harm the political interests of France. As far as Zwingli's Zurich is concerned, the situation there was again different. In Zurich one did not have to worry about the political considerations of France. But one also did not have to call for a war on the Turks. This is the main reason, why one finds little on the Turks in Zwingli, but far more in the writings of his successors Heinrich Bullinger and especially Theodor Bibliander who developed a lively scientific interest in Islam, the strongest scientific interest that can be found during the Reformation.

II

In the decisive years of the Reformation, in the decade after the Leipzig Disputation of 1519, in which the break with the traditional authorities, papacy and council, had become evident, Luther appeared openly as a heretic, who had broken radically with the medieval church. Did this heresy of Luther only touch upon inner-Christian problems? Or did it also alter the relationship of Christianity to the world around it? Was Luther's attitude toward Islam and the Jews different from the attitude of the medieval papal church?

It certainly looked that way in the beginning. Luther was declared a heretic by the Church also because of his attitude toward Islam. Among the 'Errores Martini Lutheri', which are listed in the bull 'Exsurge Domine' of 1520, we find the following assertion 'Proeliari adversus Turcas est repugnare Deo visitanti iniquitates nostras per illos' (To fight against the Turks is to resist God, who through them punishes us for our iniquities). Luther had actually written this in his resolutions to the Ninety-Five Theses (5th thesis). Furthermore, Luther rejected any idea of a crusade, any idea of a Holy War against the infidels, as it had grown in the Christian Middle Ages during the confrontations with Islam. In his most popular book *To the Christian Nobility of the German Nation* one reads: 'It has been said, that there is no finer worldly regiment anywhere, than among the Turks, who know neither religious nor secular laws, but only their Alcoran. We then have to admit, that there is no regiment that is more despicable than the one we have with our religious and secular rights'.[8] And in 1524 Luther declared that the Turks were 'ten times more sensible and pious than our princes'. The impression could arise that Luther wanted to change the negative image of Islam, which had been created during the Middle Ages and that he wanted to establish an alliance with Islam in the fight against the papacy.

Since the Diet of Worms, Luther distanced himself even more clearly from the attitudes of the medieval church in regard to the Jews. 'We should not treat the Jews so unfriendly', he writes in the *Magnificat*.[9] Two years later, in 1523, he published the treatise: *That Jesus Christ is a born Jew*.[10] It is the first one that deals with this topic. Unmistakenly clear and harsh is Luther's rejection of the traditional mistreatment of the Jews by the Christians: 'They (the Pope, the bishops and the monks) have treated the Jews as if they were dogs and not humans'.[11] Luther also rejects the medieval practice of forced baptism. The Christians should deal with the Jews in a 'brotherly' fashion. 'They are the brothers of our Lord'.[12] Luther also turns against the defamation of the Jews, against the lies, which are spread about them. He demands an end to social isolation of the

Jews. They should be allowed any kind of work; they should be allowed to be 'with us and among us'.[13] Even if this brotherly treatment did not result in a conversion, 'what does that matter? Not all of us are good Christians either'.[14] Small wonder that Luther's treatise: *That Jesus Christ was a born Jew* was received enthusiastically by the Jews as a sign of a basic change in the relationship between Jews and Christians. It was sent from Antwerp to the secret Jewish communities in Spain. Luther's treatise even reached Jerusalem.[15]

III

Luther, opponent of the Pope, ally of the Mohammedans, and friend of the Jews? Johann Eck, Luther's most famous opponent indeed presented his contemporaries with this abhorrent picture. However, this picture did not last. We will now discuss the changes in Luther's attitude toward Islam and toward the Jews. Today it is generally accepted that these are not fundamental changes in the underlying theology. But they are important in that they had far-reaching consequences for the attitude toward Islam and the Jews.

From 1529 on, Luther begins to write openly against the Turks. In the year of the siege of Vienna, the first two treatises on the Turks appear: *About the War against the Turks* (WA 30 II, 107-148) and *A War Sermon against the Turks* (WA 30 II, 160-197). At the outset of the first treatise, Luther mentions his previous contention, that one should not fight against the Turks. However, he says, that was only valid then, when he tried to counter the call for a crusade by the Pope. Not the Pope, but only the emperor was allowed to fight against the Turks. But since there now exists a widespread pacifism, which mistakenly bases its convictions on him, Luther now calls for a defensive war. In his second treatise *A War Sermon against the Turks* he identifies Islam with the little horn from the vision of the prophet Daniel (Dan. 7.8), which grows between the ten horns of the animal and tears away three. Luther views the present Turkish danger as an apocalyptic sign of the end of times. As Heinrich Bornkamm has said, Luther replaces the call for a crusade with a call for an eschatological war[16] (*Martin Luther in der Mitte seines Lebens* [1979], p. 525).

Luther retracts nothing of his previous positive evaluation of the life of the Mohammedans. Indeed, he even praises their religious practices: their prayer, fasting, monasticism, religious services; in all outer manifestations the Mohammedans are far superior to the Christians. But practices are not most important, doctrine is. Luther is not interested in perpetuating the stories which were told in the Middle Ages about the life of Mohammed: 'Personalia quae dicunt de Mahomet, me no movent, but the doctrine of the Turks we have to attack, Dogma has to be considered'.[17]

Luther views it as his task, to familiarize his fellow Christians with the teaching and with the faith of the Mohammedans. But he does not know the Koran. As he writes in 1530, he has wanted 'fervently' (*vehementer cuperem*) to learn about the religion of Islam. However, he has not been able to lay his hand on anything but the 'Confutatio Alcorani' of the Dominican Ricoldus and the 'Cribratio Alcorani' of Nicolas Cusanus. And Luther did not put much faith in these excellent examples of medieval Islam polemics. A 'Libellus de ritu et moribus Turcorum', written by an unknown Dominican monk in the late fifteenth century, appeared to him as more dependable, and he published this work with a foreword.[18] Finally in 1542, his long standing wish to be acquainted with the Koran was fulfilled. He obtained a Latin translation, probably the one made in the Middle Ages by the Abbot Peter of Cluny and circulated in manuscript. After reading this translation, the 'Confutatio Alcorani' appeared to him to be even more dependable, and he published it in a free German translation in the same year, 1542.[19] At the same time he encouraged the Zurich theologian Theodor Bibliander, who had for many years studied Islam, to publish a Latin translation of the Koran. When Bibliander encountered difficulties with the City Council of Basel and when the already printed Koran was confiscated, Luther wrote a fervent letter on October 27th, 1542, to the City Council of Basel, in which he used all his influence to have the Koran publication released.[20] Luther also wrote a foreword for the Basel Koran Edition.[21] At the initiative of Luther, who translated the Bible, the Koran also became known for the first time among European scholars. And it is again a Lutheran theologian, Abraham Hinckelmann, who 150 years later, printed for the first time the Koran in the Arabic language (an earlier edition of 1530, printed in Venice, was burned by papal decree).

It is impossible for me here to go further into Luther's Islam criticism. Compared with Nicolas Cusanus, he is far more radical. A 'Cribratio Alcorani', in which the truth is sorted out from the lies, Luther could not have written. Christianity and Islam in the whole are for him in the same relationship as Truth and Lie. The Christian God is a different God than the God of Mohammed. For our purposes, it is important that Luther, already in the decade of the Diet of Worms, shows a clear turning against Islam. From then on he sees in Mohammed and the Turks the second enemy of Christianity, after the Pope.

IV

When does Luther's attitude toward Jews change? The answer has to be that the change came much later than his change of attitude concerning Islam. Luther's pro-Jewish treatise of 1523 was followed by a whole series of similar writings by friends and followers of Luther (Michael Kramer, Wenzeclaus Linck, Caspar Güttel, Urbanus Rhegius and others).[22] The followers of Luther appeared openly as friends of the Jews. The renewal of the study of Hebrew led to close connections between reformed theologians and Jewish scholars. For instance the famous Jewish grammarian Elias Levita came from Venice to Germany and founded together with the Lutheran scholar Paul Fagius the first Hebrew printing firm in Isny. As Selma Stern, the biographer of Josel von Rosheim, points out, it was with justification that many of the Old Church at the Augsburg Diet of 1530 considered the Jews and the Protestants as secret allies of each other, and the leaders of the German Jews could not foresee that a decade later, Luther would instigate an action against them.[23]

Even seven years after the Augsburg Diet, in 1537, Josel von Rosheim wrote to Luther requesting him to use his influence with the Elector of Saxony to speak for the Jews, who one year before had been denied residency. Luther's answer[24] is the first sign of a changed attitude regarding the Jews. To be sure, the tone of the letter is still friendly. Luther addresses the leader of the German Jews with 'my dear Josel' and 'my good friend'. He assures him of his continued friendliness. 'Because I have always felt and still feel, that one should be friendly toward the Jews'. But Luther declines to interfere on the Jews' behalf. We can find the reason for this change in a treatise called *Against the Sabbaticians*, printed the following year 1538.[25] The Reformation, with its renewal of Hebrew Studies, had given the Jews a new feeling of identity. Instead of converting to Christianity, they even won new converts among the Christians, for instance in Moravia. This strengthened Jewish self-awareness, which is evident in literary attacks on the Christian creed, is the reason why the old Luther, in the last years of his life, began a campaign against the Jews. In the year 1543, three years before Luther's death, three anti-Jewish treatises appeared, entitled: *About the Jews and their Lies* (WA 53, 417-552), *About Schem Hamphoras* (WA 53, 579-648) and *About the last words of David* (WA 54, 28-100). It is in the first of these treatises, *About the Jews and their Lies*, which was caused by a rabbinic attack on Christian interpretation of the Bible, that we find the infamous advice to those in power: One should no longer tolerate that the Jews slander the name of Christ in their synagogues. One should burn their synagogues and their schools, destroy their houses and make them a migratory people like the gypsies. One should take their Talmud and their prayer books away from them, forbid their rabbis to preach, prevent their practice of usury and force them into manual labour. As the final, most severe measure, Luther proposes to follow the example of France and Spain and drive the Jews out of the country.

Unfortunately it is not possible to discuss how Luther deals with the rabbinic Bible-interpretation, which takes up a large portion of his later writings. In the last part of this paper, I confine myself to answering the question what effect it had that Luther clarified his 'anti' positions toward Islam and toward the Jews at different times of his life.

V

As far as Luther's 'anti' position toward Islam is concerned, it developed at such an early stage, that it became a fundamental part of the Lutheran doctrine and teaching. Already in Luther's Great Confession of 1528, the basis of all later Lutheran Confessions, the 'Turks and all other heresies' are mentioned—together with the Pope as the horrors of the Antichrist. Nothing is said in this Confession about the Jews. Also the *Augsburg Confession* (Art. XV,18) and Luther's *Smalcald Articles* present the Pope and Mohammed as the main enemies of Christianity. Melanchthon and Luther differ only in that Luther sees the Antichrist primarily in the Pope, Melanchthon on the other hand sees him equally represented in Islam and papacy.[26] There is no Lutheran theologian of name, who did not adopt this negative picture of Islam as it came from Wittenberg. The doctrine of the 'double Antichrist', the Pope and Islam, is the *opinio communis* of post-reformation Lutheran theology. Wilhelm Postell, whose suggestions for a unification of all religions (*De orbis terrae concordia*, Basel [1544]) were rejected sharply by Melanchthon and more calmly by Luther, occupies a position outside of the mainstream of Protestantism. In the hymnals and prayer books of the Lutheran Church of the sixteenth and seventeenth century a multitude of songs and prayers against Pope and Islam can be found, for instance the hymn written by Luther in 1541: 'Lord Keep us steadfast in your Word, Curb the murder by Pope and Turk'.

As far as Luther's 'anti' position against the Jews is concerned, matters are far more complicated. Luther's turn away from a brotherly feeling for the Jews toward a conviction which placed the Jews among the enemies of Christianity occurred at a time at which Luther no longer had much influence on the course of the Reformation. The later anti-Jewish writings of Luther did not have much literary impact.[27] The early pro-Jewish treatise *That Jesus Christ is a born Jew* was circulated in ten German editions and three Latin ones. In addition to Wittenberg, it was printed in Augsburg, Basel, Speyer, and Strasbourg. The later writing *About the Jews and their Lies* was only printed twice in Wittenberg, and there are no later printings anywhere else. Only in Frankfurt did a Latin translation appear. The response among his contemporaries was mixed. Especially in Southern Germany Luther received more criticism than agreement. And, what is even more important, the princes did not follow Luther's advice. We are familiar with synagogue burnings, book indexes, and the expulsions of the Jews as they took place in the Middle Ages until the beginning of the Reformation. Except for a short but bloodless expulsion of the Jews from Frankfurt am Main and Worms shortly before the Thirty Years War, there are no pogroms in Protestant territories for several centuries. The old Luther was not able to counteract with the anti-Jewish writings of his later years his own earlier writings and their call for a friendly, brotherly attitude toward the Jews.

One has also to recognize that the change in Luther's attitude against the Jews occurred at a time, when the *Augsburg Confession* and the *Smalcald Articles*, the basic texts of the Confessions of the Lutheran Church, were already written. The *Book of Concord* of 1580, which is the authentic collection of the Lutheran Confessions, being a *regula praedicandi* for many centuries, contains condemnations of Pope and Islam, but no condemnations of the Jews.

Therefore it is no wonder, that in the devotional literature and in the hymns of the older Lutheran Church we will not find anti-Jewish passages similar to the widespread anti-Papal and anti-Islamic passages.

To be sure, there were Lutheran theologians who tried to revive the struggle of the aged Luther against Judaism. For instance Georg Nigrinus, pastor in Gießen, with a book entitled *Enemy Jew* (1570) and Nikolaus Selnecker, pastor at Leipzig, who published in 1577 an anthology of Luther's works on the Jews. Nigrinus and Selnecker took the position of a Lutheran intolerance against the Jews. But in 1611 two Theological Faculties, the Lutheran Theological Faculties of Jena and Frankfurt/Oder had to deliver theological opinions for the City of Hamburg, on the question, whether Jews could be tolerated in Christian states. Both faculties answered in the affirmative. The Jena theologians explicitly referred to the authority of Martin Luther and his early treatise of 1523 *That Jesus Christ is a born Jew*.[28] Since then the ideas of the younger Luther became predominant in the Lutheran Church. The anti-Jewish writings of the old Luther were not forgotten at once, but in the seventeenth century they lost their function, and in the eighteenth and nineteenth centuries they were almost completely forgotten in the Lutheran Church. That is the reason, why Haim Hillel Ben-Sasson could state, that it was rather the Luther of 1523 than the Luther of 1543 who remained dominant in the view of large segments of the Protestant world until well into the twentieth century.[29]

NOTES

1. Reinhold Lewin, *Luthers Stellung zu den Juden*, Berlin (1911) (reprint Aalen 1973).

2. Heiko A. Oberman, *Wurzeln des Antisemitismus*, Berlin (1981, 2nd edn, 1983) = *The Roots of Anti-Semitism in the Age of Renaissance and Reformation*, Philadelphia (1984).

3. Walther Bienert, *Martin Luther und die Juden*, Frankfurt am Main (1982).

4. Guido Kisch, *Erasmus' Stellung zu Juden und Judentum*, Tübingen (1969).

5. Cornelis Augustijn, 'Erasmus und die Juden', *Nederlands archief voor kerkgeschiedenis* 60 (1980), pp. 22-38.

6. Reprinted in the second edition of Walch, St. Louis (1890).

7. Weimar Luther edition (cited: WA), Briefe vol. 8, 89.

8. WA 6, 459, 24 ss.

9. WA 7, 600, 32 s.

10. WA 11, 314-336.

11. WA 11, 315, 3 s.

12. WA 11, 315, 22.27.

13. WA 11, 336, 32 s.

14. WA 11, 336, 34.

15. Cf. Pinchas E. Lapide, 'Der Mann, von dem alle sprechen'. Der junge Luther aus zeitgenössischer Sicht', *Lutherische Monatshefte* 14 (1975), pp. 527-30.

16. Heinrich Bornkamm, *Martin Luther in der Mitte seines Lebens*, Göttingen (1979), p. 525.

17. WA Tischreden vol. 5, 221, 4 ss.

18. WA 30 II, 205-208.

19. WA 53, 272-396.

20. WA BR 10, 160-163.

21. WA 53, 569-572.

22. Cf. Lewin, *op. cit.* p. 34.

23. Selma Stern, *Josel von Rosheim*, Stuttgart (1959), p. 84.

24. Luther to Josel von Rosheim 11.6.1537 (WA BR 8, 89-91).

25. WA 50, 312-337.

26. Cf. H. Brenner, 'Protestantische Orthodoxie und Islam. Die Herausforderung der türkischen Religion im Spiegel evangelischer Theologen des ausgehenden 16. und 17. Jahrhunderts', Diss. theol. Heidelberg (1968).

27. Cf. Lewin, *op. cit.* p. 97.

28. Georg Dedekenn, *Thesauri Consiliorum et Decisionum Volumen I*, Hamburg (1623), pp. 139-43.

29. Haim Hillel Ben-Sasson, *Geschichte des Jüdischen Volkes*, II, München (1979), p. 323.

13

SOME REFLECTIONS ON
MODERN JEWISH BIBLICAL RESEARCH

Benjamin Uffenheimer

In this essay I intend to point out some characteristic qualities of modern Israeli biblical studies in comparison to Jewish medieval Bible commentators on the one hand and to modern Protestant studies of the Old Testament on the other hand. My exposition will culminate with a critical juxtaposition of two different theologically minded trends, which found their classical expression in the biblical opera of Yecheskel Kaufmann (1889-1963) and Martin Buber (1878-1965)—both scholars of the preceding generation, whose main activities embraced five and six decades of this century respectively.

I

Modern Jewish biblical research in terms of the historical-philological method is a relatively late phenomenon in Jewish intellectual history. It reached its acme only during this century. This does not imply that Judaism was not interested in biblical studies during its long history. On the contrary, the Bible is its very foundation, and the great medieval Jewish Bible commentaries are a source of deep inspiration to the student and scholar down to the present. But besides the philological trend, the midrashic method had its deep impact on medieval Jewish Bible interpretation. *Inspiratio verbalis* being their main tenet, these scholars approached the biblical text as a meta-human language containing an unlimited multiplicity of meanings. The Rabbinic saying שבעים פנים לתורה, 'The Tora has seventy faces',[1] is the classical expression of this exegetical mentality. This belief was the main incentive to their interpretive creativeness which resulted in the course of time in a variety of sophisticated hermeneutical methods. In many cases these were tantamount to a re-interpretation of the Bible according to the changing conditions of life, thus adapting biblical law to the new historical setting of the second commonwealth and afterwards to the fluctuating situations of the diaspora.

The first encounter with Greek philosophy during the Hellenistic age and afterwards the spiritual symbiosis with Moslem and Christian Scholasticism resulted in the allegorical and symbolic exegesis of the philosophers and mystics. When reading their new ideas into the text they claimed to have revealed the hidden meaning of the Holy Scriptures, the Tora, unknown to preceding generations.

The development and the dynamic changes in Judaism were evaluated as the gradual unfolding of the full meaning, or the full meanings, of the Tora. During this conference we had the opportunity to study some aspects of these hermeneutical methods, which forged both Judaism and Christianity together. The classical evidence of the flexibility of these methods is found in Maimonides' magnum opus *The Guide of the Perplexed*, part II, chapter 25. The subject matter he dealt with in the preceding chapters pertains to the problem of *creatio ex nihil* and the eternity of matter. He opts for the theory of creation out of nothing, despite the fact that in his view there are no compelling rational grounds for choosing between the opposing views. However, he makes a strong and explicit point by saying that if there were any decisive philosophic scientific evidence for the eternity of matter, he would accept it without hesitation, and would be able without difficulty to interpret Scripture accordingly. He assures his readers 'that our shunning the affirmation of the eternity of the world is not due to a text figuring in the Tora according to which the world has been produced in time. For the texts indicating that the world has been produced in time are not more numerous than those indicating that the deity is a body. Nor are the gates of figurative interpretation shut in our faces or impossible of access to us regarding the subject of creation of the world in time. For we could interpet them as figurative, as we have done when denying his corporeality'.[2] Here the point is made openly and without any ambiguity: the flexibility of the figurative interpretation is unlimited. So whenever we have arrived at any new rational knowledge we may interpret Scripture—no, it is our duty to do so—in such a way that it accords with this new philosophic understanding and scientific knowledge.

II

The rise of critical-philological research on the Bible, beginning with Spinoza and culminating during the nineteenth century in the work of Wellhausen and his school, reflects a completely different approach. The Bible was regarded as literature with its linguistic and semantic limitation; its books were assessed as historical documents, thus putting clear-cut limits to interpretive intuition and to arbitrariness. The biblical scholar considers himself as historian who is in search of historical truth, striving for detached objectivity in relation to his subject matter. Yet whenever he proceeds to describe a period, person, event etc. in their general context, i.e. in terms of cause and effect, he necessarily has to have recourse to his personal philosophical convictions, to his leanings and interests; in other words, he becomes aware that Ranke's statement that the historian tells us 'wie es eigentlich gewesen ist' (how it actually happened) is in fact a utopia. It is precisely some of these underlying presumptions, aspirations and interests of modern Jewish biblical scholarship which I am going to trace in this paper.

The present situation is characterized by the fact, that there is no 'Israeli school' in the sense of the Scandinavian school, the German historical-philological, the school of Form Criticism or that of 'History of Tradition', nor is there the slightest prospect of such a school emerging in the foreseeable future. Ideological and methodological pluralism is still far too diverse to be reduced to a common denominator. This is also due to the positivist mentality of a greater part of this generation, whose main interest is focused on biblical realia, i.e. on archaeological, geographical, linguistic, historical detail, which is being accumulated and analysed with special regard to the affinity of the world of the Bible to the cultures of the ancient Near East, in particular to Canaan-Ugarit. It is their daily renewed contact with the landscape of this country which enabled Israeli scholars to enrich and deepen this tangible living aspect of the Bible, thus opening new vistas to the research of historical geography, of biblical agriculture, the flora and fauna of the Land of Israel,[3] and to a deeper insight into military and strategical problems which can be traced in the historical books of the Bible.[4] The major collective achievement of this positivist, empirical approach, which showed relatively little interest in the theological setting of the Bible, is the *Encyclopedia Miqra'it* (*Encyclopedia Biblica*), the first volume having been published in 1955, the eighth and last in 1982.

Despite the aforementioned pluralism, it seems that a common consensus is crystallizing pertaining to a basic critical problem regarding the Pentateuch; I mean the dating of the priestly tradition or the priestly source contained in it. Indeed, three outstanding Jewish biblical scholars of the preceding generation paved the way for this approach: the Jewish-German liberal Rabbi, Benno Jakob, the Italian-Jerusalem scholar Moshe David (Umberto) Cassuto and the sociologist and Bible scholar Yecheskel Kaufmann. Benno Jakob published his comprehensive commentary on Genesis (*Das erste Buch der Tora*, Berlin, 1934) simultaneously with Cassuto's monograph (*La Questione della Genesi*, Firenze, 1934). Both these scholars who were reasoning independently of each other, were trained philologists, far from any fundamentalist approach; both developed exegetical methods, which were tantamount to a full-fledged repudiation of the Wellhausenian source hypothesis. Both arrived at the conclusion, that the book of Genesis, far from being the product of late editors, living during the Babylonian exile, dates back to the beginning of the united Monarchy. Cassuto contended that this book like all the other books of the Pentateuch reflects an ancient Epic which was transmitted by oral tradition from time immemorial. On the other hand, Yecheskel Kaufmann[5] accepted the source hypothesis in principle, but had strong reservations regarding the nature, number and chronological interrelationship between the sources. He maintained that what is considered J and E is a single narrative source which should not be divided or subdivided, as common in western scholarship. Secondly, he made a strong case for the early dating of the Priestly source, arguing that it was edited during the early monarchy, centuries before Deuteronomy, and not during the Babylonian exile as Wellhausen would have it. As to Deuteronomy, in his view it crystallized between the eighth and the seventh centuries, between the days of King Hezekiah and Josiah. Eventually he emphasizes that the bulk of Deuteronomic legislation, namely those laws which do not refer to the centralization of cult, go back to the most ancient period preceding the establishment of the monarchy.

So we may contend that Kaufmann's underlying assumption is, that the Pentateuch, in particular its laws and codes, far from being a late fanciful creation of priests and prophets, who lived during the Babylonian Exile, as the Wellhausian school argued, is the organic outgrowth of Israel's folk-culture during the first commonwealth. He maintains that this culture was not polytheistic as we read in the textbooks down to the present; it was monotheistic. In other words: monotheism is the creation of the so-called 'national spirit' of Israel; moreover, it is the formative element in Israel's culture and religion. This is diametrically opposed to Wellhausen, who referred the creation of monotheism to an elitist group, the classical prophets, who allegedly shaped it in a long process of evolution from Amos to Deutero-Isaiah.

In Kaufmann's opinion the peculiarity of the prophetic faith is the conception of the priority of morals over the cultic commandments, saying that the observance of the moral code would be of crucial importance to the survival of the nation. This, however, does not imply that they rejected cult as such, as Wellhausen had claimed, for a cultless religion is the invention of modern scholars. He argues that this ethical reinterpretation of ancient monotheistic tradition together with prophetic eschatology denotes the zenith of biblical monotheism. As to the historical assessment of the prophetic writings. Kaufmann argues with great eloquence and perspicacity for their basic authenticity, contending that almost all the prophetic books were edited according to chronological principles, additions and extensions by late editors being only marginal.

This amounts to a new critical approach to biblical literature and faith, intended to be a polemical response to Protestant scholarship of his time. As these scholars assessed the Hebrew Bible only as Old Testament, i.e. as a prelude to the New Testament, they were keen to unveil the assumed preceding evolutionary process, which in the fullness of time culminated in the religion of the NT. So it is natural that the main point in their commentaries and introductions was the emphasis on this presumed evolutionary process, sometimes even at the expense of the concrete text itself. Again, the pejorative assessment of the Hebrew Bible by the writers of the NT, in particular of its legal positions, being one of the underlying tacit premises of the German Protestant school, their analysis of the Pentateuch was haphazard. They contended that the laws of P reflect the spiritual decline of 'late Judaism', which emerged during the Babylonian exile. This religion, after having abandoned the universal and spontaneous elements of the prophetic heritage, degenerated into a formalistic legalism with particularistic tendencies—the forerunner of the much hated Pharisees, according to their view. In their analysis of the prophetic literature they claimed that the authentic portions contain only admonitions and oracles of woe and disaster, whilst the consolations and the eschatological sections were additions and inventions of late Jewish scribes. Indeed, this conception dresses in terms of modern scholarship some major prejudices of the NT and the early church fathers, who considered Israel as *massa damnata*, whom God had driven out of their country and disowned from their being His nation, the people of God. Kaufmann's presentation reflects the secular Jewish national response, emphasizing that the Jewish nation, far from being idolatrous, contributed to human culture the monotheistic dimension. The universal outlook of prophetic eschatology is based on the future ingathering of the exiles, the restoration of the temple service and the Davidic dynasty with Jerusalem and Zion as the spiritual centre of mankind. The universalism inherent in this faith is paradoxically based on the restoration of Jewish nationhood and simultaneously on the acceptance of monotheism by all nations. The spiritual centrality of Jerusalem and Zion is tantamount to the reshaping of the nations by the word of God (Isaiah 2).

Thus, Kaufmann draws a quite different image of Israel being a monotheistic nation from its very beginnings, who despised idolatry as a primitive fetishistic worship of wood and stone. Moreover, Israel was devoid of any understanding of mythology, this being the spiritual basis of paganism. An unbridgeable gap divides pagan consciousness, which is mythological, and the a-mythical monotheistic mentality of Israel. This chasm cannot be done away with by the assumption of gradual evolution. Consequently, he contends that there was never in Israel an intermediary stage like syncretism, as commonly assumed.

III

Before investigating the spiritual roots of Kaufmann and before presenting our critical remarks on his view, let us return to his dating of the priestly tradition which had a deep impact on this generation of Jewish scholarship, as I already pointed out. This problem was dealt with for the first time in the sharp polemic anti-Wellhausian booklet written by an orthodox Rabbi, David Hoffmann, at the beginning of this century: *Hauptinstanzen gegen die Graf-Wellhausen'sche Hypothese* (1902/3). Despite the harmonistic and apologetic tendencies of this research, it entails very substantial exegetical arguments against Wellhausen's late dating of the Priestly source—arguments which were taken up by Kaufmann in a critical context and in our generation by M. Haran. These were enlarged by recent linguistic research to the effect that P was written during the united monarchy before D; this linguistic research refers to two additional aspects:

1. The close affinity of priestly cultic terminology to ancient NE cultic language, as has been demonstrated recently by Jacob Milgrom ('Priestly Terminology and the Political and Social Structure of Pre-monarchic Israel', *JQR* 69 [1978] pp. 65-81; *Studies in Levitical Terminology I*, Berkeley/Los Angeles/London [1970]).

2. The fact, brilliantly demonstrated by A. Hurvitz (*A Linguistic Study of the Relationship between the Priestly Source and the Book of Ezekiel* [Cahiers de la Revue Biblique, Paris, 1982]), that the Hebrew style and language of P is part and parcel of ancient classical Hebrew of the first commonwealth. This Hebrew style is completely different from the style and structure of late biblical books like Ecclessiastes, Ezra and Nehemiah, Chronicles, Esther, which stem from the Babylonian exile and the period of restoration. These books reflect an intermediary linguistic stage, which resulted in post-biblical Hebrew of the Mishnah. It was Moshe Zvi Segal who analysed at the beginning of this century the particular features of Mishnaic Hebrew in his pioneering work: *A Grammar of Mishnaic Hebrew*, Oxford (1927). So the linguistic analysis of late biblical Hebrew, which gained momentum with the discovery of the Dead Sea Scrolls, is actually the completion of this work. In this context the book by E.Y. Kutscher, *The Language and the Linguistic Background of the Isaiah Scroll*, Jerusalem (1959) (Hebrew), should be mentioned; there we find for the first time a comprehensive analysis of late biblical Hebrew, being the transitory stage from the classical-biblical language to that of the Mishnah.

It was no lesser scholar than the Jewish historian Heinrich Grätz, who drew our attention for the first time to this basic philological reality in his acrimonious attack on Wellhausen in the *Jewish Chronicle* 5 (1887). There he accuses Wellhausen of antisemitism and charlatanism. He writes:

Wellhausen is a blunderer in the elementary facts of Hebrew and his criticism is largely influenced by his antisemitism, which he takes no pains to disguise ... and then the nonsense of making Ezra the author of the Pentateuch, or of a part of it! The critics should be ashamed of such idle chatter. Ezra's Hebrew style which we know well, is to the artistic diction of the Pentateuch as the Greek style of a Byzantine writer is to that of Plato. Ezra could not have written a single complete verse of the Pentateuch. Besides which, Ezra's bitter enemies, the Samaritans, have accepted the Pentateuch in its entirety as their holiest book. Would they have done this if it had been the work of Ezra? (p. 9).[6]

I cannot endorse this furious, unbalanced statement that Wellhausen was a blunderer; nevertheless, Grätz's argument as to the deep stylistic gap between the classical Hebrew of the Pentateuch, including the Priestly source, and the Hebrew of Ezra's days is an indisputable fact. This trend in Jewish scholarship which assesses P as the reflection of the concrete cultic conditions of the first commonwealth or even the period preceding it, is the most serious challenge to Wellhausen's historical structure, based on his biased evaluation of P as the artificial legalistic artifact of late priests and scribes, who were the forerunners of Pharisaic Judaism.

IV

And now to the sources of Kaufmann's hermeneutic approach: two conflicting elements are discernible which Kaufmann inherited from the romantic trend which dominated Yiddish and Hebrew literature during the first decades of this century, on the one hand, and from the rationalist disposition of the 'Wissenschaft vom Judentum', which flourished during the nineteenth and the beginning of the twentieth century in the German speaking world, on the other hand. Let us briefly dwell on these trends: it is a well known fact that the rise of modern Jewish biblical research coincides with the rise of Zionism, the Jewish renaissance movement, most of whose exponents were from Eastern Europe, where Hebrew and Yiddish literature flourished around the turn of the century in an unprecedented way. The men who created this literature were engaged in a conscious search for the expression of Jewish popular culture. This trend considered Jewish religion as a function of national culture or the so-called folk spirit: the stories of Yehuda Leib Peretz and the collection of Jewish legends by Micha Josef Berdyczewsky (=Bin Gorion; also published in German translation: *Die Sagen der Juden I–V*, 1912-27; and *Der Born Judas I–VI*, 1916-1923), depict this element with great love. The same stress on the organic link between nation, land, culture and religion, with its markedly romantic overtones, is reflected also in Berdyczewsky's theoretical essays, in Simon Dubnow's ten-volume *Weltgeschichte des jüdisches Volkes*, and in the early writings of Buber. Under the impact of this romantic trend Kaufmann coined his sociological framework, in particular the concept 'national spirit', which he conceived as an empirical historical fact. Herewith he did away with Wellhausen's derogatory evaluation of Israel's ancient popular culture, which allegedly was of pagan character.

The second element of Kaufmann's theory is taken from Jewish raionalist tradition, the outstanding medieval representative of which was Maimonides. Kaufmann's immediate precursor in this respect was Hermann Cohen. In his posthumous work *Religion der Vernunft aus den Quellen des Judentums* (1919), Cohen preceded Kaufmann emphasizing the unbridgeable gap between the mythological and pantheistic character of polytheism and monotheism, which by definition is a-mythological, its central idea being the absolute otherness of God, his transcendence, and the absolute superiority of his will. Cohen also connects the spirit of the Jewish nation with the monotheistic idea, thus trying to divorce it from the concept of evolution. But here emerges the basic difference between both: as a liberal religious Jewish thinker with pronounced assimilatory tendencies, Cohen explained Israel's uniqueness in terms of its universal monotheistic mission. Kaufmann, the secular historian and sociologist of the Jewish national revival, translated this idea into the language of empirical historical research, contending that the basic feature of Israel's culture is its monotheistic nature and mentality. As I pointed out before, the rationalistic tradition to which he belonged, goes back to Maimonides, who objected to any corporeal concept of God. The exegetical tool, which Maimonides used, was allegorical Midrash, by means of which he identified the anthropomorphic images of God with the abstract concepts of the Aristotelian system. H. Cohen, on the other hand, who was forced to acknowledge these images as they were, belittled them as desiccated remains of a pre-monotheistic stage. Kaufmann, the historian and sociologist, made a fundamental distinction between abstractness and transcendence. He maintained that biblical faith, borne out of popular intention, is far from conceptual thought, abstraction of any kind being foreign to it. The instrument by which the Bible expresses the monotheistic idea is the legendary popular tradition.

In this way Kaufmann draws our attention to the inner paradox of biblical monotheism, which despite its militant attitude towards pagan myth, expresses its basic ideas in the pictorial anthropomorphic language of myth. He tries to play down the importance of the paradox in two ways:

1. by accepting the limited definition of the term myth as denoting only stories about gods;
2. by avoiding the term 'myth' or 'mythological' expression when describing the inner world of the Bible. Instead he uses the words 'symbolic expression' when discussing the basic idea of monotheism, and so bypasses the problem of mythological thought in the Bible.

V

In this context, one cannot avoid raising two questions:

1. Does the rationalistic definition of Monotheism as an a-mythological creation accord with historical reality?
2. Does the monotheistic image of ancient Israel, which he sketches, take into account all the historical facts?

Let us begin with the second question: the repeated and detailed denouncement by biblical writers of the pagan inclinations of the masses bear clear evidence that idolatry was a serious problem during the first commonwealth. Kaufmann argues against his critics that two literary sources clearly indicate that idolatry, as described in the historical books, was forcibly imposed on the people by the royal court. The first is the Elijah cycle (2 Kgs 18–19) which bears clear evidence that the Phoenician cult was forcibly introduced by the foreign queen Jezebel; the second source pertains to Manasseh King of Judah who forcibly ushered in the Assyrian cult (2 Kgs 21.1-18). But this argument is only half the truth, for prophets like Hosea, Jeremiah and Ezekiel repeatedly condemn the idolatrous inclinations of the masses. It was only after the destruction of the Temple and the State of Judah, that idolatry ceased to be a national problem. Then the exiles of Babylonia, shocked by the idea that the unfaithfulness towards YHWH and the idolatrous behaviour of their forbears, had brought about the national disaster, did away with foreign cults once and for all.

And now to the nature of monotheism as such: I am afraid that the gap between monotheim and pagan worship is not so absolute as

Kaufmann would have it, for the Bible itself describes many transitory phenomena. It was Cassuto who defined this strand, where the biblical writers try to assimilate in various ways Canaanite traditions to their own conception.[7]

Moreover, the problem of myth is far more vexed and complicated than presented by Kaufmann. The arbitrarily narrow definition of mythology as tales about gods does not comply with this universal phenomenon, which pervades all strands of human culture, from the most primitive to the most sophisticated religions. Myth is rather a meta-rational category of thought and expression, which is beyond the limits of conceptual, discursive thought, both these modes being the major forces shaping human consciousness and creativeness.

The structure of mythical thought has been largely dealt with in modern philosophical, psychological and anthropological literature.[8] In this context it will have to be sufficient only to mention briefly that myth contains a direct perception of reality, of human situations and relations, in terms of pictorial, personal and dramatic presentation. Already at the beginning of this century Buber proclaimed the existence of mythological Judaism in his famous speech 'Vom Mythus der Juden'. This was the starting point of an anti-intellectual reassessment of Judaism, which had its deep impact on Jewish studies of the twentieth century, the most outstanding contribution in this respect being doubtlessly Scholem's opus on Jewish mysticism. Again, it is Buber who sketched with a masterly hand the central myth of the Bible, i.e. the ancient utopian concept of the Kingdom of God in his book *Königtum Gottes* (1936).[9]

VI

Consequently the question arises: what are the special qualities of monotheistic myth in contrast to pagan myth? Buber himself was deeply involved in the philosophical issue pertaining to the problem of myth. Time and again he tried to come to grips with this problem during his lifetime, as can be learned from many of his philosophical essays, which I analysed elsewhere.[10] However, he never raised the question as to the differences between pagan and monotheistic myth. Precisely this is the problem which emerges from his writings in the mind of the attentive reader. Indeed, Franz Rosenzweig in his great philosophical oeuvre *The Star of Redemption* attempted for the first time to deal with this problem when distinguishing between the pagan and the Judeo-Christian approach. He maintains there that the categories, man, world and God are perceived by the mythical mind in their dissociation, while Judaism and Christianity place them into relation with each other. But neither the classical Greek sources, nor those of the ancient Near East warrant such a presentation of the problem, for every myth bears evidence of the close relationship between man, gods and world. What makes the real difference between biblical monotheism and pagan myth is the very nature of the relationship between God, man and the world. Pagan myth is based on the belief in an ontological continuum, which means that the world of man and the gods are hewn from the same matter. To be more precise, the human world is derived from divine matter, which is sometimes explained by 'divine biology' i.e. by theogony, and sometimes by theomachy, that is, the struggle between gods, the final outcome of which is the slaying of a monstrous god or goddess and the creation of the earth and sky from his or her body (the Babylonian myth of creation). This means that the world and everything in it, as well as the gods, was formed from the same material substance, which is divine per se. Consequently there are frequent transitions between the three spheres: the divine, the human, and the natural. Gods, who fell or were overthrown, became mortal; gods and goddesses engaged in sexual intercourse with human beings and gave birth to semi-gods, giants, heroes etc. Outstanding human heroes (Utnapishtim etc.) were elevated to the divine sphere and attained immortality. Nonetheless, despite the divine substance of the universe, and the frequent transition from one sphere to another, the creators of pagan myths were aware of the fact that ordinary human beings could not rise above their mortality.[11] But this failure of man is conceived as an accident or as the personal mistake, miscalculation or error of the hero involved. Thus, the myths of creation like those which tell about human efforts to attain immortality, simply illustrate the principle of the ontological continuum, which is explained as the universal rule of biological-organic vitality.

The whole picture changes fundamentally in the Bible. The ontological connection between God and his world, including man, is disrupted. God is outside the world and totally different from it; he and his celestial host are devoid of any material or biological substance whatsoever. His uniqueness is his Almightiness, his unlimited power and will. Everything and everybody in this world derives his very existence from him. An unbridgeable ontological gap separates him from his creation. As against the abstraction of Greek philosophy the God of Israel is a living personality, his relations with the world and man being the result of his free decision. Gone is the biological-ontological continuum, which is the backbone of paganism, for the God of Israel reveals his will to his people, and man is called to respond. In other words, the core of the monotheistic myth is the awareness that the God-man relationship is based on mutual free decision. This should be the starting point of a new theological assessment of the Bible; under this aspect the assimilation of the ancient Near Eastern idea of incarnation by young Christianity indicates a very substantial concession to paganism and pagan myth—a problem which has been dealt with by Christian philosophy from the beginnings up to the present.

To sum up in a few sentences, I maintain that modern Jewish biblical research came into existence as a polemical response to Protestant scholarship. The majority of present Jewish biblical scholars, however, being deeply steeped in the material setting of the Bible, have lost their interest in the theological aspect of the Bible. This, however, was one of the main issues dealt with by two representatives of the preceding generation: Kaufmann and Buber. In the course of their discussion two systems were developed, which opened new vistas to the theological understanding of the Bible: the rationalist trend represented by Y. Kaufmann and Buber's anti-rationalistic approach, which attempted to take into account the irrational mythological elements of biblical faith. Indeed, this is the only possible point of departure for a future Jewish theological approach to the Bible, the first signs of it being already discernible. Again, this discussion between two philosophically minded scholars had also a deep impact on modern Jewish philosophy, on Jewish studies and on the Jewish-Christian dialogue which gained momentum during our generation.

NOTES

1. On this trend see Gershom G. Scholem, 'The Meaning of the Tora in Jewish Mysticism, in: *On the Kabbalah and its Symbolism* (translated from German by Ralph Mannheim), New York: Schocken Books (1960, 1965, 1972), pp. 87-117. (Geman original: 'Der Sinn der Tora in der jüdischen

Mystik', in: *Kabbala und Symbolik*, Zürich: Rhein Verlag [1960], pp. 49-116.)

2. Moses Maimonides, *The Guide of the Perplexed*, vol. II, translated and with an introduction and notes by Shlomo Pines, Chicago (1963), pp. 327f.

3. M. Avi-Yonah, *Historical Geography of the Land of Israel*, Jerusalem (1950) (Hebrew); F.S. Bodenheimer, *Animal Life in Palestine*, Jerusalem (1935). Hebrew edition: *Animal Life in Biblical Lands*, Tel-Aviv (1950); Y. Aharoni, *The Land of Israel during the Biblical Period*, Jerusalem (1963) (Hebrew); Y. Felix, *Agriculture in the Land of Israel during the Period of the Mishnah and the Talmud*, Jerusalem; Y. Pers, *Eretz-Israel, Topographical-Historical Encyclopedia*, 4 vols., Jerusalem (1946-1956) (Hebrew).

4. Y. Yadin, *The Art of Warfare in Biblical Lands in the Light of Archeological Study*, Jerusalem (1963).

5. Yehezkel Kaufmann, *Toledot ha-Emunah ha-Yisre'ēlit* (8 vols. in 4), Tel Aviv (1937-1957). Seven volumes translated and condensed by Moshe Greenberg, *The Religion of Israel* (1960). Beginning of the eighth volume translated by C.W. Efroymson, *The Babylonian Captivity and Deutero-Isaiah* (1970); Y. Kaufmann, *The Biblical Account of the Conquest of Palestine* (1953) (Hebrew original, 1956); *idem, Mi-Kivshonah shel ha-yezirah ha-mikra'it* (1966) (a posthumous collection of studies in the Bible).

6. Quoted according to M. Weinfeld, *Shnaton* 4 (1980), p. 83.

7. D.M. Cassuto, *Biblical and Canaanite Literatures*, I, Jerusalem (1971), pp. 20-54, 55-61, 62-90. English translation under the above name. See also A. Ohler, *Die mythischen Elemente im alten Testament*, Düsseldorf (1969); F.M. Cross, *Canaanite Myth and Hebrew Epic*, Cambridge, Mass. (1973).

8. The diverse aspects of the problem are dealt with in a short and informative way in a booklet edited by George F. McLean, *Myth and Philosophy*, Proceedings of the American Catholic Philosophical Association, Vol. XLV (1971).

9. The reader will find a critical assessment of this important contribution to biblical studies in my book, *Ancient Prophecy in Israel*, Jerusalem (1973), pp. 121-37 (Hebrew).

10. 'Buber and modern biblical scholarship', in H. Gordon and J. Bloch (eds.), *Martin Buber—A Centenary Volume*, Ben Gurion University of the Negev (1984), pp. 163-214. All bibliographical information pertaining to the topic can be found there.

11. B. Uffenheimer, 'Biblical Theology and Monotheistic Myth', *Immanuel* 14 (1982), pp. 7-25; *idem*, 'Myth and Reality in Ancient Israel', in: S.N. Eisenstadt (ed.), *The Origins and Diversity of Axial Age Civilizations*, State University Press of New York (1986), pp. 135-68.

14

HUMANISTIC EXEGESIS: THE FAMOUS HUGO GROTIUS

H. Graf Reventlow

Today the name of Hugo Grotius is known, if at all, only as the founder of international law (by his work: *De iure belli ac pacis*),[1] and perhaps as a politician. Much less noted is his theological opus, collected in four voluminous infolios.[2] Grotius was a lawyer, he was a politician, a statesman, a member of the Remonstrant community in Holland, and as such he was involved in the fierce political and religious struggles of his time.[3] But he is best regarded as the last representative of the European movement starting in the fourteenth century commonly known as Humanism,[4] which found a last heyday in Holland in the first half of the seventeenth century. He united in his person all the qualities of a humanist: an all-embracing classical formation, the knowledge of several ancient and modern languages, including biblical and mishnaic Hebrew and Syriac (possibly also English, though this is uncertain), the interest in classical philology and ancient sources (he edited several Greek and Latin authors) and history (he also wrote historical works).[5] Remarkably enough he seems to be completely untouched by the enormous progress in natural sciences reached in his lifetime, by KEPLER, GALILEI, BACON and others,[6] untouched also by the growing movement of philosophical empirism. Standing on the eve of a new epoch, he is seemingly looking back to the ancestors. And yet, a careful observer will detect in his works time and again the vestiges of a changing view, leading over to the period which we are used to call modernity. Best known is his important step to found an independent fundament of law 'etiamsi daremus . . . non esse Deum',[7] arguing for the autonomy of ethics that has been defended later by his follower LEIBNIZ.[8] The inclination to a self-sustained morality is a characteristic layer in the substructure of humanistic thinking, one that would prove especially important for the following period of enlightenment.

Though a layman, GROTIUS was also a theologian of fame. His endeavours for the reunification of the church are not yet forgotten.[9] His proposals for a settlement between the confessions, including the Roman Catholics, were made possible by the same humanist view which took the central credentials of protestant confession—*sola fide* (by faith alone), *sola scriptura* (the scriptures alone)—to be less important, indeed, openly added tradition, a second way of ensuring the reliability of the apostolic message.[10] In his exegetical work we are surprised by the recurring citations of patristical sources: Hieronymus, Augustine, Chrysostom, Justin and others are called over and over again in support of the explanation of a certain passage of Scripture. He was very much at home with the church fathers.[11] But he had also a comprehensive knowledge of the Jewish exegetical tradition, beginning with 'the rabbis', Philo and Josephus and ending with Ibn Ezra, Kimchi and Maimonides, who are his witnesses in countless textual and philological details. 'In understanding the sense of the books belonging to the Old Covenant the Hebrew authors can contribute a lot, especially those who know the words and customs of their fathers the best.'[12] Besides these he used to cite classical writers abundantly, sometimes in illustrating sentences, sometimes in historical remarks. Humanistic exegesis was first of all a philological programme. This aspect of his work occupies much space in GROTIUS's Annotations to both Testaments which he began when he was confined in the Castle of Louvestein in 1619-21 (for being an adherent of the party of Oldenbarneveld) and finished shortly before his death.[13] The system is a verse-by-verse exegesis of the whole Bible in the manner of the time,[14] in famous chapters explaining nearly every word, sometimes including an excursus on a specific topic, otherwhere leaping from one chapter to the next more or less superficially. But the impression of the whole is overwhelming for its richness and originality. No wonder that GROTIUS became famous as an interpreter for more than a hundred years after his death.[15]

In his philological explanations of single words he is fond of his profound knowledge of Hebrew (and Aramaic), besides the more common but not universally understandable Greek.[16] Proceeding from the Vulgate in explaining the Old Testament he usually looks back to the original Hebrew term, following this with the different Greek versions for a better understanding. To give an example: In Gen. 3.1 the snake is called the most cunning of all creatures, callidior omni animali. 'Sic et Aquila (similarly also Aquila)', remarks GROTIUS: πανοῦργος ἀπὸ παντὸς ζῴου. This translation is also backed by Paul, who ascribes πανουργίαν to the snake in 1 Cor. 11.3. Furthermore, the Hebrew צרום is translated by the Greeks everywhere in Job and Proverbs by πανοῦργος. But in Gen. 3.1 the LXX gives φρονιμώτερος, *prudentior*, more clever, intelligent. Lk. 16.8 shows that the term can be used *in bonam et in malam partem*, and in Mt. 10.16 the Christians are exhorted to be clever like snakes. There follow remarks on the manner in which snakes creep on the earth, and on a special kind of snakes living on trees, taken from the classical authors SERGIUS and LUCANUS (giving a passage out of the latter's poem). The Greek name of these snakes, ἀκοντίαι, is given by Agarthachides, Strabo, Diodorus Siculus. The last observation notes that also the devil (called Samael among the Jews) can be called the old serpent (Rev. 12.9; 20.2), who is the most cunning (1 Cor. 2.11 etc.) and proud creature (1 Tim. 3.8). So the reader receives a wealth of information.

In this case GROTIUS just describes the different possibilities of translating a word. There are other examples where the versions do not represent the same text as the Hebrew original. For instance, in Exod. 33.13 the Latin has: *ostende mihi faciem tuam*, 'show me your face', that means: δόξαν (so some Greeks). But in the Hebrew the clause says: make known to me your way, 'what the Rabbis interpret concerning the divine qualities which they call מדוא, but the passage shows that what is here spoken of is the manner in which God rules the whole, which Moses wanted to imitate'. Here we have remarks on the correct (original) reading and how it has to be correctly understood.

A second group of remarks relates to text-critical questions. Here GROTIUS notes differences between the Hebrew text and the versions, for instance in Exod. 31.4, where the LXX has some words more than the Hebrew and some codices even an additional clause. Conclusions, as regards the original text, are not drawn. The major problems of the LXX, for instance the different structure of the book of Jeremiah, or the beginning of the book of Ezra, are not mentioned. Obviously GROTIUS regarded the differences between the Hebrew text and the versions as not crucial; on the contrary, he once mentions the accordance of the Greek translations with the original in all historically important points as one of the proofs for the reliability of the textual tradition.[17] In the New Testament he justly observes a completely different situation as regards the textual tradition: 'Who compares the codices experiences that the variations are countless in the scriptures. . . To discern what is true in that is an immense labour, and not always successful'.[18] But these questions do not trouble too much; the apostolic tradition as a whole is backed by many trustworthy witnesses and the broad *consensus ecclesiae*. Questions of literary criticism are completely out of sight, as we shall see later still more strikingly. We have to remember that we are still far away from the period of historical-critical exegesis which fully developed no earlier than in the nineteenth century.

In his widely known apologetic work '*De veritate religionis Christianae*'[19] GROTIUS defends the truth of the Christian religion in Book III by the truthfulness of the scriptures. Among the first arguments is the sentence, '*Libros qui nomina praescripta habent eorum esse quorum nomen praeferunt*', 'the books which have names in the superscription belong to those whose names appear there'.[20] To begin with, books of the New Testament are meant, but later on the same is said about the books of the Old Covenant.[21] GROTIUS knows that some books of the New Testament were disputed and not accepted as genuine by all churches (for instance, the letters of James and Jude, the letter to the Hebrews), but as they were recognized by most churches and contain nothing that cannot be found abundantly in other books which are not doubtful, the scepticism is not well founded.[22] As regards New Testament books which are without the name of an author, or even those whose authorship is open to doubt, such as the Apocalypse of John, that would not matter, either, because the intrinsic value of the product of an author is the important thing, not whether his name is known.[23]

The reliability of the New Testament books can be shown, too, because they relate what their authors were personally informed about. Matthew, John, Peter, Jude belonged to the Twelve, Luke lived near the places where Jesus had lived himself and had the opportunity to contact eye-witnesses of his work. Paul could not have been deceived by the revelations he had received from Jesus out of heaven.[24] Besides, all these writers had no intention of lying, and no reason to do so.[25] If God has the aim to care for mankind and to guide them to honouring and adoring him, he would not tolerate their being deceived by lying books.[26] Similar additional arguments are adduced to plead for the trustworthiness of the Old Testament books:

Hi autem quorum nomina praeferunt aut Prophetae fuerunt, aut viri fide dignissimi; qualis et Esdras, qui eos in unum volumen collegisse creditur.[27]

Those people whose names they bear were either prophets or very trustworthy men; such a one was also Esdras who is believed to have collected them into one volume.

Besides the reputation of the authors of the biblical books ancient oriental history can also confirm the reliability of Old Testament traditions. Above all the names of several Babylonian kings such as Nabuchodonosor, and other historical details, are preserved in the fragments of Berossos; Pharaoh Apries is mentioned by Herodotus. Much more information about the Persian kings is contained in Greek authors.[28] The historical interest of the humanist is visible here and we are standing at the inception of an apologetical approach to historic testimonies which has not yet died out. In the prolonged notes, covering several folio-pages, which explain these remarks one gains a vivid insight into the enormous difficulties a seventeenth-century author had to cope with in trying to collect information about the history of the ancient Near East. The sites of the ancient capitals and their clay tablet libraries would still lie covered, for more than two hundred years, by the debris of the past. All one could do was to collect the second-hand news that classical and early church authors had passed on from remote and often distorted traditions. In connection with Isaiah 13 GROTIUS on one occasion remarks:

> We could expound this prophet and others more clearly and exactly if we had the Assyriaca of Abydenos and the Babyloniaca of Berossos. But now in the holy scriptures little of this is touched upon and most of what relates to the Jews, and profane histories are lacking.[29]

Far away from the apologetic aims of his *De veritate*—though not on the basis of other convictions—GROTIUS in his Annotations to both Testaments offers besides the philological and grammatical a historical exegesis of the whole Bible. In order to value this enterprise adequately we must be aware of the fact that this is the first comprehensive commentary on the Bible which tries to explain the scriptures systematically against their historical background. As we saw, the intention is not to question their authority—that is the basic difference from the Deistic criticism a hundred years later—but in a way it was a radical new approach compared with the orthodox view of most of GROTIUS's contemporaries.

The orthodox standpoint—represented by GROTIUS's antagonist A. RIVET—had developed the dogma of verbal inspiration to the extreme, so that it regarded even the masoretic vowal points as inspired. GROTIUS had a rather different standpoint on the question of inspiration. In his discussion with RIVET he declares about himself:

> That the prophets did speak what they spoke, did write what they were ordered to write (driven) by the spirit of God Grotius acknowledges wholeheartedly. The same is his judgment on the predictions of the apocalypse and of the apostles. That all words of Christ are words of God it would be a crime to doubt. On the historical books and the moral sentences of the Hebrews he has another opinion. It is enough that they were written with a pious attitude, with the best faith and on the highest subjects... Neither Esdras nor Luke were prophets, but earnest and wise men who did not want to deceive, nor to be deceived, either.

Citing the first words of the gospel of Luke, he adds: 'How did he (Luke) receive (what he wrote)? From the witnesses themselves, not by revelation'.[30] Here we observe an important step from a dogmatic to a historical-critical approach. 'Did Luke say: "The word of God same to Luke and God said to him: write!", as the prophets did? Nothing like that!'[31] GROTIUS takes the verbal sense of the Bible in earnest. He observes that in the prophetic books the direct transmission of the word of God is explicitly mentioned. To this extent the dogma of verbal inspiration has its, albeit restricted, right. According to SCHLÜTER[32] GROTIUS knows only a personal inspiration, not the inspiration of whole books. But in other books of the Bible, for instance in the Gospel of Luke, the circumstances are completely different.

> Rightly I have said that not all the books which are in the Hebrew canon are dictated by the Holy Spirit. That they are written by a pious movement of the heart, I don't deny... But there was no need that histories should be dictated by the Holy Spirit; it was enough that the author had a strong memory about things he had seen, or intelligence in copying the commentaries of the Ancients.[33]

Therefore each book has to be handled according to its peculiar origin; global theories are not useful for an historical understanding.

Also for GROTIUS, the canon is just an historical problem, not a theological one. In fact, to his conservative standpoint, the canon is no problem at all: 'Quos libros tales judicavit Synagoga, ii sunt Canonici Hebraeis. Quos tales Ecclesia Christiana, ii sunt Canonici Christianis'.[34] He mentions the decision of the 'Great Synagogue', including the majority vote regarding Kohelet, 'which I readily sign', though not all Old Testament authors were prophets or had the Holy Spirit.[35] The books which the synagogue considered as such belong to the Canon for the Hebrews; which the Christian church (considered) as such, belong to the canon for the Christians. The authority of the tradition is sufficient to warrant the extent of the canon.

In commenting upon single chapters and verses of the Old Testament GROTIUS sees one of his most important tasks in explaining the historical background of names and events that are mentioned. We take as an example the book of Isaiah. Chapter 7 of this book was widely known for the mysterious name of the child Immanuel, whose birth was announced to king Ahaz as a sign of the soon approaching end of the imminent danger during the Syro-Ephraimite war. For Christians the messianic interpretation was the usual one, starting with the citation of the verse in Mt. 1.22-23. In his annotations on the Gospel of Matthew, GROTIUS provides a long excursus[36] on Isaiah 7, in which we find the following identification of the child:

> The child. . ., as can be deduced from the following, seems not to have been Hezekiah, as many of the Hebrews think . . . because he, if the dates are rightly valued, had already reached a certain age before the reign of Ahaz, as rightly is annotated by Rabbi Solomon, though what is said at the beginning of chapter nine below can rightly been referred to him; but rather this child is the son of Isaiah himself. . .[37]

In this manner GROTIUS tries to explain also other details of the text. The sixty-five years in Isaiah 7.8 he regards as a mistake in the Hebrew text, 'addito ם ad שש'. 'For from this time to the deportation of the ten tribes which Shalmaneser made, 2 Kings 17, are six and five years, that means, eleven'.[38] The fly from uppermost Egypt which is announced to Ahaz in v. 18 is Pharaoh Necho, the bee from Assur Sennacherib. At this point we already perceive the effect of one of GROTIUS' principles mentioned above: as far as prophecy is concerned he has the greatest imaginable confidence that any prediction is possible, since a prophet speaks under the guidance of

God's own spirit. This basically dogmatic presupposition renders
him blind to constellations that are obviously historically improbable.
That the son whose birth is announced in Isa. 9.6—GROTIUS takes
the verbs as denoting the future—means the future king Hezekiah,
and that the mention of defeat of the enemies referred to the
destruction of Sennacherib's army around Jerusalem that would
occur in the year 701, are still conceivable. Chapter 11 is likewise
taken as referrring to Hezekiah; the 'remnant' coming home from
far-off countries (v. 11) are refugees out of the ten tribes returning
under Hezekiah to Judah/Jerusalem, an explanation occasionally
offered also in recent times. After having read more or less likely
identifications of historical events in other chapters of Proto-Isaiah,
the reader is curious as to how GROTIUS will explain the background
of Deutero-Isaiah. One should remember: it was DOEDERLEIN in
1775 (and, following him, EICHHORN) who first uttered the thesis
that chapters 40ff. of Isaiah are a separate book and the work of an
anonymous prophet who lived 150 years later than the first Isaiah.
GROTIUS was inhibited from discovering this because in a conservative
way he saw the prophets as proclaimers of a possibly also distant
future. He already has a tendency of trying first to find out a nearby
historical occasions for a word[39]—that is his humanistic impetus—
but the dogmatic legacy in his thinking causes him to stop halfway.
As far as ch. 36, in his opinion, Isaiah's predictions are restricted to
the time of Hezekiah, from ch. 29 to ch. 36 for instance in prophecies
spoken two years before the arrival of Sennacherib.[40] But in ch. 13 he
had already met with a prophecy on Babylon, which he took to have
been fulfilled in the period between Sennacherib and Nebuchadnezzar.
From ch. 40 onwards he sees himself confronted by prophecies which
largely transcend Isaiah's lifetime. Not only the exile under
Nebuchadnezzar and the return of the exiled Jews after the end of
the Babylonian rule, but even the Maccabean period and afterwards
are predicted by the prophet in the second half of his book. 'For God
did not want that anything honorable which would happen to the
people should not be mentioned in order to console the pious who
would be exiled for the guilt of others'.[41] This theory enables him to
cope also with some striking details: for instance that the name of
Cyrus is mentioned in Isa. 44.28:

> It is really astonishing that so long before, more than two hundred
> and ten years, as Josephus states, the name of this king should be
> openly mentioned. . . But God, who had predicted this, gave this

name into the minds of those people who had the right to give the
name, so that they should give this name, not another.

At other places GROTIUS is free in his identifications. So he sees in
the Servant of the Lord in the first three Servant-songs Isaiah
himself, a type of explanation that is still discussed. The last Servant-
song (of course the designation does not appear) concerns Jeremiah.
Isa. 57.1ff. is about king Josiah, ch. 62 about Cyrus, 63ff. about Judas
Maccabee and the Jews in the time of Antiochus IV.

Given the totally fragmentary knowledge about the history of the
ancient Near East in GROTIUS's day and the obscurity of many
passages in the later parts of the book of Isaiah itself, it is no wonder
that many of these conjectures have proven erroneous in the
meantime. More important is GROTIUS's consistency in seeking these
historical identifications. And as is well known, the Maccabean
setting of most of the psalms was still in vogue some sixty years ago.
The impact of humanist exegesis—represented by GROTIUS—on
modern interpretation of the Bible, with regard to the stress laid on
the search for the historical setting of a text, cannot be overrated.

For the reasons already mentioned, in the main GROTIUS does not
yet arrive at historico-critical observations. There are some exceptions: in spite of his declared belief in *De veritate* that all biblical
books are from the authors whose names they bear he is sceptical in
some cases. So in the case of Qohelet:

> I do not think that it comes from Solomon, but it is written later
> under the name... of this king. As reason for that I point to the
> many words which are only found in Daniel, Esra and the
> Chaldean interpreters.[42]

Remarkably enough the philological reasons are decisive. The same
reason is also given in the case of Job, a book that GROTIUS wants to
date in the period of the Babylonian exile.[43] GROTIUS is also already
aware of a gradual development of revelation in the Bible: 'As the
times progress, God shows things more openly to his people. So
Daniel saw more than Ezekiel; Ezekiel and Jeremiah more than
Isaiah'. The same can be said also about New Testament authors:
'The destruction of the Roman Empire was revealed to John; that it
was revealed to Paul cannot be made likely by any argument'.[44]
Important also is an observation that the apostolic letters are written
for specific occasions, 'and what the time brought with them', that
they are not intended as a corpus of doctrine or on the regiment of

the church.[45] In GROTIUS's day this was a revolutionary opinion.

He caused a sensation and met embittered opposition by disputing the hitherto almost unanimous identification of the Antichrist with the Pope by the Protestants, introduced by LUTHER.[46] In a separate investigation of the relevant New Testament passages (Mt. 24.24; 1 Thess. 4.14; 2 Thess. 2.8; 2 Cor. 15.22; 1 Jn 2.22; Rev. 13.1)[47] he showed that all are to be explained in a contemporary context. His intention was to promote peace in the church and to further a hoped-for reconciliation with the Roman Catholics. He caused instead a fierce opposition which he tried to answer by a second essay.[48]

In his view of the theological relevance of the Old Testament GROTIUS takes the typical standpoint of a Christian humanist. When we see him using both Testaments as a source of law (in his *De iure naturae et gentium*), this cannot surprise us, as he is following a long tradition, alive since the early church, which tried to combine the Stoic natural law with the Christian authority of the Bible. Nor does GROTIUS see any problem in taking natural law as having its source in God, who willed these principles to dwell in the human soul. He does not hesitate to cite in support the opinion of Chrysippus and the Stoics that the origin of law is to be sought with Zeus.[49] This attitude corresponds to the typical humanistic theory of a basic true religion common to all mankind, consisting of four notions: 'First, that God exists and is one. Second, that God is nothing visible, but something more sublime. Third, that God cares for human affairs and judges by the most fitting scales. Fourth, that God is the creator of all besides himself'.[50] GROTIUS sees these four principles contained in the commandments of the decalogue, which are binding for all mankind, because the same precepts were already given to Adam and Noah and through them to their posterity.[51] But his judgment of the importance of the Old Testament for law is nuanced, trying to steer a middle course between two extremes: the one equating the Old Testament completely with the law of nature, the other arguing that since the time of the New Covenant the Old Testament has become totally useless. The first opinion is wrong in so far, 'as many of them (of the Old Testaments commandments) come out of the free will of God, which nevertheless nowhere contrast with the true law of nature', it is right in so far 'as we distinguish between the law of God—which, however, God executes by men—and the law of men among themselves'.[52] This must be seen against the background of contemporary Puritanism, which considered Old Testament prescriptions as to a large extent binding also for Christians, some Christian sects in Holland even being converted to Judaism.[53] On the other hand GROTIUS was called by his opponents a Judaizer in connection with his exegetical methods, but in his evaluation of Old Testament law he follows the usual distinction between particular Jewish law (not valid for Christians) and moral law (binding on everyone). He refers also to the New Testament,

> because it is the nature of the New Covenant, that it teaches the same things which in the Old Testament are commanded relating to the moral virtues, and greater ones; and we see the ancient Christian writers in this way using the witnesses of the Old Covenant.[54]

In all this GROTIUS has the rationalistic idea of a basically moral religion regarding Jesus as a model to follow; on this foundation he also hoped to ground the reunification of the churches.[55] It is no surprise that he refused to acknowledge Jewish traditions after Christ: 'in this time the spirit of God left the Synagogue, as was predicted'.[56]

In relating the words of the Old Testament prophets to contemporary events and circumstances GROTIUS had to answer the question what he thought about the traditional Christian approach, which found in them predictions of the coming Messiah, predictions which already the first Christians and the Evangelists in the New Testament regarded as fulfilled in Jesus Christ. He embarks on this problem in the aforementioned excursus in his Annotations on the Gospels, where he comments on the formula in Mt. 1.22 ἵνα πληρωθῇ 'in order that be fulfilled'. Taking as his starting-point above all the sentence in 1 Cor. 10.11, 'that all happened to them (the Israelites) τύπικως', and similar utterances, he develops a theory very similar to modern typological reflections. 'There are two sorts of signs, those that can be heard, and visible ones. And the things that are signified are past ones, present ones and future ones'. 'Thus the Passover lamb was a visible sign of a past thing, namely the liberation from slavery in Egypt. But this liberation is the type of our liberation from sins. Therefore 1 Cor. 5.7 shows that Christ was adumbrated in the Passover lamb'. Another visible sign are the thirty silver coins mentioned in Zech. 11.13, which foreshadowed the treachery of Judas Iscariot (Mt. 27.9). A sign to be heard was the prophetic word Hos. 11.1, being likewise a sign of the past liberation from the Egyptian slavery and the greater liberation by Jesus Christ.

> The history of Christ itself admonishes us that the mind of the prophet was so directed by God that what was said by him about the Israelite people corresponded no less correctly, indeed possibly even with more right, to Christ, Mt. 11.15.

On the basis of this hermeneutical principle—which he also detects as a method in Jewish exegesis[57]—he is able to explain the various prophetic words from their respective contemporary background and at the same time as foreshadowing the saving deeds of Jesus Christ. Many examples of this can be found in the commentary on Isaiah. For instance on Isa. 9.6: 'A son is given to us': 'Hezekiah who was very different from his father. But that this can relate also and much better to the Messiah is acknowledged not only by Christians, but also by the Chaldean (commentator) on this place'. Or on the Servant of the Lord, Isa 42.1: directly Isaiah himself is meant, as we mentioned already. 'But in a higher sense this is fulfilled in Christ, whose figure Isaiah foresaw, as far as he could, as also Jonah, Jeremiah and some others'. In the case of the Song of Songs he follows the opinion of the Targum (Chaldaeus) and MAIMONIDES, 'that Solomon, in order that this scripture would exist the longer, had composed it so artfully that in it, without distortion, allegorical senses could be found which express the love of God towards his people'. The Christological explanation is the consequent next step.[58] Being attacked by RIVET for his method, he defends it resolutely:

> Does it mean to falsify a passage if one acknowledges in one place a popular and a higher sense as well? But Grotius showed that this has to be done indeed in many Old Testament passages. He showed likewise that the same words frequently have a meaning in the popular sense, another in the higher sense.[59]

He is ready to drop the usual opinion: 'The resurrection of Christ is rightly believed, and has to be believed, in view of so many fitting witnesses, but it is not predicted by the prophets, if you take the direct words, the first sense only'.[60]

One would misunderstand GROTIUS, if one saw in this second level of interpretation a mere subterfuge or a concession to the official opinion. There is no reason to assume that he was not in earnest. The two-level understanding of a prophetic word points to deeper hermeneutical problems with which every believer handling of the

Bible will have to struggle. For taking a text of the past as authoritative also for the present and meaningful for the future means at any case opening up a new perspective in it, which a unilinear historical understanding will not see. I just hint at these problems; they need further discussion.[61]

GROTIUS is well aware that typological explanations are no means of convincing anybody who is not already a believer.

> All these things . . . are not employed in the real force of an argument, but for illustrating and confirming a matter already believed.[62]

> It has to be noted that the Apostles do not fight with the help of these supposed evidences against the Jews in order to prove that Jesus was the promised Messiah. There are few oracles which they usurp to this end, for the rest being content with the miracles and the resurrection of Christ.[63]

> But they wanted to show those to whom it was already clear that Jesus is this Messiah how the whole economy of God in the earlier time always precisely had this Christ and his deeds before its eyes like a most beautiful and perfect picture, so to speak, and formed all the other things after this design.[64]

In taking the miracles as an irrefutable proof for the truth of the gospel,[65] GROTIUS was a child of his time, untouched still by the intellectual revolution of the enlightenment. But on the exegetical field he opened up methodological ways which were to influence work on the Bible up to the present day.

NOTES

1. *De iure belli ac pacis libri tres*, Paris (1625); we have used the critical edition, ed. P.C. MOLHUYSEN, Leiden (1919).
2. *Opera omnia theologica*, Vols. I, II.1.2, III, Amsterdam (1679). We have used the London, 1679 edition.
3. Only few modern biographies of GROTIUS can be mentioned. Cf. especially W.S.M. KNIGHT, *The Life and Works of Hugo Grotius* (The Grotius Society Publications, 4; London [1925]); A. HALLEMA, *Hugo de Groot*, The Hague (1942); the biographical sketch by W.J.M. van EYSINGA, *Hugo Grotius* (German translation Basel [1952]), is written in the loose style of an essay.— On the theological thoughts of GROTIUS cf. esp. J. SCHLÜTER, *Die Theologie*

des Hugo Grotius, Göttingen (1919); A.H. HAENTJENS, *Hugo de Groot als godsdienstig denker*, Amsterdam (1946) (on the exegetical work esp. pp. 27-65); A. CORSANO, *U. Grozio. L'umanista—il teologo—il giurista*, Bari (1948) (excluding the exegetical work).

4. On his humanistic predecessors from ERASMUS and MELANCHTHON to SCALIGER and CASAUBONUS cf. CORSANO, *op. cit.*, pp. 3-44.

5. Cf. esp.: *De Antiquitate republicae Batavicae*, 1610; *Historia Gothorum Vandalorum et Longobardorum*, 1655.

6. On GROTIUS's utterances relating to GALILEO and KEPLER and his position as to the modern worldview cf. SCHLÜTER, *Theologie*, pp. 21f.

7. *De iure belli*, ed. MOLHUYSEN, p. 7.

8. Cf. esp. A. DROETTO, *Ugone Grozio e l'"avversario" di Cartesio nella questione delle verità eterne*, in: *idem, Studi Groziani* (Torino, 1968), pp. 35-63; cf. also *idem*, 'I Prolegomini al "De iure belli ac pacis"', *ibid.*, pp. 292-308.

9. Cf. esp. *Via ad pacem ecclesiasticam...* (1642) = *Op. omn. th.*, III, pp. 535-636; *Votum pro pace ecclesiastica...* = *ibid.*, pp. 653-76. Also CORSANO, *op. cit.*, pp. 159-230.

10. Utterances in favour of the traditions of the early church are frequent with GROTIUS; cf. esp. his preface to his *Annotations to the New Testament*, *op. omn. th.* II.1, p. 2: 'Testor autem, si quid usquam a me scriptum est pugnans cum iis Sacrae Scripturae sensibus, quos Ecclesiae Christianae a prima aetate acceptos perseverante consensu tenuere... me id pro non scripto habere ac mutare paratissimum'. Cf. also *Votum pro pace, op. omn. th.*, III, pp. 653, 675ff.; *Rivetani apologetici discussio, ibid.*, pp. 679-745, pp. 723f., etc. K. KROCH-TONNING (*Hugo Grotius und die religiösen Bewegungen im Protestantismus seiner Zeit*, Cologne [1904]), an oldfashioned Catholic apologist, takes all these traits as signs that GROTIUS was close to being converted to the Roman church! Cf. also regarding the broader background of the dialogue between the two communities: P.H. WINKELMAN, *Remonstranten en Katolieken in de eeuw van Hugo de Groot*, Nijmegen (1945).

11. A problem is, however, that sometimes his references are not exact enough, cf. MOLHUYSEN, Preface, in *De iure belli, op. cit.*, p. xiii.

12. *De iure belli*, p. 17.

13. *Annotationes ad Vetus Testamentum* (1644); now in *op. omn. th.*, I; *Annotationes in quatuor Evangelia* (1641), now in *op. omn. th.*, II.1; *Annotationes in Novum Testamentum*, II (1646), III (1650), now in *op. omn. th.*, II.1 and II.2. On the different stages of this work cf. HAENTJENS, *op. cit.*, pp. 31f. For the following examples cf. GROTIUS's annotations on the respective biblical passages.

14. On the method used in the philological Annotations commentary (as opposed to the theological commentary) see also H.J. de JONGE, *De bestudering van het Nieuwe Testament aan de Noordnederlandse universiteiten en het Remonstrants Seminarie van 1575 tot 1700* (VNAW, 106; 1980), pp. 39ff.

15. His *Annotationes in Vetus Testamentum* were re-edited as late as 1775-76 in Halle by J.C. DOEDERLEIN, who writes in his foreword to the admirers of the 'immortal Grotius': 'Whoever used almost any of the theological commentaries which were worth their price without perceiving that all . . . have drawn out of these books whatever they have of good material in philological matters?' (*op. cit.*, II, p. 3). J.G. HERDER (*Briefe, das Studium der Theologie betreffend: Sämtliche Werke*, ed. B. SUPHAN, vol. X; Berlin [1879]) (reprint Hildesheim/New York [1967/8]). Letter 22, p. 253, mentions GROTIUS's as the only commentary for a suggested reading by a student. A. KUENEN, one of the heroes of the historical-critical method in the nineteenth century, still regarded GROTIUS as an outstanding protagonist of modern Bible criticism; cf. *Hugo de Groot als uitlegger van het Oude Verbond* (VAW r. II, d. 12; 1883), pp. 301-32.

16. In the final edition of the *Annotationes*, he therefore adds the Latin translation to each Greek clause.

17. *De veritate religionis Christianae*, III/16, *op. omn. th.*, III, p. 61b.

18. *Votum pro pace* = *op. omn. th.*, III, p. 673a. GROTIUS did not yet have the textual material at his disposal as we now have; cf. HAENTJENS, *op. cit.*, 32f.

19. 1627 and about 70 later editions. For convenience's sake, we use the reprint in *op. omn. th.*, III, pp. 1-96.

20. *De veritate*, III/2, superscription, *op. omn. th.*, III, p. 50a.

21. III/16, *ibid.*, pp. 56b-62b.

22. III/3. *ibid.*, p. 50b.

23. III/4, *ibid.*, pp. 50b-51a.

24. III/5, *ibid.*, pp. 51a-b.

25. III/6, *ibid.*, p. 51b.

26. III/9, *ibid.*, p. 52b.

27. III/16, *ibid.*, p. 56b.

28. *Ibid.*, pp. 56b-60a.

29. *Annotationes, ad loc.*

30. *Rivetani apologetici discussio* = *op. omn. th.*, III, pp. 677-745, 722b-723a.

31. *Ibid.*, p. 723a.

32. *Theologie*, p. 27.

33. *Votum pro pace* = *op. omn. th.*, III, p. 672b.

34. *Discussio* = *op. omn. th.*, III, p. 723a.

35. *Animadversiones in animadversiones Riveti* = *op. omn. th.*, III, pp. 637-50, 647b.

36. *Annotationes in quattuor evangelia* = *op. omn. th.*, II.1, pp. 11a-14a.

37. *Ibid.*, p. 13a-b.

38. *Annotationes ad Vetus Testamentum* = *op. omn. th.*, I, *ad loc.*

39. Cf. for instance ad 33.1: 'Nihil hic de Nabuchodonosoro, multoque

minus de Alexandro Magno cogitandum. Omnia enim haec vaticinia inter se cohaerent, & ad tempora proxima pertinent.'

40. Ad Isa. 30.1.

41. Ad Isa. 40, prooem., *op. omn. th.*, I, p. 308a.

42. Ad Eccl, prologue, *op. omn. th.*, I, p. 258b Cf. the similar utterance on Wis.Sol., prologue, *op. omn. th.*, I, p. 588a.

43. *Ad librum Hiob*, prologue, *op. omn. th.*, I, p. 203a.

44. *Appendix ad interpretationem locorum N. Testamenti quae de Antichristo agunt* . . . = *op. omn. th.*, III, pp. 745-504, p. 482b. Another example is the expectation of Paul that he would possibly (not certainly) live to see the last day, *Votum pro pace* = *op. omn. th.*, III, p. 671b.

45. *Votum pro pace* = *op. omn. th.*, III, pp. 673b.

46. Cf. G. SEEBASS, art. 'Antichrist IV. Reformationszeit', *TRE* III, pp. 28-43.

47. *Commentatio ad loca quaedam Novi Testamenti, quae de Antichristo agunt aut agere putantur* = *op. omn. th.*, III, pp. 457-74.

48. *Appendix*. . .; cf. note 44.

49. *De iure belli*, Prolegomena, *op. cit.*, p. 7.

50. *De iure belli*, *op. cit.*, p. 399. Also in his *De veritate* the 'consensus omnium gentium' about God's existence is one of the most prominent reasons adduced in its favour, which is the cornerstone of the whole apologetical argumentation (*op. omn. th.* III, p. 4a). Van EYSINGA (*op. cit.*, pp. 81f.) reminds us of HERBERT of CHERBURY's 'notitiae communes' as a similar theory. GROTIUS met CHERBURY in Paris (where the latter was British ambassador) and recommended the publication of the famous deist's 'De Veritate'.

51. *Rivetani apologetici discussio* = *op. omn. th.*, III, p. 707a.

52. *De iure belli*, *op. cit.*, p. 17.

53. Cf. KNIGHT, *Life*, p. 255.

54. *De iure belli*, *op. cit.*, p. 17. Cf. also *Rivetani apologetici discussio* = *op. omn. th.*, III, p. 706a: 'Those Jewish customs GROTIUS at last renders free of blame which were received universally and by Christ who was sent to correct all defects, not to reproach.'

55. Cf. F.-J. NIEMANN, 'Die erste ökumenische Fundamentaltheologie. Zum 400. Geburtstag von Hugo Grotius', *Cath* (M) 37 (1983), pp. 203-16.

56. *Animadversiones* = *op. omn. th.*, III, p. 648a.

57. Ibn Esra on Cant. 5.12, cf. ad Mt. 1.22 (*op. omn. th.*, II.1, p. 11b).

58. *Ad Canticum*, *op. omn. th.* I, p. 267a-b.

59. *Rivetani apologetici discussio* = *op. omn. th.*, III, p. 725b.

60. *Ibid.*, p. 726a.

61. At any cast the judgment of H.J. KRAUS (*Geschichte der historisch-kritischen Erforschung des Alten Testaments* [3rd edn; Neukirchen-Vluyn, 1982], p. 52)—'The authority of the Deus loquens has been cancelled . . . The words of the text are therefore not only protected against an

orthodox theory of inspiration and dogmatic prejudices, they are also blocked against the possibililily that God himself could speak in these texts'—is anachronistic, because it is spoken out of the presuppositions of his own age, in this case of Barthian theology.

62. Ad Mt. 1.22, *op. omn. th.*, II.1, p. 12b.
63. *Ibid.*, p. 11a.
64. *Ibid.*
65. Cf. also *De iure belli*, *op. cit.*, p. 404.

PANEL DISCUSSION

INTRODUCTION

B. Uffenheimer

During this conference we dealt with problems quite different from those which interest professional biblical scholars. Our main topic was the formative influence of the Bible on the development of Jewish and Christian cultures. This panel discussion which is the final session is intended to sum up the existential relevance of our deliberations, in the Jewish-Christian context.

It was at the beginning of this century when a post-assimilatory believing Jew discussed this question with a converted Jew who had become a believing Christian. I mean the significant exchange of letters between Franz Rosenzweig and Eugen Rosenstock-Huessy, which is today available in a booklet, *Judaism despite Christianity* (1969). Rosenzweig, who was at the verge of conversion to Christianity in July 1913, suddenly changed his mind three months later after attending the Yom Kippur service in a small orthodox synagogue of an east European Jewish community in Berlin. After this experience he became the foremost Jewish philosopher of this century. But it was not until between the autumn of 1918 and the spring of 1919 that he wrote his opus magnum *Der Stern der Erlösung* (1921, 2nd edn 1930, 3rd edn 1954) (English translation by W.W. Hallo, *The Star of Redemption*, 1971), where he presented his own philosophy which had grown out of his observations during World War I, when his faith in German idealism was smashed to pieces. The exchange of opinions reflected in the above mentioned booklet is the first step towards his return to his Jewish heritage. Its importance for the present-Jewish Christian dialogue cannot be overrated.

Far from being a dogmatic discussion in the manner of the middle ages, its point of departure is the personal existential crisis of the believers, who strive to understand their common heritage without blurring the differences of their respective own ways of life.

Rosenzweig was the first Jewish thinker of standing who allotted to
Christianity a positive role in the process of salvation, leaving the
Jewish people outside the vicissitudes of history, in the orbit of
eternity.

In the meantime, fundamental changes have taken place in the
wake of the holocaust. The Jewish people have made an adventurous
leap into history, which is no longer something to be contemplated
by the passive Jewish onlooker, but has to be acted upon. Eschatology
has become a living political factor in our activities. Ben-Gurion
coined it in the biblical terms of 'ingathering of the exiles' in the land
of their fathers, in Eretz-Israel, and in the establishment of the
society of justice and equality. Simultaneously we became aware
during this generation of Auschwitz, that the forces of evil are very
concrete and have to be met by force in the field of history; otherwise
we will have no chance of surviving.

Again, we cannot participate in the individualistic adventure of a
thinker like Rosenzweig, for whom Judaism was first and foremost a
private, personal problem, not to mention Kierkegaard, whose
Christian approach was tantamount to an escape from the responsibility to this world. For us the adaptation of Jewish religion and
culture to this new situation is essential for our national and cultural
survival. Our living interpretation of the Bible is the response to
these conditions of life.

Professor Raiser told us about a parallel situation in the Christian
world. As far as I understand, the underlying problem he dealt with
is relevant not only to the third world. It is the problem of the
Christian, western world as well.

The question we want to talk about is the following: what are the
repercussions of this concrete situation upon Jewish and Christian
Bible-reading? When speaking about Jewish and Christian reading I
am aware that in both camps there are widely different approaches.
The Christian variations were presented today by Professor Dubois
on the one hand and by Professor Frey on the other hand. In the
Jewish domain the differences fluctuate between the orthodox, the
religious liberal and the secular attitudes. What is that common
ground of both the Jewish and Christian approaches? What are the
differences?

JEWISH AND CHRISTIAN UNDERSTANDING OF THE BIBLE

Ze'ev W. Falk

This coming Sabbath we are going to read in the Synagogue Gen. 46.1, which I would like to choose as the motto of my presentation:

> So Israel took his journey with all that he had and came to Beer Sheba and offered sacrifices to the God of his father Isaac.

During the first part of the third century Rabbi Joshua ben Levi remarked that he had visited all the sages of homiletics in Judea to ask them for the interpretation of this verse and that nobody could give a satisfactory answer. He then stayed with Judah ben Pedayah, nephew of Ben Qappara, who interpreted the verse by the following rule: If a teacher and his disciple are on their way, one should first greet the latter, who usually comes first, and then the former (*Gen. Rab.* 94.5).

R. Joshua ben Levi's problem was the description of the God of Jacob as the God of Isaac and not as the God of Abraham and Isaac; Judah ben Pedayah gave the explanation that you usually turn to the disciple, who goes before the teacher to arrange for his reception. The people therefore first see the disciple and come to understand the teacher through the disciple. Likewise, Jacob first perceived God as the God of his father Isaac, and only in the second stage came to perceive Him as the God of Abraham.

Let me continue the line of thought of this metaphor. For each of us, Jews and Christians, God is perceived in the first instance as that of our direct parents and teachers and only indirectly as the God of Scripture. Therefore, we start the first benediction in prayer by mentioning God as our God and the God of our fathers, only hence we call Him the God of Abraham, the God of Isaac and the God of Jacob. First comes the personal experience, then the last links of the tradition, and finally the original concepts of the Patriarchal faith.

Likewise, Jewish understanding of the Bible is largely conditioned by the impact of the last links of tradition. I would like to mention the commentaries of Rabbi Jacob Tsevi Mecklenburg (1785-1865), Rabbi Naphtali Tsevi Judah Berlin (1817-1893), Rabbi Meir Loew ben Yehiel Michel (1809-1879) and Rabbi Samson Raphael Hirsch (1808-1888). The common purpose of these teachers was the restoration of the unity between the legal and homiletic tradition, on the one hand, and the scholarly study of Scripture, on the other hand. The same tendency can be found in the commentary of Rabbi Samuel David Luzatto (1800-1865), though already engaging in textual criticism and making use of Christian scholarship.

The latter author, again, extended Jewish exegetics by paying attention to the Christian understanding of the Bible. In order to appreciate his stand, we should go back to Rabbinic reaction towards Christian beginnings, as reflected in the Talmud and Midrash. Let us mark a number of stages in the development.

At the end of the first century, Rabbi Tarfon delivered an opinion that Christian tracts should be burnt, for Christians perceived God but denied some of His attributes as taught by Jewish tradition (*Tosefta Sabbath* 13.5). The reference was probably to the belief in incarnation and the concept of the 'Son of God'. Rabbi Tarfon must have been afraid that Christian interpretations of Scripture, e.g. Isaiah 53, would lead the Jewish listeners to apostasy and illegal behaviour.

Indeed, the preaching of Paul, for instance 2 Cor. 3.14-16, denied the legitimacy of Rabbinic exegesis, so that the Rabbis were led to fight the Christian message by fire.

On the other hand, Rabbi Meir, in the middle of the second century, declared a gentile who was engaged in the study of Scripture to be as laudable as the High Priest (*b. Sanhedrin* 59a; *Avodah Zarah* 3a). According to this opinion, Christian exegesis was therefore legitimate, at least as far as it did not deny the validity of Jewish tradition.

Around 225 we hear Rabbi Jonathan ben Elazar talking with a Samaritan about the sanctity of Mount Gerizim and Jerusalem, respectively (*Deut. Rab.* and Deut. 7.14). By way of analogy, a similar tolerance may be presumed on the part of the rabbis vis-à-vis Christian exegesis.

Rabbi Simlai (c. 250), by explaining the use of the plural in the creation story (*j. Berakhot* 9.1, 12d) probably answered a Christian argument in the line of Trinity (cf. E.E. Urbach, *The Sages; their*

Concepts and Beliefs, Jerusalem, ch. 9). This reflects a positive attitude towards Christian study of Scripture and a need for serious consideration of its results.

Around 275 Rabbi Abbahu replied to Christian arguments against the Jewish belief in election (*b. Avodah Zarah* 4a; Urbach, *The Sages*, ch. 16). The discussion included the exegesis of Amos 3.2, and illustrated the common ground of Jewish and Christian teachers in the understanding of the Bible.

On the other hand, Rabbi Johanan (c. 180-279) opposed the common study of Scripture by Jews and Christians. In his view, a Gentile engaged in Torah forfeited his life (*b. Sanhedrin* 59a), for his study was a kind of plagiarism against Jewish tradition.

However, his view was transmitted subject to that of Rabbi Meir, and both were harmonized with each other by the assumption that Gentiles had to study the seven Noachic commandments. A common interest was therefore established between the rabbis and Christian scholars, to elucidate the universal elements of Scripture. Indeed, Maimonides in his code mitigated the rule established by the Talmud in two ways: he omitted the idea of capital punishment for the unauthorized study of Torah, and he explained the reason of the prohibition to prevent the creation of a new religion (*Mishneh Torah*, *Hilkhot Melakhim* 10.9).

In any case, Jewish biblical scholars maintained contacts with Christian theologians and related to their exegesis. As a rule, they followed the literal meaning of the text, which they felt to have been intended by Moses and the other authors of Scripture. Figurative interpretation was accepted only when the literal sense was un-acceptable (cf. Sa'adyah ben Joseph, *Emunot we Deoth*, ch. 7; Joseph Kimhi, *Sefer Habrit*, quoted in F.E. Talmage, *Disputation and Dialogue; Readings in the Jewish Christian Encounter*, New York [1975], p. 117).

Nevertheless, Jewish scholars were often open-minded enough to discuss the meaning of Scripture with Christians. Hai Ga'on (939-1038), for instance, consulted the Catholicus of the Syrian Church regarding a verse of the Psalms. Allegorical interpretations of the text were used to harmonize philosophical insights with the Bible (cf. A. Altmann: 'Bible—Allegorical Interpretation', in *Encyclopedia Judaica*, IV, pp. 895-99). The same method became prevalent among mystics and was developed through the Hassidic hermeneutics: *benaqel lilmod ulefaresh* (*Iggeret hacodesh*), which can be roughly translated: simple sense, study and allegory.

In the following an attempt will therefore be made to present a Jewish attitude towards Christian exegesis and towards Jewish-Christian study of the Bible.

The divine teaching and commandments were originally addressed to all human beings. They were to be written upon stone *very plainly* (Deut. 27.9), which was interpreted by the rabbis as *in seventy languages* (*m. Sotah* 7.5). Thus an invitation was extended to each nation to develop its own understanding and to participate in the discussion of the meaning.

Indeed, the Word of God had been described as a fire and as a hammer breaking the rock into pieces (Jer. 23.29), which was taken to refer to the plurality of interpretations. Likewise, though the divine revelation was one, its understanding was multiple (Ps. 62.11), i.e. various ideas could be derived from one verse and no verse should be taken as a mere repetition of the other (*b. Sanhedrin* 34a). The principle was also expressed by the statement that God gave one word and that great was the company of those who bore the tidings (Ps. 68.12). According to a rabbinic view, this meant that every single revelation was transformed into seventy versions (*b. Shabbat* 88b).

Thus, there is no limit to the interpretation of the Bible and all nations are invited to participate in the endeavour. The number seventy represents obviously the seventy nations of mankind as listed in Genesis. This idea corresponds with that of the 600,000 senses of divine revelation, which are published through the variety of understanding among the Israelites (R. Samuel Eliezer Edels [1555-1631]: *Commentary, b. Berakhot* 58a). Just as the full meaning of the divine message depends on the participation of all Israelites, bringing in their individal understanding of the text, so the exegesis of the seventy nations may enrich and extend our own understanding. The study of Christian theology and the dialogue with Christian scholars are therefore part of the Jewish search for the meaning of the Bible. It may be included in the parameter of the study as defined by the great Talmudist and Biblicist: 'I, Samuel son of Meir, who was son-in-law of *Rashi*, argued with the latter and he admitted that if he had still time, he would have to write "new Commentaries according to the simple sense of the word as innovated every day"' (R. Samuel ben Meir [c. 1080–c. 1174], *Commentary*, Gen. 37.2).

Even Christological interpretation of Scripture can be meaningful for Jewish self-understanding. Just as the Jewish sermon tried to create a link between present-day experience and Scripture, the

Christian speaker did the same. Homiletical exegesis was the method of granting legitimation to the present and discovering new dimensions in the past.

We cannot accept Christian spiritualization of Israel's teaching and commandments. For us, God enters into celestial Jerusalem only after having entered into the terrestrial one (*b. Ta'anit* 5a). However, we are in need of a reminder, from time to time, that the spiritual vocation of Judaism is not to be forgotten.

Christianity has realized the universal aspiration of Judaism, which has otherwise been neglected. A Jew has become teacher to a great part of humanity and could be called by them 'Saviour' and 'Messiah'. This event is not only of universal significance but also plays an important role in the self-understanding of the Jewish people.

Let us, Jews and Christians, complement and listen to each other. There is a creative tension between us which can help the world to prepare for the Kingdom.

ROMAN CATHOLIC UNDERSTANDING OF THE BIBLE

Marcel Dubois

First of all we have to state which kind of Catholic position we are speaking about, because there are, within Catholic theological scholarship, different positions and orientations. We would not receive the same answer from Hans Küng, Urs von Baltasar, Xavier Léon-Dufour, Yves Congar, Cardinal Martini, Cardinal Ratzinger or Archbishop Lefevre! I think that it will be more interesting, especially for our guests and perhaps also for our Israeli friends, to present the experience of a Christian living in Israel among the Jewish people. What is the benefit of such a situation for his understanding of the Bible?

There are two areas of discovery. First I shall summarize what are the discoveries that a Christian can make reading the Bible in this country. Later on I shall introduce these discoveries within the framework of a permanent problematic, that of the difficulties or even the crisis of hermeneutics in our time, as they appear in every field but especially in biblical exegesis.

Let us begin by a presentation of the advantages of a reading of the Bible in this land and among this people, Israel.

If I had to summarize my discoveries in this country, I would use three words: Jews have taught me or have given me the living example of an *existential*, a *traditional* and of what I call—because I did not find any other suitable term, even if my Jewish friends do not always understand what I mean—a *sacramental* approach to the Bible.

Existential	synchrony of the language
	synchrony of the landscape
Traditional	*Torah she bikhtav—Torah she be'alpeh*
	Scripture—tradition
Sacramental	Event—text—memory—faith

First of all: *existential*. I shall begin with a practical experience. As Christians living in Israel, in October 1973, during the Yom Kippur War, we were struck by the way our Jewish friends opened the Bible. They were not looking for spiritual sentences or moral inspiration like Christians when they read so-called books of spirituality. It was with a kind of existential anxiety, a spiritual emergency. 'What does this book which is the summary of our history and our wisdom, say about the present day situation? What about our people today? What about our country? What about the city of Jerusalem?' I call such an approach existential, because of the practical, immediate, realistic relationship between the history written in the book and the events of present life.

We were struck and challenged by this example, for this book contains also for us the word of God, the word of life, yea, of eternal life. We felt challenged to ask ourselves: Do we read the Bible and the Gospel during such an emergency with such historical realism? Now, here it is clear that we are touching on a very important and difficult problem. If I live in Jerusalem as a member of the people, it is quite easy to be anxious about the destiny of the people and the country. That is the every-day reality. It is more difficult to do so about what we call spiritual realities. Unfortunately, we are not so realistic when we think of the Kingdom of God and the celestial Jerusalem! From this point of view, we can say that we receive from the Jewish people a living example of a realistic and existential approach to the Bible. It is interesting to see that, here in Israel, this existential link with the text is kept alive by two elements which belong to culture and daily life. Using a structuralist vocabulary, I would call them the synchrony of the language and the synchrony of the landscape.

Synchrony of the language. I hope that you will visit the Shrine of the Book in Jerusalem, and more precisely, I hope that you will meet there children from Israeli schools. If you see these kids at the scrolls of Qumran, you will discover that the 'cultural distance' between the slang they speak in Dizengoff or in the Katamonim and the language of the biblical texts, is much smaller than the 'cultural distance' for a child of Paris between the 'argot' of Clichy or Aubervilliers and the language of Proust, not to mention Chateaubriand or Racine! On one side are two or three centuries, but on the other, more than two thousand years! These children can hear the Bible on the radio every day, and even read the text every evening on television. It is not exactly the same colloquial language, but nevertheless they feel at home. They use the same roots, the same system. I could give many examples of this synchrony of the language and of its existential or its cultural significance.

Now, another interesting fact is that this synchrony of the language is supported by a *synchrony of the landscape*. Just try to imagine what it can mean for a child living here, when he reads the signposts: Beersheva (Abraham) 60 km, Jericho (Joshua and the trumpets) 30 km, and so on. The framework and the settings of daily existence are those of the Bible. We discover, here, in Israel, that the sacred history took place within a sacred geography the map of which remains the same for people living here today. The discovery of the synchrony which unites this land, the landscapes and significant places, the Book, the Bible, and History is without a doubt a singular experience for a Christian who lives here.

This introduces my second consideration: the *traditional* approach to the Bible. Here again, we receive from the Jewish approach an example and a justification for the Christian reading of the Scripture.

It is an aspect that may, perhaps, be surprising, for it is most often put forward as the touchstone of the separation between Christian and Jewish tradition. I refer to the fundamental distinction between *Torah she bikhtav* (written law) and *Torah she be'alpeh* (oral law). It is true that, in the eyes of our brethren, a Christian reading of the Bible appears congenitally infirm and mutilated, for it only considers written law (as a Jewish sect, the Karaites, did). A religious Jew, for his part, attaches as much importance to the Talmud and to the oral tradition of the Sages, as to the letter of the written text. This original difference covers an immense and difficult problem into which I cannot enter here, for this is not the point of my argument. If I have drawn your attention to it, it is, paradoxically, to invite reflection on the exemplary value of this dichotomy: Torah as a written record and oral tradition, which in spite of appearances is not a text added to the first. It is not an oral Bible augmented alongside the other, nor a verbal message employed to compete with the written one! Familiarity with Jewish tradition reveals that the true nature of oral tradition is rather one of flair, a capacity of understanding, a kind of divine trust to be acted upon, an affinity given by God to His people which aims at the comprehension of His word and its practical application. Indeed, it illuminates the condition of any approach to Scripture according to faith, and it announces in particular the necessary complementarity between *Scripture* and *Tradition* in a Christian reading of the Bible. Is it not, for the Church, the most suggestive example of the gift of faith, as *affinity* with the *revealed* message, and of the role of *tradition* as a Christian subjectivity? More precisely, of the subjectivity of the Christian community and its faith throughout history. In other words, the Jews give us the example of a reading of the Word of God within the subjectivity of the community according to the memory of its tradition.

In this regard, a Christian who looks at Jewish existence, especially if he lives in Israel, in the midst of the Jewish people, in the Land of the Bible, discovers with wonder that the heritage he has received from the Jewish people does not consist only of a book, or a treasure of truths which it would be wise to study, but in the very attitude of Israel toward God's gift and toward the One who gives this gift, and in the very way in which this people has received this book, has kept and transmitted it.

My dear Christian friends, what would we do if we had to give an account of who we are, in front of all those who don't share our faith—not so much an account of the content of our creed but of our attitude, facing God, under the movement of the Spirit?—It seems to me that we could do it by drawing a sketch with some simple, pure and strict characteristics in the manner of Matisse. I see at least six characteristic features.

As Christians, we listen. God has spoken, God is speaking, we pay attention to what He says. We listen to the Word of God. Faith is listening.

As Christians, we remember. We not only remember what God has said and done, but we actualize, we represent through memory the actuality of his initiatives.

As Christians, we are not alone: we have a multitude of brothers and sisters who listen as we do, and share our memories. We belong to a community, to a people.

As Christians, gathered in a living community, we are faithful to a tradition, we live according to the tradition of the people we belong to.

As Christians, we thank God for the certitude of the Word we have received and for the traditions which we live by. Without the Word, without our traditions, we could not speak, we could not sing.

As Christians, we believe that the One who has spoken has promised to come or to come again; therefore, we live in permanent hope, an eschatological expectation.

Listening, remembering, community, tradition, thanksgiving, hope: these are the features of our spiritual portrait. But what originally inspired these attributes? Who is the model? We too often forget that the characteristic dimensions of our attitude toward God and toward His Word are a heritage which we have received from Israel. Through Jesus, a son of the Jewish people, we have received the attitude, the behaviour, the subjectivity of Israel facing the gift of God. So the Jewish people gave us the Word, which he has heard and by which he has called us to life: and he has shown us how to be attentive, to listen, to receive, to keep alive and to live according to this message. *Shema Israel*: Listen, hear, Israel. We have inherited from the people of the Covenant this invitation and the relation with God which it implies.

If I were the Minister of Education, or the Minister of Tourism, or even the Minister of Foreign Affairs, I would organize every visit in this country, for scholars like you or for pilgrims, be they Jews from Brooklyn or students from Paris or seminarians from Rome, according to the three components of Jewish identity: Torah Israel, Am Israel, Eretz Israel—the book, the people and the land. I think we could organize every programme in the following way:

The first period which would require a week, a month, or even better a year, would demonstrate the link between the book and the land. We would read the Bible on location. Thus we could make the link between the Bible and its settings, between sacred history and sacred geography! More and more pilgrims have discovered the importance of this approach to the land. They do not come to kiss the stones of the holy places, but to remember sacred history within the framework of the Bible.

In the second period here we would show the link between the people and the book. As I told you, the Jews did not give us only the text of the Bible but also the living example of reading it. More and more Christians are coming to Jerusalem in order to share this Jewish approach to the book, taking advantage of what I have called the Jewish subjectivity.

And finally, we discover that there is a link between the people and the land, in the name of the book. This link is much deeper than any kind of political Zionism. It belongs to Jewish identity.

Hence one discovers an existential reading of the Bible as well as a traditional reading of it. That is precisely what we could call the 'interior hermeneutics of Jewish interpretation'. The Jewish people reads the book according to its own experience within the framework of its history and tradition.

This consideration brings us to the third point which I have put forward for discussion, i.e. the *sacramental* reading of the Bible.

To make it short, let us begin with an example. I see the most striking and the most typical illustration of what I call 'the sacramental approach' to the Bible, in the *Haggadah* of *Pesah*.

'In every generation everyone is duty bound to see himself as if he came forth out of Egypt.' This sentence, let us say more precisely this affirmation, which is at the very centre of the *Seder* of *Pesah*, is the expression of the significance of the original *event* of the Exodus for both the memory and the actual faith of the Jewish people. This proposition is at the same time an act of remembrance, uniting memory and hope in the awareness of a permanent and continuing identity. Jews recall, during the *Seder*, a transcendent event as a mighty deed of the past, but above all, as a divine gesture which remains constantly present to the Jewish consciousness. The event of the Exodus is at the origin of the adventure of the Jewish people and remains actually present in every instant of that people's unrolling in time, assembling the community in the same act of memorial throughout its memory. We are here in the presence of a paradoxical dynamic process, that of the development of a permanent identity, a progressive discovery of an identity revealed in a divine initiative, an increasing identification to the original vocation, through an activity of remembering which is at the same time a remembrance both of the past and, more importantly, of God Himself. In the theology of Augustine, we find a concise and strong expression which summarizes what we have just observed in the *Haggadah* of *Pesah*: *meminisse sui, meminisse Dei*: to remember myself, to remember God. So we are invited to discern the twofold dimension of memory. The first dimension we could call the historical or psychological memory, that is to say the capacity of remembering the events of the past as they are recorded on the tape of time. The other, on a much deeper level, we could call the substantial or ontological memory: the very presence of oneself to oneself, throughout time. It is clear that the latter is the basis and the source of the former. We remember the events of our past life because we are aware, in the depth of our conscience, of the permanence of an 'I', a self which reminds and recalls all the facts of which it has been the subject. The memory of the past is the occasion and the matter of remembering what actually is and finally what is given by God.

This is exactly the structure of the spiritual attitude manifested in the celebration of the *Seder*: 'In every generation everyone is duty bound to see himself as if he came forth out of Egypt'.

We have inherited this fundamental structure. It is not by chance that Jesus has chosen precisely this moment to say to his disciples and to us: 'Do this in remembrance of me'. Here and there, the structure is the same, that of a progressive integration of an identity, election or vocation, given at the very beginning by the initiative of God.

What is true for the *Haggadah* is true for every reading of the Bible. The question is not any more to read the text, so to speak, from the outside, but to read it from within and to be present in the original event and finally to listen to God Himself who speaks through it. Therefore it can be said that a Christian reading of the Bible finds in the *Haggadah* of *Pesah* and in the Jewish approach to the biblical events, an example of what might be called a sacramental approach to the Scripture.

These considerations seem to me sufficient in order to show how the spiritual attitude implied in the existential, traditional and sacramental approach of the Jewish people to the Bible effectively proposes a living example in which a Christian reading of the Scripture could find a permanent source of health and renewal.

Having said that, let me add one remark which seems to me very important as well as paradoxical: I have found comfort for my faith in the Resurrection of Christ, here in Israel, among the Jews who by definition don't believe in it! Not at all because I had to defend myself against a kind of spiritual aggression! On the contrary. I have received an example for my own faith, in the way in which my Jewish friends refer to the original events of their faith.

Here, again, the Jewish experience and attitude contain both a unique and an exemplary value. In the commemoration of the Exodus, there is, for the Jewish consciousness, a vital link between the original *event*, the *community* which has experienced this event, the *texts* in which the report of the event was written and transmitted by the community, and the *faith* by which this community has adhered to these facts throughout the centuries. As a Chistian, I think that many false problems would have been avoided and many crises resolved if the key of all Christian reading of the Word of God could be found in this living attitude. Again, the Church has inherited this fundamental structure. The mystery of Resurrection finds a decisive application of it. The *happenings* of Easter, the *texts* of the New Testament which relate it, the *witnesses* who have written and transmitted them, and the faith of the Church by which we cleave to these texts, are merely the aspects of one and the same structure of memory.

Having come this far, my purpose is now to show how the structure we have discovered in this exemplary of the Jewish approach to the Bible could propose a kind of solution to the problems which we find in present-day hermeneutics, whatever is the field: poetry, drama, philosophy, Scripture.

It would be possible to present the two contemporary ways of approaching a text, any text (Bible, poetry, myth or philosophy) according to two great methodological lines. On the left is an objective approach, that of logical positivism, philosophy of language or structural analysis, and the approach represented on the right is that of existential philosophy or hermeneutics.

Logical positivism	Existential
Phil. of language	Philosophy
Structuralism	Hermeneutics

Erklären—Verstehen (Dilthey)
(Saussure) Language—Speech
Historie—Geschichte (Heidegger)
(Frege) Sense—reference
Was—Dass (Bultmann)
meaning—significance

As you can see, it is striking that, on both sides, the great witnesses of these two different streams have perceived the same fundamental opposition.

Dilthey introduced, long ago, the distinction between *erklären* and *verstehen*. Even if this dichotomy has passed, it played a very important role at the beginning of the existential hermeneutics.

In a quite different pespective we find in F. de Saussure a distinction which is the key to his linguistic theory: the opposition between *langue* and *parole*. The first is nothing more than a network of words and rules, a closed synchrony in which all the elements are referred to one another, like a dictionary or a grammar. The other depends on the usage of this system of language when he wants to say something to somebody. It is the same opposition between two methods or even two mentalities which is expressed by Heidegger in his famous distinction between *Historie* and *Geschichte*. The former depends on a naturalistic conception of the events, historical facts being considered out of any kind of subjective references; the latter, on the contrary, implies an existential view according to which the events of the past become historical phenomena only when they have a significance for a *Dasein*: man creates history in which he is involved and on which he depends. On a more analytical level, Frege makes a distinction between *meaning* and *reference*, that is to say between the logical or grammatical structure of any sentence and the reality to which it refers which actually exists. Coming back to the right we find in Bultmann as a good disciple of Heidegger, a distinction between the objective knowledge of a *Was*, a content of meaning given to theoretical analysis, and the existential perception of a *Dass*, an event which is involved within an experimental perception and which requires from the subject an existential *Entscheidung*, a decision.

I have recalled these distinctions in order to show their parallelism. The simple comparison of both sides is sufficient to suggest the radical difference between the two mentalities. The crisis of contemporary thought, in every field, consists in this fact that we have to find our way between these two decisions. If we call *meaning* the objective dimension of the language or of the symbols in their synchronic structure, and if we call *significance* the transcendent dimension, the reference to the thing which the speech wants to express, it seems that we can summarize the situation, in our time, saying that every interpretation is condemned to oscillate between two dangers or two temptations. Either a meaning, analytical and abstract, without any attention to an external reference, *erklären* without enough *verstehen*. Or, at the opposite, a *significance* which does not pay enough attention to the rules of meaning.

Now, if you remember what we have discovered, considering the benefits of the Jewish traditional interpretation, we see that the way in which the Jewish people approach the Bible is a beautiful example of the balance we are seeking by a transmission through memory and tradition, within the synchrony of the community, of the book and of its contents. Meaning and significance are transmitted together as if the synchrony of the faith were the condition of the synchrony of the text, throughout the diachrony of tradition.

My only intention was to invite you to think about the exemplary value of this fact.

PROTESTANT UNDERSTANDING OF THE BIBLE

Henning Graf Reventlow

The question to be answered—What is the Protestant position in the interpretation of the Scriptures?—is not to be answered in a single way because there is no single Protestant position. In a way you can only explain what your personal position is as a Protestant, perhaps in the tradition of Protestant Bible understanding, and it could be that what I declare differs from the opinions of some of my colleagues who are here and others who are absent, because of course Protestantism is also a larger community embracing different confessional traditions. There is a Lutheran tradition, but there is also a Reformed tradition and there are not very easily detectable differences between them. Nevertheless, we have a common path in the Reformation and the first thing one would have to say is that one of the most important points in the programme of the Reformation was to reform the church according to the Scriptures. This was conceived as a reform against the statutes of the contemporary church which comprised Scripture and tradition, in opposition against mingling both and regarding tradition as partly decisive for the interpretation of the Scriptures. When I am saying this you will see at once that in a way the programme was a Utopian one because you have to have a tradition and you have to have presuppositions for explaining the Scriptures. You have to put questions and only your questions will be answered. The Protestant standpoint had also other more dogmatic components. The second rule was the *sola fide/ sola gratia* (by faith alone/through grace alone), in the Pauline and Augustinian tradition of understanding the Bible. I think the second rule is also very important.

Of course Protestants interpret the Old Testament from the New Testament because for all Christians both parts of the Bible are equivalent. There have been times when the New Testament was the preponderant and even the only important part of the Bible, but I

think the way back to regarding both parts of the Bible as equally
important is the first step to a common understanding of the Bible by
both Judaism and Christianity. We see a movement back to the
common basis in what we call the Old Testament and you call our
common Bible. And we see a way back to acknowledging our
common heritage in the tradition of interpreting the Bible.

Perhaps the basic difference between a Christian and a Jewish
standpoint is that we are theologians: we try to find out a centre for
the Scriptures. That means a viewpoint which enables us to
understand the whole word of God as a unity which has a detectable
(or not detectable) centre. Luther formulated it in his doctrine of
justification, because he himself in the experiences of his life had
seen that to be saved is the work of God alone and cannot be won by
human endeavours alone. In this he was in opposition to the position
of the Church—not a theoretical position, I think, but a practical one
which Luther had experienced as a monk when he was trying to gain
the favour of God by ascetic exercises and by trying to do the will of
God completely. This was his experience as a reformer: God saves
man before he has earned this favour. He does it by his own word. I
think this is the main topic, the basic dogma of the Reformation as
we still have it, and all other topics: where ethics has its place and
how the Bible has to be read are dependent on this central position of
the Reformation.

And now something about Bible criticism. Bible criticism is in my
view not the original outcome of the Reformation. The aims of the
Reformation lay in a way on a dogmatic level and were not
dependent on a critical view of the Bible, but a critical view of the
Bible was possible under the circumstances of a reformed and
Evangelical understanding of the Bible. The motives for criticism
came from outside, mostly from a humanistic impetus, at first on the
philological level, later on a historical level. All these questions were
put into the discussion not for dogmatic reasons, not for specifically
Protestant reasons, but they could be put because no Church
authority hindered it, there was no Papal authority forbidding
anything.

I think a problem remains because in my view all that we do on the
basis of a historical understanding or a philological understanding of
the Bible helps to understand the verbal sense. It was also the aim of
Luther and the Reformation to go back to the literal sense and in this
way the critical explanation of the Bible is built upon the ground of

the Reformation. Both have in common the resoluteness to refuse any predetermined sense, to go back to the verbal sense of the Bible and to see the Bible as an expression of the work of God on man in history. And now the problem is that when we have done all this, when we have understood the historical sense and have solved all our critical problems the central question of the Reformation is still open. Luther did not regard the written word as the critical, as the most important matter, but the proclamation of the word of God is for him decisive. The Bible is only thought of as containing the word of God, but the word of God does its work only when it is preached to people, that means, only when you hear the word of God and answer it in your soul, with your whole existence. The word of God has to be preached: that is central for the standpoint of the Reformation. Therefore, all critical and scientific work on the Bible starts as a preparation to the central office of the Church.

The theory of verbal inspiration crept in at a certain period in the history of Protestantism after the period of the Reformation in the late sixteenth and mostly in the seventeenth century and can be thought of as a reappearance of a scholastic system. By some scholars it was pushed to the extreme of maintaining the verbal inspiration even of the vowel pointing of the Hebrew Bible. Because you know that the whole Bible is inspired nothing can not be inspired. You cannot even exclude the vowel points. But this was in a way a deviation and had to give way later. Other periods followed in the history of Protestant exegesis.

I think Protestant orthodoxy was in danger of losing the central aspect of Luther, taking the book again as the most important thing and forgetting that preaching the word is decisive.

INDEX

INDEX OF BIBLICAL REFERENCES

INDEX OF AUTHORS AND EXEGETES

JOURNAL FOR THE STUDY OF THE OLD TESTAMENT
Supplement Series